D1255029

Literary Lives
General Editor: Richard Dutton, Reader in English,
University of Lancaster

This series offers stimulating accounts of the literary careers of the most widely read British and Irish authors. Volumes follow the outline of writers' working lives, not in the spirit of traditional biography, but aiming to trace the professional, publishing and social contexts which shaped their writing. The role and status of 'the author' as the creator of literary texts is a vexed issue in current critical theory, where a variety of social, linguistic and psychological approaches have challenged the old concentration on writers as specially-gifted individuals. Yet reports of 'the death of the author' in literary studies are (as Mark Twain said of a premature obituary) an exaggeration. This series aims to demonstrate how an understanding of writers' careers can promote, for students and general readers alike, a more informed historical reading of their works.

Virginia Woolf

A Literary Life

John Mepham

St. Martin's Press　　　New York

© John Mepham   1991

First published in the United States of America in 1991

Printed in Hong Kong

ISBN 0-312-06204-4

Library of Congress Cataloging-in-Publication Data
Mepham, John, 1938–
Virginia Woolf:a literary life/John Mepham.
p.   cm. — (Literary Lives)
Includes bibliographical references and index.
ISBN 0-312-06204-4
1. Woolf, Virginia, 1882–1941—Biography.   2. Novelists,
English—20th century—Biography.   I. Title.   II. Series:Literary
Lives (New York, N.Y.)
PR6045.072Z8164   1991
823'.912—dc20   91–9081
                                                              CIP

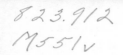
Contents

List of Abbreviations

WORKS BY VIRGINIA WOOLF

BA   *Between the Acts* (Penguin, 1953).

CE I–IV   *Collected Essays* ed. Leonard Woolf 4 vols. (Chatto & Windus, 1966–67).

CSF   *The Complete Shorter Fiction* ed. Susan Dick (Triad/Grafton, 1987).

D I–V   *The Diary of Virginia Woolf* ed. Anne Olivier Bell 5 vols. (The Hogarth Press, 1977–84).

E I–III   *The Essays of Virginia Woolf* ed. Andrew McNeillie, 3 vols. to date (The Hogarth Press, 1986–88).

JR   *Jacob's Room* (Triad/Granada, 1976).

L I–VI   *The Letters of Virginia Woolf* eds Nigel Nicolson and Joanne Trautmann, 6 vols. (The Hogarth Press, 1975–80).

MB   *Moments of Being: Unpublished Autobiographical Writings* ed. Jeanne Schulkind (Chatto & Windus for Sussex University Press, 1976).

MD   *Mrs Dalloway* (Penguin, 1964).

ND   *Night and Day* (Triad/Granada, 1978).

O   *Orlando* (Penguin, 1942).

P   *The Pargiters: The Novel–Essay Portion of The Years*, ed. Mitchell Leaska (The Hogarth Press, 1978).

RF   *Roger Fry* (Penguin, 1979).

RN   *Virginia Woolf's Reading Notebooks*, ed. Brenda Silver (Princeton University Press, 1983).

RO   *A Room of One's Own* (Penguin, 1945).

TG   *Three Guineas* (Penguin, 1977).

TL   *To the Lighthouse* (Triad/Granada, 1977).

TL/MS   *To the Lighthouse* Holograph draft, ed. Susan Dick (The Hogarth Press, 1983).

TY   *The Years* (Penguin, 1968).

VO   *The Voyage Out* (Triad/Grafton, 1978).

W   *The Waves* (Penguin, 1951).

OTHER SOURCES

LW   Leonard Woolf, *An Autobiography* vol. 2 (Oxford University Press, 1980); this volume contains *Beginning Again, Downhill All the Way* and *The Journey not the Arrival Matters*, which were originally published as separate books.

MHP   Monks House Papers, University of Sussex Library.

MM   *Virginia Woolf: The Critical Heritage*, eds R. Majumdar and A. McLaurin (Routledge & Kegan Paul, 1975).

QB I–II   Quentin Bell, *Virginia Woolf: A Biography*, 2 vols. (Triad/Paladin, 1976).

TLS   *Times Literary Supplement*.

List of Tables

Acknowledgements

I acknowledge with gratitude, permission, given by the Trustees of Virginia Woolf's literary estate, to print passages from her unpublished writings and permission, given by the Hogarth Press and Harcourt Brace Jovanovich, to print passages from her published works and to use material from Leonard Woolf's *Downhill All the Way*.

On many occasions over the years that I have worked on this book, I have received generous help from Bet Inglis of the University of Sussex Library and from the staff of the British Library and I would like to record my gratitude to them. I would also like to thank my friends at Bennington College for their support and encouragement and the Dean of Faculty for providing help with the preparation of the manuscript. Early versions of some portions of this book were read to audiences at Middlesex Polytechnic in London, the Institute of Modern Biography at Griffith University in Brisbane, and at Macquarie University in Sydney, and I am grateful for the discussion and advice offered on those occasions. I have learned a great deal about Virginia Woolf over the years from conversations with Andrew McNeillie who was also kind enough to read through the manuscript correcting errors and discussing important points of interpretation. I am very grateful to him. Of course, only I am responsible for the book and whatever errors remain in it.

My deepest gratitude is to Janet Rée from whom I have learned, and with whom I have shared, more than I can say: to her, 'that word known to all men'.

Harcourt Brace Jovanovich, Inc. and renewed 1959 by Leonard Woolf, reprinted by permission of the publisher.

Excerpts from *Orlando*, copyright 1928 by Virginia Woolf and renewed 1956 by Leonard Woolf, reprinted by permission of Harcourt Brace Jovanovich, Inc.

Excerpts from *To The Lighthouse* by Virginia Woolf, copyright 1927 by Harcourt Brace Jovanovich, Inc. and renewed 1955 by Leonard Woolf, reprinted by permission of the publisher.

Excerpts from *Moments of Being* by Virginia Woolf, copyright 1948 by Harcourt Brace Jovanovich, Inc. and renewed 1976 by Harcourt Brace Jovanovich, Inc. and Marjorie T. Parsons, reprinted by permission of the publisher.

Excerpts from *Jacob's Room* by Virginia Woolf, copyright 1922 by Harcourt Brace Jovanovich, Inc. and renewed 1950 by Leonard Woolf, reprinted by permission of the publisher.

Excerpts from *Essays of Virginia Woolf, Volume III* by Virginia Woolf, copyright © 1988 by Quentin Bell, Angelica Garnett, reprinted by permission of Harcourt Brace Jovanovich, Inc.

Excerpts from *Collected Essays, Volume II* by Virginia Woolf, copyright © 1966 by Leonard Woolf, reprinted by permission of Harcourt Brace Jovanovich, Inc.

Excerpts from *Night and Day* by Virginia Woolf, copyright 1920 by George H. Doran & Co. and renewed 1948 by Leonard Woolf, reprinted by permission of Harcourt Brace Jovanovich, Inc.

Excerpts from *Voyage Out* by Virginia Woolf, copyright 1920 by George H. Doran and renewed 1948 by Leonard Woolf, reprinted by permission of Harcourt Brace Jovanovich, Inc.

Excerpts from *The Letters of Virginia Woolf, Volume I* by Virginia Woolf, ed. Nigel Nicolson, Joanne Trautmann, copyright © 1975 by Quentin Bell, Angelica Garnett, reprinted by permission of Harcourt Brace Jovanovich, Inc.

Excerpts from *The Letters of Virginia Woolf, Volume IV* by Virginia Woolf, copyright © 1978 by Quentin Bell, Angelica Garnett, reprinted by permission of Harcourt Brace Jovanovich, Inc.

Excerpts from *The Letters of Virginia Woolf, Volume VI* by Virginia Woolf, copyright © 1980 by Quentin Bell, Angelica Garnett, reprinted by permission of Harcourt Brace Jovanovich, Inc.

Excerpts from *The Diary of Virginia Woolf, Volume V* by Virginia Woolf, ed. Anne Olivier Bell, copyright © 1984 by Quentin Bell, Angelica Garnett, reprinted by permission of Harcourt Brace Jovanovich, Inc.

Excerpts from *The Diary of Virginia Woolf, Volume IV* by Virginia Woolf, ed. Anne Olivier Bell, copyright © 1982 by Quentin Bell, Angelica Garnett, reprinted by permission of Harcourt Brace Jovanovich, Inc.

Excerpts from *The Diary of Virginia Woolf, Volume III* by Virginia Woolf, ed. Anne Olivier Bell, copyright © 1980 by Quentin Bell and Angelica Garnett, reprinted by permission of Harcourt Brace Jovanovich, Inc.

Excerpts from *The Diary of Virginia Woolf, Volume II* by Virginia Woolf, ed. Anne Olivier Bell, copyright © 1978 by Quentin Bell, Angelica Garnett, reprinted by permission of Harcourt Brace Jovanovich, Inc.

Excerpts from *Down Hill All The Way*, copyright © 1967 by Leonard Woolf, reprinted by permission of Harcourt Brace Jovanovich, Inc.

Introduction: The Will to Write

In this book I tell the story of Virginia Woolf's literary life. However, in her case, more than in most, it is impossible to separate out her literary life from all her other lives. We must take seriously her claim that writing, making up phrases, contriving scenes, was 'the greatest rapture' known to her (D III, 22 October 1927). She had the will to write in very extraordinary measure. As E. M. Forster said after her death, 'She liked writing with an intensity which few writers have attained or even desired'.[1] Writing was not an addition to her life but its foundation. It was essential to the integrity of her personality. Without it she would have been quite lost. Her writer-self was like a conductor who kept, not always but for the most part, all her other selves in order. So the story of her life as a writer intersects at innumerable points with the stories of her mental health and her breakdowns, of the sexual abuse to which she was subjected as a child and then again as a young woman, of her passions, loves and marriage, of the traumas she suffered when so many of the people on whom she depended died, of her friendships and social life as a member of the Bloomsbury Group, and of her convictions as a feminist and critic of society. Nevertheless, I have tried to bring her life as a professional writer and the story of her career into focus. I have given particular emphasis to her life as an author and publisher, and to the publication history of her work. I have described the family and cultural conditions which both obstructed her career and yet eventually made it possible. I have emphasised the unusual degree of control over the production and publication of her own work which she exercised as a consequence of owning her own press. I have examined the sales of her books and her income, and have charted her very slow progress to success in terms of money and reputation. In a word, I have told the story of the material and psychological obstacles and rewards of her life as a writer. It is a way of looking at a writer's life which she herself pioneered in *A Room of One's Own*.

In addition, however, I have emphasised that the story of her work was also a story of a series of *choices*, choices about how to write, and specifically choices of experimental narrative forms. For perhaps the most remarkable feature of her work is that, though she has a recognisable style of sentence which we find in all her writing, in other respects her work constantly changed. She moved from one experiment to another, in both fiction and non-fiction. Her work is astonishing in its formal variety and inventiveness. Not only did she not write the same book twice, she did not even write the same *kind* of book twice. A study needs to be written on the subject of Virginia Woolf's narrators. It would trace in detail the different narrative techniques and modes of representing consciousness and life stories which she developed from *The Voyage Out* in 1915 to *Between the Acts* in 1941, both in her fiction but also in her autobiographical work, her biographies, her essays and polemical books and diaries. The present book can only sketch the main lines of that particular inquiry. Phyllis Rose has written that, '*Every choice of form makes a statement about the way life is*'.[2] I emphasise this because I have chosen to tell the story of Woolf's literary life as the story of her choices of form, and consequently of her many implicit statements about what life is. What does it mean that she chose a new form for every book that she wrote and never settled on one statement about the way life is? I think she constantly held in mind different ways of thinking about what life is, and needed ever new techniques in order to give voice to them all. She invented many different forms, and each was like a container within which could be held in suspension a variety of different statements about what life is, in constant agitated motion.

Everything about Virginia Woolf was unstable. Nothing was ever settled. Even her most deeply felt and apparently unchanging opinions, for example about women's lives and men's power, sometimes gave way to their opposites, or at least to a different perspective. For example, *A Room of One's Own*, a book about the need to write as a woman, finishes with a celebration of androgyny, and with her myth of herself as a manly-woman writer. In her characters' minds meanings assemble at moments of insight, but then break up again as life rushes on. There is nothing solid that one can hold onto, there is no discovery which one can point to and say 'This is it' (D III, 27 February 1926). The movement towards integration, meaning and belief is always counterbalanced by a movement towards disintegration and scepticism. Trust searches for a resting place. It never settles on one ground for long.

The story of her choices and experiments in form, which tells of her unwillingness to settle for any final statement as to what life is, at the same time reflects her lack of any stable definition as to who she was herself. Her works, she said, created a series of fictional identities for herself, 'each one accumulates a little of the fictitious V. W. whom I carry like a mask about the world' (D V, 28 July 1940). We might say that her writing was a series of experiments in partial self-definition. To borrow again from Phyllis Rose, her life story does not follow the standard plot of organic development and consolidation of character, culminating in a stable, final identity. She never ceased to use her writing as a way of experimenting with different selves, trying out successively, for example, the naive and sexually damaged Rachel Vinrace, the 'unwomanly' artist Lily Briscoe and the eccentric solitary Miss La Trobe. According to this way of thinking about identity, life involves a 'series of crucial adjustments and self-definitions'. The self is made, unmade and remade through adult life in a series of tentative, temporary creations.[3] The identity which Virginia Woolf clung to most constantly was that of a writer, though this itself went through different interpretations, different views about the values and purposes served by a writer's life. I come back again and again in this book to the question as to what she herself understood her purposes as a writer to be. Why write? It is after all not the most obvious way of spending a life. Why write, as Virginia Woolf did, obsessively, passionately, as if her life depended on it? What did she herself think her motivations and her purposes were? In her own eyes, what values did her art serve?

I do not believe that there is any single answer to these questions. I do not think that Virginia Woolf's understanding of her own life was either singular or coherent. At different times she emphasised different ways of thinking about her projects as a writer. In some cases these comfortably co-existed, but in others she was at war with herself. Her story is one of self-contestation. She used her fiction, and her essays, to create different partial self-portraits and different fables or accounts of what it was that she was attempting to do. In one famous statement she talked about the delight of using writing to bring 'the severed parts together' (MB 72). She had the idea that people do not have single selves. We are multiple, dispersed across many different zones of our being. We want, sometimes very painfully, to bring our parts into coherent relation with each other and in some moments of peace can feel that we have achieved this. But in her novels, as I have already said, moments of integration are always balanced by moments of disintegration. There is no final settlement, except death. Virginia Woolf's lack of coherence, in this sense, was not a failure but was her great strength. She resisted the temptation to make a final statement about life, about what it is to be a person, except the statement that to be a person is always to be riven inwardly by divisions and differences. The partial settlements that we make, and which we call 'character', are always provisional. Her fictions have neither characters nor endings, in the traditional senses of these things. This is because the point of her writing was not to resolve contradictions but to contain them and display them. Her integrity as an artist can be seen in her adoption of inconclusiveness as a principle. As she said when writing about the inconclusiveness of the Russian writers she admired so much: 'It is the sense that there is no answer, that if honestly examined life presents question after question which must be left to sound on and on after the story is over in hopeless interrogation that fills us with a deep, and finally it may be with a resentful, despair' ('Modern Fiction', CE II 109).

I have therefore not promoted any one of her statements of purpose as a writer into a central explanatory principle. In particular I have given detailed reasons why her definition of the purposes of modern writing as expounded in her essay 'Modern Fiction' should not be treated as the key to her work, as it has unfortunately been treated by very many academic commentators. She was not an 'impressionist' writer or a 'stream of consciousness' writer, as she has so often been made out to be. I have tried to bring into focus successively her many different definitions of purpose and to examine the conflicts between them, as registered in the story of her temptations and her choices. Her concerns do not always pull in the same direction and the contesting parts of herself surge successively into prominence. For example, her feminism and her modernism at times work together and at other times lead her in different directions. In many places she emphasised her concern to write 'as a woman'. At other times her concern was of a more mystical or visionary nature. Or else she set herself the goal of writing about the destiny and meaning of life, or of recording and describing 'moments of being' and the 'true reality'. At yet other times her interests might be called more materialist; she takes pleasure in expressing a disenchanted view of the stupidity of nature, the alien instincts of the human body, the absurd accidents of illness and death. She wanted to find forms of fiction and non-fiction that could chart some of the invisible forces, both social and psychological, which determine the shape of our lives. She wanted to explore the dark places of psychology, the complex, unverbalised material of our inner lives, of fantasy, memory, sensation, which drove her to attempt to extend what it is possible for language to articulate. 'There is a silence in life, a perpetual deposit of experience for which action provides no proper outlet and our words no fit expression.'[4] In short, she wrote as a woman, as a psychologist, as an 'Outsider' and social critic, as a poet and as a visionary. I have wanted to keep all of these meanings of her work alive and active and to resist the tidiness and impoverishment of a single definition.

So what are the main outlines of the story of Virginia Woolf's career as a writer? Almost always, in telling her story the emphasis is placed on the period from 1925 to 1931. In these years, with her novels *Mrs Dalloway, To the Lighthouse* and *The Waves*, she established her reputation as a serious experimental novelist to be reckoned with. At the same time she found a wider audience with *The Common Reader, Orlando* and *A Room of One's Own*. She became famous and financially successful. Before these years she was an apprentice, and after them her work went into a decline, it is said, with time wasted on unfinished or unsatisfactory works, culminating in the final, ambiguously valued work *Between the Acts*.

While not wishing to minimise the importance of the books of this middle period of her life, I have wanted to tell her story so as to place the emphasis elsewhere. I have tried to give some prominence to some of her other achievements, to other books, however unfinished or unresolved they may have been. In the last years of her life, when she herself tried to understand the value of and limitations of her achievements as a writer (in 'A Sketch of the Past'), she did so in terms of the categories of 'being' and 'non-being'. Her strengths, she thought, were in putting moments of being into words. She was less successful when it came to conveying non-being. However, of all her works, I myself value most highly those in which, against the grain, non-being is given its due. They are the works in which she escapes most from the obsessive tidiness and over-control of that triumphant trio of modernist novels, with their Bloomsbury aspiration to significant form. They are those in which her formal ingenuity gives way to a

less elegant, more riotous composition, in which greater prominence is given to social criticism and material reality. The works I
have in mind are those in which she most strongly resists the
temptation to be consequential. I have tried to bring these other
works more into the light; for example, that rhapsody of disconnection, *Jacob's Room*, which is an anti-war novel; *The Years* with its
aesthetics of interruption; *Between the Acts*, with its emphasis on
dispersal and on 'orts, scraps and fragments'. I have also wanted
to highlight some of her non-fiction, in particular 'A Sketch of the
Past', in which self-composition battles with self-doubt and under-
mines the conventions of autobiographic writing, and the profuse
Diary, in which we read the poetry of everyday life.

1

1882–1903: Virginia Stephen Becomes a Writer

'I cannot remember a time when Virginia did not mean to be a writer.'
(Vanessa Bell)[1]

Adeline Virginia Stephen was born on 25 January 1882. However far back in her life we look, we find that she was already a writer. She did not choose to write in the same way that others might choose to lay bricks or to become doctors. Writing, and specifically the writing of fictions, was already, even when she was very young, essential to her way of being, with her family and in the world. Long before it became a career, writing was already an essential part of her identity, of her sense of self. In her adult life it became a vital necessity, without which she would fall to pieces; the integrity of her personality depended upon it.

At the age of five she told a story to her father every night. This initiated a tradition of communal family story-telling. She made up a serial story for her brothers and sisters. She had, and never lost, an unusually fertile narrative imagination. She concocted ever more fanciful and outrageous tales about the Dilke family next door. All her life she was alarmingly liable to launch into extravagant narratives, accompanied by wild hoots of laughter, whether to entertain her niece and nephews or at the dinner table with friends. It was hilarious fun, but also dangerous. As her nephew explained, her mind had an accelerator but no brakes.

She began to write down her stories for *The Hyde Park Gate News*, a 'newspaper' which the Stephen children (but mostly Virginia) produced weekly for their parents, between 1891 and 1895. It contained family news and drawings by Vanessa as well as Virginia's stories. The writing mattered to her, both as an offering to her parents but also, in a very unchildlike way, as a craft that she wanted to master. In her late fifties she was puzzled about her 'concern for the art of writing', by which she meant her meticulous care for detail, and she recalled that she had had it even as a child.

1

The art of writing has, she wrote in her diary, 'been absorbing ever since I was a little creature, scribbling a story in the manner of Hawthorne on the green plush sofa in the drawing room at St Ives while the grown ups dined' (D V, 19 December 1938).

In a letter to his wife of July 1893 Leslie Stephen said: 'Yesterday I discussed George II with Ginia . . . She takes in a great deal & will really be an author in time'.[2] Virginia was eleven years old, and it seemed already to be established that she would be a writer. Certainly, her stories in the *Hyde Park Gate News* are remarkable in their narrative skill, vocabulary, ingenuity and charm. 'A Cockney's Farming Experience' (1892) tells of a farmer's misadventures. The plotting is nicely managed, there is some entertaining mimicry of voices, including lower-class servant's voices, and it is very funny. For example, the hero's carthorse breaks his gold-handled cane.

> I tried not to let my wife know of the little episode of the former evening. She soon found out however and scolded me unmercifully for breaking 'the only thing by which any one could know I was a gentleman.' I replied only by a look of scorn which I thought would answer as well as my most indignant repartees. But Harriet only said 'What are you squinting like a sick rabbit for.' I said nothing but stalked out of the room.[3]

The scene of this precocious fabulation was a family home which was, even by Victorian standards, an unusually intense emotional hothouse. The tall building, squeezed into its narrow site in Hyde Park Gate, housed Virginia's parents Leslie and Julia Stephen, eight children (four of them from previous marriages) and numerous servants. It was cramped, dark, saturated with family history, a maze of spaces, with each of which ludicrous or fearful stories were associated. There was a servants' sitting room in the basement, dark, as if under water, green light shining through the leaves that covered the window, 'a dark, insanitary place for seven maids to live in'.[4] There was a wood cupboard where the children might be startled by lurking wild cats. In the living rooms upstairs, gloomily furnished in black and dark red plush, the girls later had to entertain visitors at tea. Half-brother George Duckworth would look teenaged Virginia up and down as if she were a horse, snort in disgust at her home-made dress and angrily order her to go and take it off. In the hall there was pinned over a fire-place the message: 'What is it to be a gentleman? It is to be tender to women, chivalrous to servants'. On the first floor was the parents' bedroom. This, said Virginia, was 'the sexual centre, the birth centre, the death centre of the house'.[5] In it she was conceived and born. In it her mother died when she was thirteen. She visited her mother as she was dying and her mother said, 'Hold yourself straight, my little Goat'. The origin of this nickname seems to have been Virginia's uncontrollable rages, which her sister and brothers liked to encourage and were able to trigger for their entertainment. Entering her parents' bedroom to see her mother's body for the last time she saw the ghostly figure of a man at her mother's bedside. In this same room some years later she nursed her father through the long illness of which he died in 1904.

There were three higher storeys to the house. On one lived the three Duckworth children, George, Gerald and Stella. Above them lived the Stephen children, Thoby, Vanessa, Virginia and Adrian. Above that were the servants' bedrooms and, most important, Leslie Stephen's study, completely lined with books. Somewhere in the upper reaches of the house lived Laura, daughter of Leslie Stephen's first marriage, an unfortunate girl who was so handicapped in her mind that she was treated as an idiot and eventually sent away to a home. Into Virginia's bedroom, for many years after her mother died, George would creep at night to subject her to some unknown degree of greatly damaging sexual abuse. Her other half-brother Gerald had already interfered with her sexually when she was only six.

The house was full of appalling disturbance. The family was visited by the tragic J. K. Stephen, known as Jem. He was Leslie's favorite nephew, a handsome, talented boy who was well launched upon a dazzling career at Cambridge when he injured his head and became deranged. Virginia remembered him rushing into the nursery and lunging at a loaf of bread with his sword-stick. He became wild, manic, depressed. He is said to have pursued Stella Duckworth. He was eventually forcibly confined to an asylum.

Later, Jack Hills courted Stella Duckworth (this started at St Ives and was, said Virginia, her first acquaintance with passionate love) and then, after a stormy engagement (the storms were the outrageous furies of Leslie Stephen who raged against being abandoned by his 'housekeeper' Stella) they married and moved to a house just up the street. After no more than a few months Stella took ill and died.

This was the context of the young Virginia's early years as a writer: she lived in an atmosphere of chronic emotional turbulance. She was sexually abused, traumatised by the loss of her mother and her half-sister, and acquainted with many varieties of mental disturbance and insanity. The house contained all of this emotional intensity, each episode marking its own part of the house. It became a metaphor for the separation of parts, the dis-integration of life into disconnected fragments. A person would undergo metamorphoses, and be required to play different parts, in going from one room to another. There was no one room in which the parts came together, made sense of each other. Upstairs, George was a sexual hog, wallowing in his emotional excess ('Kiss me, kiss me, you beloved' he would cry), while downstairs he was the very model of social decorum, pursuing his lazy career as a courtier and a snob. Up in the study Leslie was a cool, radical sceptic, reasoning his way through the intricacies of utilitarian theory and quietly supporting Virginia's efforts to educate herself among his books. But downstairs, when Julia died, he would act out his melodramatically inflated grief. He would outrage his daughters by his displays of anger over the weekly accounts. Yet at other times, at tea with visitors, he could be charming and liked to flirt with the women. Virginia was forced to play many parts – a hostess, a debutante, a nurse, a student. Vanessa was an art student (she refused to play along with George's efforts to launch her into society) and a housekeeper. Different parts, different worlds, and between them Virginia was 'quite unable to make any connection' (MB 137). She could make nothing coherent of all this. Moreover, the intense emotions which endlessly surged up within this family scene were insupportable and were mostly rapidly repressed – grief, anger, love, loathing, fear, all tangled up into incomprehensible and destabilising knots. Writing was the only place where things could be first disentangled into intelligible threads of feeling and secondly made to hold together into a coherent story of her life. There was be an unusually intimate relationship between her life, especially this early family life, and her writing, in which she made a lifelong effort 'to put the severed parts together' (MB 72).

Becoming a person, developing a personality, is a long hard process which we all have to attempt, some of us in conditions less favorable than others. To grow up involves developing structures of personality that allow desire to coexist with reality within the

contingencies of adult life. There are many obstacles which prevent this happening smoothly but also many cunning ways around
them for those who have the resources to find them out. The
obstacles in the path of the infant Virginia Stephen were formi-
dable, almost insurmountable. Most damaging was the fact that
people on whom she most depended for emotional support, for
love and recognition, died – in 1895 her mother, in 1897 her
half-sister Stella, in 1904 her father and in 1906 her favorite brother
Thoby. Her adult life was in the end possible because there were
two people to whom she turned for mothering who were able to
provide it for her over thirty years, her sister Vanessa and her
husband Leonard Woolf. Perhaps as damaging for her was the
sexual abuse she received at the hands of her half-brothers which,
as she later said, spoiled her life before it had begun. Of all the
means of overcoming these terrible obstacles to stable adulthood,
the one which became the most crucial was of course writing. We
will see how at various crucial stages the story of her career has to
be told as the story of her lifelong attempt to build, preserve,
modify or hold together her identity, her personality.

When Virginia Stephen was thirteen her mother died. We know
that until she was in her forties she was haunted by her dead
mother. She would talk with her every day, would feel her presence with her constantly. 'The presence of my mother obsessed
me. I could hear her voice, see her, imagine what she would do or
say as I went about my day's doings . . . She obsessed me, in spite
of the fact that she died when I was thirteen, until I was forty-four'
(MB 80). She reduced the force of this obsession by writing *To the
Lighthouse*. In this novel Julia Stephen is transfigured by her
daughter's imagination thirty years after her death and after thirty
years of uninterrupted and unfinished conversation with her. This
book stands between us and the other sources of information
about Julia Stephen and makes it quite hard to imagine her differently. She was famous for her beauty. Photographs of her as a
young woman show how attractive she was, though perhaps in a
style that is quite difficult for modern taste to feel comfortable
with.[6] She is portrayed as passive and soulful, never as intelligent
or active or competent. She is never shown laughing, or even
smiling. She gazes off into another world. The photographer
wanted each picture to show the soul shining through the face,
and in her conception Julia's soul was deeply melancholy, and is
turned towards a higher realm, though her soulfulness was not of

an orthodox religious kind, for after the death of her first husband she became 'the most positive of disbelievers' (MB 32). Her face expresses also that favorite Victorian form of love, which was self-sacrificing devotion to duty. The adult Virginia, for whom these conceptions and values were the targets of a lifetime's battle, who saw the angelic woman as the deadly enemy of the living individual woman writer, could hardly have viewed these images of her mother without ambivalence, without a confusing and painful mixture of needy love and furious rejection. Photographs of Julia Stephen at the time of Virginia's childhood show that by this time she had become a more exhausted woman. She was now not so much soulful as severe, almost frightening. Her face is settled into permanent unsmiling gloom. She is worn and thin. Her eyes are hollowed out. Her hair is now pulled back very tightly around her head as if she is inviting us to see the skull beneath the skin.

She was in some ways a very old-fashioned woman. She was against women's suffrage and against education for women. In the Stephen family her views on the appropriate upbringing for a girl prevailed over those of her husband. In his opinion, failing to educate young women was to waste their lives. 'I hate to see so many women's lives wasted simply because they have not been trained well enough.' To which Julia's reply was that 'To serve is the fulfilment of woman's highest nature'.[7] If women should be trained, then it should be for service. When she agreed to marry Leslie Stephen she insisted that she should carry on the charitable work to which she had devoted so much of her life as a widow. She visited the poor and the sick, often staying away from home to tend to them. She wrote a short booklet on the management of the sick room. She was, more than anything else, busy. Apart from the huge demands that she placed on herself nursing the sick, she ran the large Stephen household with all those children, servants and guests. She comes across as a rather grim and joyless figure and to the infant Virginia she must have seemed rather inaccessible.

She died young, aged 48. *Hyde Park Gate News* was heard of no more. Virginia suffered her first breakdown. She was taken in hand by Stella who became her surrogate mother and they went together to visit the sick and the dying, to hospitals and work-houses. Virginia became pathologically shy and could not bear to be with people. If required to speak she would become extremely flushed, like a scarlet sweet pea according to her sister. In these two years after her mother's death, for the only time in her entire life, she lost the will to write. 'I was terrified of people. Used to turn red if spoken to. Used to sit up in my room raging – at father, at George. And read and read and read. But I never wrote. For two years I never wrote. The desire left me; which I have had all my life, with that two year break.'[8]

Virginia was placed under the medical supervision of one Dr Savage, and his view of the matter was that a pubescent girl could not spare resources for intellectual activity.[9] She would risk starving her reproductive parts of vital nutrients and hence risk a failure to become a real woman. So he made an attempt, with the cooperation of the family, to resocialise Virginia into a more conventional model of a young woman. Her father deprived her of her lessons and bought her gardening tools. She became anorectic. She lost the will to write. When she emerged from this two year hiatus it was with her rejection of her mother's views on femininity strengthened; her determination to be a writer was confirmed.

Leslie Stephen was already in his fiftieth year when Virginia was born. For her to choose to be a writer was to choose to be like him. He was an unorthodox Victorian, sceptical of many of the religious and social doctrines of the age. He is remembered now mainly for his work on the intellectual history of the eighteenth century and, above all, for his work as editor of that great Victorian edifice, the *Dictionary of National Biography*. He was a renowned but privately disappointed man. He had wanted to make a significant contribution to philosophy and thereby (for philosophy was then still thought to have such powers) to the cultural and moral life of his age. This he never achieved and he had by his late middle age, when Virginia knew him, settled for an intellectual role that was managerial rather than creative. But he was an attractive figure to many of his progressive contemporaries for he was a man of integrity (he had given up a career at Cambridge University rather than dishonestly seek ordination in the Anglican Church), and an unworldly man, quite uninterested in social elevation and reward. He was a pioneering Alpinist and even into old age would find pleasure in walking vast distances. He liked to take on challenges that were strenuous and invigorating, that would call on his 'manly' qualities, though he also tended to be brought down by them. Both he and his father before him went through crises severe enough to be called mental breakdowns. His oldest son Thoby once, weakened by influenza, threw himself from a window in his delirium. To some degree Virginia's later episodes of mental ill-health could be seen as being in the family tradition. Leslie Stephen liked to think big – big mountains, a big family, an extremely big *Dictionary* (it reached an amazing 65 volumes by the time of its completion in 1903). If he saw something big he wanted to control it, to be master of it. He suffered terrible anxiety whenever this proved difficult to achieve. If things seemed to be getting out of his grasp he would rage with a dreadful, mad anger or else collapse into impotent self-disgust. He raged at his contributors and subordinates when he was editor of the *Cornhill Magazine*, and at his daughter Vanessa when she dealt with the family's weekly accounts. He raged at his sister-in-law, Anne Thackeray, whose life of serene chaos defied all his attempts at control. He loved to exercise power. He was a patriarch. He related to women by infantilising them and disciplining them like naughty children, or by worshipping them as angels in his house.

He was a typically Victorian amalgam of bluster and panic, of self-assertion and collapse. He swung between thinking that he was intellectually master of the universe and horribly out of his depth. His own strong emotions sometimes threatened to get the better of him and he was particularly rigidly determined not to give in to sexual lust or to horror at the human condition. To allow the latter is to be 'morbid' and this is the opposite of 'manly' though 'Stephen sometimes seems to use the word to mean almost any emotion not kept rigidly in control'.[10] One can understand his private feelings of failure for his life combined a public image of 'intellectual power under perfect control',[11] with a private reality of serious mental breakdown, an immature, almost vampirish relationship with his wife after her death and a more or less total incomprehension of the needs of his rebellious daughters.

If Leslie Stephen's way with insubordinate females was to turn them into naughty children, Virginia Woolf's way with difficult adults was to turn them into animals (was her mother the only person on whom she failed to perform this rhetorical trick?) Towards the end of her life, by which time her ambivalent feelings were no longer so confusing to her, she composed a portrait of her father and his work. 'I, at 15, was a nervous, gibbering, little monkey, always spitting or cracking a nut . . . he was the pacing, dangerous, morose lion; a lion who was sulky and angry and injured; and suddenly ferocious, and then very humble, and then majestic; and then lying dusty and fly pestered in a corner of the cage.'[12] As for his work, her estimation of it in this same sketch is surely very accurate.

> I find not a subtle mind; not an imaginative mind. But a strong mind; a healthy out of door, moor striding mind; an impatient limited mind; a conventional mind entirely accepting his own standard of what is honest, what is moral, without a shadow of doubt accepting this is a good man; that is a good woman; I get a sense of Leslie Stephen the muscular agnostic; cheery; hearty; always cracking up sense and manliness; and crying down sentiment and vagueness. . . .[13]

He presented an ambiguous model for his daughter as she aspired to a career as a woman of letters. There were positive points – his courage, outspokenness and honesty. On the other hand, in some respects he was hopelessly conventional. Most unattractive to his daughter must have been his certainty, his inability to doubt most of what he believed in, and his patriarchal attitudes. Virginia launched herself into her career simultaneously trying to imitate him and rebelling against much of what he stood for. She knew that she could never have become a professional writer as long as he lived, so strong was his power to silence her (D III, 28 November 1928).

What contribution did Leslie Stephen make to his daughter's preparation for her literary career? The question is much debated. His biographer claims that he decided that she was to be his literary heir and set about educating her accordingly in biography and history. Yet he withheld from her the university education that he and his sons had all enjoyed, and she resented this all her life. He liked her to read in his library, and he read her essays and chatted with her about them. He was supportive and encouraging. So she was both unworthy of university and yet worthy of patriarchal education. Almost certainly he had no comprehension at all of the confusing, contradictory meanings that his regime offered his daughter, who was invited to internalise simultaneously the ideals of 'angel in the house' and independent professional writer, a mix of self-denial and self-assertion that Virginia found unbalancing all her life. In the years after her mother died, she seems to have lost her affectionate, tolerant relationship with her father. When she picked up her education and her writing again from 1897 it seems to have been without very much active guidance or help from him.

Her relationship with him and his contribution to her training in those last six years before he died is much disputed. One scholar sums it up thus: 'Woolf's education had been hit or miss and had prepared her for little more than ladylike reviews of ephemeral novels which, she wryly noted, "don't take much brains"'.[14]

She attended lectures on Greek and history at King's College, London. Later Janet Case, who was to become an important friend and an ally against George Duckworth, gave her Greek lessons. Most importantly, in 1897 she started to write again. She wrote a series of diaries and essays. Later she described both these essays and some of her reading.

> It was the Elizabethan prose writers I loved first & most wildly, stirred by Hakluyt, which father lugged home for me – I think of it with some sentiment – father tramping over the Library with his little girl sitting at H[yde] P[ark] G[ate] in mind. He must have been 65; I 15 or 16, then . . . I used to read it & dream of those obscure adventurers, & no doubt practised their style in my copy books. I was then writing a long picturesque essay upon the Christian religion, I think; called Religio Laici, I believe, proving that man has need of a God; but the God was described in process of change; & I also wrote a history of Women; & a history of my own family – all very longwinded & El[izabe]than in style. (D III, 8 December 1929)

In her 1897 diary she made a detailed note of the books she was reading. It is a long and very impressive list.[15] What is remarkable, apart from the sophistication of reading and writing for an 'uneducated' 15-year-old, is that her thinking settled so early onto themes which were to concern her throughout her life: attempts to think unconventionally about religion, the history of women and the history of her own family. Perhaps it is not surprising that this young woman, uncertain of her identity, unsure about just what it is possible for a woman to be and therefore uncertain about the possibilities for her own life, should turn to these fields of speculation. She was using reading and writing as her laboratory and her workshop, in which to investigate what women have been and so to find out how she might become what she knew she wanted to be, a writer.

If she were to reject her mother's views about what a woman should be and aim to earn a living as a writer, then there were some role models she could look to in her own family. Researching her family's history she would have studied the life of Julia Margaret Cameron (1815–79), the photographer who had an important place in the family story not only as the one who had preserved in photographs her mother's beauty but as a remarkable character in her own right. Virginia Woolf later published as essay about her and gave her a place as one of the main characters in her play *Freshwater*.[16] She was a wonderfully eccentric woman whose life departed dramatically from the conventionally accepted scripts for women's lives at that time. She began her successful career as a photographer at the age of fifty. She must have been a heartening reminder for the young Virginia Stephen of those *other* Victorian values, unconventionality, eccentricity and determination, in the pursuit of her chosen art.

Equally unconventional was Aunt Anny (Anne Thackeray, later Lady Ritchie, 1837–1919). She was the daughter of the novelist Thackeray and sister of Leslie Stephen's first wife. She acted as her famous father's secretary and wrote biographical introductions to his works. She became a professional writer herself and wrote many essays and eight novels. Both Stephen and Thackeray circles were literary and Virginia Stephen was as a young girl brought up among successful men and women in a culture in which writing was a normal activity. However, Aunt Anny may herself have been a confusing model for the adolescent Virginia, adding to all the doubts and ambiguities about what was possible for a woman which her parents had created in her mind. For she was treated in a patronising way by Leslie Stephen, who was convinced that she had very feeble intelligence and that her works were not worth a great deal. She was, at least in family lore, a scatter-brained woman given to great good humour and cheerful exaggeration, traits which sent Leslie Stephen into a fury (just as they do Mr Ramsay in *To the Lighthouse*). She was a familiar face on the family scene when Virginia was young. She was a support to the children when Julia Stephen died and again was a great help to Virginia when her father was ill and in the years after his death. Leslie Stephen was exasperated and frightened by her uncontrollable spending, her wild talk and her muddle. She did finally win his respect and affection. She scandalised everyone by marrying Richmond Ritchie who was both her cousin and seventeen years her junior. Virginia might have found her an off-putting example of the difficulty a woman writer might have in being taken seriously by the patriarchs. Yet she came to appreciate her and to value her highly. She is the model for the delightful Mrs Hilbery in *Night and Day* and the subject of Woolf's very affectionate essay of 1924, 'The Enchanted Organ' (E III). Her example helped to define for Woolf the value of the independent woman, the Outsider, who could refuse society's definitions and triumph over the condescension of powerful men.

2
1904–1909: Journalist

'I dont in the least want Mrs L's candid criticism; I want her cheque!'
(L I, 11 November 1904)

On 28 November 1928 Woolf wrote in her diary: 'Father's birthday. He would have been 96, yes, today; & could have been 96, like other people one has known; but mercifully was not. His life would have entirely ended mine. What would have happened? No writing, no books; – inconceivable'. It is true that it was his death that made her birth as a professional writer possible. He died in February 1904. Until then his daughter had been an inexperienced student with no defined role in the world and no immediate hope of achieving anything. By the end of that year she was a published journalist, an apprentice, but now earning money and determined to make a career for herself as a woman of letters.

She was also within a year established with her sister and brothers in Bloomsbury. They flew as fast as they possibly could from the dark, crowded Victorian house in Kensington and all that it stood for. They broke with the family aesthetic style. Their Bloomsbury apartments would have white walls and airy open rooms. They were also liberated from the Duckworth brothers and their unwanted attentions. The changes in the lives of the Stephen sisters in the course of this one year were quite remarkable. For Virginia the transition was a testing one. She was much harder hit by her father's death than was her sister.

She went to stay with Violet Dickinson (1865–1948), who was to be for some years Virginia's closest friend, apart from her sister. They travelled together and there was a large correspondence. She suffered a terrible breakdown and Violet arranged for three nurses to attend her. This was the year of which her biographer said that 'all that summer she was mad'. She threw herself from a window. She listened to the birds speaking to her in Greek and to the mad King George shouting obscenities from behind a bush. Virginia's attitude to her sister became insupportable, becoming suspicious and angry and filled with hatred. Violet Dickinson, seventeen years older than Virginia, a high-spirited woman, full of vitality and fun though sometimes rather conventional by Stephen standards, played an essential motherly role. More than any other person it was Violet Dickinson who smoothed Virginia's way into her profession.

In 1904 Virginia stayed in Cambridge with another woman who had a deep influence on her life, helping her through this hard year and more generally providing her from within her own family with another model of the woman author. This was her father's sister Caroline Emelia Stephen (1834–1909). She had had tense relations with her brother for their values and ways of thinking were entirely different. He disparaged her 'little books' and thought her an unappealing failure. She pitied his lack of imagination and lack of natural piety. She dedicated her life to the service of others, remained unmarried and became a significant writer on Quaker religious thought. She built and ran homes for the servant class, the Hereford Houses, in Chelsea, London in 1877, and in this became a model for Eleanor Pargiter in *The Years*. In later years she established herself in a solitary life in her cottage, known as 'The Porch', in Cambridge, where she wrote books that were of some importance in the Quaker tradition, *Quaker Strongholds* (1890) and *The Light Arising: Thoughts on the Central Radiance* (1908).

When Virginia stayed with her aunt in 1904 there were at first difficulties between them. They had utterly different feelings about Leslie Stephen and his death. 'I cant tell you how she maddens me when she begins to talk about Father' (L I, 24 October 1904). Virginia, who had nursed him through his final illness and who had come to have great affection for him towards the end of his life, was already angry with Vanessa, who regarded their father's death as unambiguously liberating. Caroline Stephen was also unable to summon up much by way of regret for his passing, partly because she had not much liked him, but more perhaps because she regarded death in a positive light, as a release from our suffering bodily state. So in this year Virginia's descriptions of her aunt were intolerant and even cruel. 'She is soporific, and leisurely to an excess, and my desire begins to be to blow her up with gunpowder, and see what would happen! . . . I hear the Quaker trumpeting like an escaped elephant on the stairs, which means that it is near lunchtime' (L I, 22 October 1904).

While staying with 'the Nun' and partly in order to disprove her views about Leslie Stephen, Virginia wrote a memoir on him for his biographer, F. W. Maitland ('Impressions of Sir Leslie Stephen', E I). Although this was not eventually published until 1906, it was her first piece of writing successfully written for publication. Her writing career thus opened as it was to go on, with a very intimate relation between her writing and deep and difficult feelings, as if through writing she attempted to put her feelings in order. In the course of writing this memoir she went through correspondence between her father and mother which was judged to be too private for her biographer to read. She re-read these very same letters again in the last year of her life, at a time when she was again writing about her father and mother (in 'A Sketch of the Past'). It is as if her entire writing career were enclosed by these returns to her parents, between her first and her last attempts to write them into some satisfactory shape. In her entire life as a writer she never really escaped from their embrace.

As time went by, Virginia's feelings about her father became less painful. She came to estimate Caroline Stephen much more highly and to feel more affection for her. There were many things about her life which appealed to her, which she could incorporate into her growing understanding of the history of women's lives and the importance of the differences between men's and women's values. For one thing, it is significant that Caroline Stephen overturned received opinions with such serenity. Also she came to feel very positively about her solitude. Perceived by society as a lonely spinster, she was in her own eyes an autonomous, free spirit. The trap of loneliness could be transformed into a space for creativity, a room of one's own. In these years, Virginia Stephen was often quite isolated and without much prospect of marriage. Her aunt enabled her to contemplate the possibility of being a woman without being married, of seeing virginity lived as inviolability rather than as failure.

Caroline Stephen represented, as Anne Thackeray had done, the positive spirit of unconventionality. She rejected the masculine voice, Leslie Stephen's for example, as an over-confident, aggressive voice, a preaching voice. As a Quaker, she was against preaching and one remembers her when reading Virginia Woolf's later work, especially *Three Guineas*, in which 'preaching' becomes a general figure for everything that she loathed about a certain kind of religion and politics. Caroline Stephen was a visionary. She heard voices. The two women shared so much that it is not surprising that within a few years they had established a very close relationship. In 1906 Virginia wrote to her friend Madge Vaughan:

> We talked for some 9 hours; and she poured forth all her spiritual experiences, and then descended and became a very wise and witty old lady. I never knew anyone with such a collection of stories . . . natural or supernatural. All her life she has been listening to inner voices, and talking with spirits; and she is like a person who sees ghosts, or rather disembodied souls, instead of bodies. (L I, July 1906)

Was Caroline Stephen's mysticism influential in Virginia Woolf's work? There is certainly a strong and consistent theme in Woolf's writing that is often labelled mystical, and which represents an aspiration to a vision of something greater than human reality, something unseen and eternal.[1] This is central to her writing. But it is never given by Woolf an interpretation in terms of religious doctrine. There was here, I think, a very clear difference between the ways in which these two women viewed the world.[2] Caroline Stephen's contemplation of 'things unseen and eternal' (the focus of her niece's obituary notice of her in the *Guardian*), was conceived by her in unequivocally theistic terms, terms which her niece would never accept. Caroline Stephen believed in Divine Presence, Divine Order, Divine Providence. Virginia Woolf believed that emphatically there is no God, and her soul suffered no tendency to be elevated in that direction.

> . . . the Quaker has a well worn semi religious vocabulary; left her by the late Sir James [Virginia's paternal grandfather], I think; and when she talks of chaff and grain and gold and ore, and winnowing feelings, and upward tending lives, and yielding to the light, and bearings of fruit, I slip and slide and read *no more*. (L I, 24 August 1906)

Therefore, although Caroline Stephen was undoubtedly important to Virginia Woolf, and perhaps as significant an influence on her as the more celebrated men of the Bloomsbury Group, yet there remained a very fundamental difference of perspective between them. When she died in 1909 her niece wrote an affectionate, respectful obituary (printed in E I). In what could be seen as her most important contribution to Virginia Woolf's career her Aunt Caroline left her sufficient capital to give her an income of something approaching the famous £500 a year, enough for her financial independence, a vital condition for the autonomy of the woman writer.

This then was the setting for the opening years of Virginia Woolf's career as a writer. She threw herself into the work of making a professional writer of herself with fierce determination. She was already *existentially* a writer: she could not help writing. What she needed was to learn the basics of writing as a job. This was a craft to be learned and this would involve application, concentration and, above all, practice, hour upon hour of practice, not unlike the practice that is necessary for a young musician, going again and again through the basic moves, beginning to get the feel for the different possibilities, different sentences, rhythms, genres. She needed to learn the disciplines of deadlines, polishing for publication, word length, precision and tact. For ten years she stayed on the very lowest rung of the professional ladder, publishing nothing except essays, reviews and obituaries. It was a long, hard apprenticeship. All the time she was experimenting with other, more ambitious forms of writing, trying her hand at stories, fantasy, biography and autobiography. It was a very different, far more arduous and in the end more valuable, route into a career as a writer than that travelled by those privileged young men Lytton Strachey and Clive Bell, who would later become her friends, whose careers were built on their education at Cambridge University and large amounts of unearned income.

After encouraging her and then nursing her back to health, Violet Dickinson then supplied yet another vital service: she provided a contact. She introduced her to Margaret Lyttleton, editor of the Women's Supplement of the *Guardian*, this being, says Andrew McNeillie, 'a pretty dull clerical newspaper' (E I Introduction). The *Guardian* was an unlikely place for her to start, given her atheistical heritage and the free-thinking culture of her friends. It was a weekly newspaper for High Church clergy. She sent Mrs Lyttleton an essay she had written about her holiday with her brothers and sister, and wrote to Violet Dickinson as she waited, nervously, though with a certain swagger, to hear if the world of journalism was to open up for her.

I dont think my chances are good. I dont in the least want Mrs L's candid criticism; I want her cheque! I know all about my merits and failings better than she can from the sight of one article, but it would be a great relief to know that I could make a few pence easily in this way – as our passbooks came last night, and they are greatly overdrawn. It is all the result of this idiotic illness, and I should be glad to write something which would pay for small extras. I honestly think I can write better stuff than that wretched article you sent me. Why on earth does she take such trash? – But there is a knack of writing for newspapers which has to be learnt, and is quite independent of literary merits. (L I, 11 November 1904)

Mrs Lyttleton responded by inviting Virginia to write an article of 1500 words for the Women's Supplement. She submitted 'Haworth, November, 1904', written she claimed in less than two hours while she was staying with her friend Madge Vaughan in Giggleswick, and a review of a novel, 'The Son of Royal Langbrith'. This latter was to be her first publication (4 December 1904) and the essay followed soon after (21 December 1904) (both in E I). They were both published anonymously, as was everything she wrote for many years, which, given the fears about exposure that she suffered, must have made these apprentice years easier for her. She was twenty-two years old and her career had begun.

As an apprentice essayist Virginia Stephen had no specialised education to call upon. She had no training in any discipline in the modern sense – no introduction to the conceptual foundations of any field of scholarship, no knowledge of methods of research. On the other hand she was unusually widely read, in literature, history and biography. She could write essays about almost anything. She also rapidly extended her knowledge through travel. Before her father's death she had hardly travelled at all. By 1909 she had seen much of Europe. She was in Italy in 1904. In subsequent years she visited France, Germany, Spain and Greece. She went to Constantinople, a very ambitious trip for that time. She went to Bayreuth to hear Wagner and to Dresden to visit galleries. She went on a boat trip to Portugal with her brother Adrian, an experience that she drew upon in *The Voyage Out*. As she travelled she wrote, mostly unpublished travel journals, some like 'A Dialogue Upon Mount Pentelicus' (1906)[3] important experimental stories containing ideas that were important to her later work. She established a habit that was to last through her life, of constant writing, as if she could not absorb an experience until it was transcribed on paper. Some of her work, on an extraordinary range of topics, was published; for example, 'An Andalusian Inn' in the *Guardian*, 'Impressions at Bayreuth' and 'The Opera' (a preview of the forthcoming season at Covent Garden) in *The Times*. Her regular output of essays and reviews covered history, memoirs and volumes of letters as well as literature. In 1909 she even wrote a review of a cookery book.

If she looked ahead to a time when she might write something more ambitious, it was not yet clear just what that might be. For two years she taught classes at Morley College, an adult education college in south London, in history and then in essay composition. 'By the way', she wrote to Violet Dickinson, 'I am going to write history one of these days. . . . I always did love it; if I could find the bit I want' (L I, May 1905). Her Aunt Caroline tried to persuade her to write a 'solid historical work' (L I, 11 December 1904).

She wrote thirty essays for the *Guardian* through 1905–6. She hunted for other outlets, and had some, temporary, success with *Academy and Literature* in 1905–6, *The Speaker* in 1906 and the *Cornhill* in 1908. This latter, a prestigious magazine of which her father had been editor from 1871–82, offered her the possibility of writing longer, signed articles. By far the most important of her new contacts was that with Bruce Richmond, editor of the *Times Literary Supplement*. With him she established a professional relationship that was to last, with only a few periods of interruption, until his retirement in 1938. He was her main professional teacher in journalism, believing in her, supporting and encouraging her work through her apprentice years. In April 1905 he rejected a review she had written about the French Revolution, on the grounds that it was not written sufficiently in the academic spirit. But in order not to discourage her in these crucial early months of her career he sent her instead three books on Spain to write about. Looking back over their thirty year working relationship when he retired she wrote in her diary: 'I learnt a lot of my craft writing for him: how to compress; how to enliven; & also was made to read with a pen & notebook, seriously' (D V, 27 May 1938).

Astonishingly, in her very first year as a professional writer, she had 35 pieces published. The details of her output between 1904 and 1915 are summarised in Table 2.1. Recent research has revealed that in the four years 1905–8 she published 122 essays

TABLE 2.1   *Essays, 1904–15*

Year	number of essays published	
1904	2	both in the *Guardian*
1905	35	including 22 in the *Guardian*, 9 in the *TLS*
1906	23	including 5 in the *Guardian*, 12 in the *TLS*
1907	35	of which 34 in the *TLS*
1908	29	23 in the *TLS*, 6 in the *Cornhill*
1909	17	including 14 in the *TLS*, 2 in *The Times*
1910	4	all in *TLS*
1911	2	all in *TLS*
1912	2	all in *TLS*
1913	5	all in *TLS*
1914	0	
1915	0	

Sources: *The Essays of Virginia Woolf*, ed. Andrew McNeillie: the figures given in this table include 44 Woolf essays (the majority from 1907) which have been discovered in the *TLS* archives since the publication of E I–III (personal communication from Andrew McNeillie).

(mostly reviews), a very remarkable average, of over 30 each year.[4] From 1909 the *TLS* became the exclusive outlet for her reviews and essays (with minor exceptions) for ten years.

Between 1904 and 1909 Virginia Stephen learned what it is to write for money and to write under somebody else's orders, lessons that were to be very influential in the way that she later organised her life as a writer. She learned that the conventions of reviewing can be confining and irritating. She learned that they sometimes prevent one from writing the truth. Writing for money means obeying conventional prohibitions and rules of courtesy and this can impose a certain superficiality. She was forced to tolerate having her work altered by the men who had power over it. Her essays for the *Cornhill* suffered unnegotiated cuts and additions which led her to threaten to resign. Her review of Henry James's *The Golden Bowl* for the *Guardian* was cut and thereby, she claimed, ruined: 'It was quite good before the official eye fell upon it; now it is worthless, and doesn't in the least represent all the toil I put into it' (L I, mid-February 1905). Perhaps it is also important that in these years she read for review a constant stream of mediocre novels and became very aware of the conventionality of fiction. I mean by this not conventionality of attitude but the fact that fictions are built according to conventional rules, most of which are not visible to the ordinary reader. Fiction is a matter of artifice, and the writer is an artificer whose craft consists in the apparently effortless manipulation of rules of plotting, of character stereotypes, of happy endings and narratorial commentary. She learned that in her fiction, as in her life, conventions can be challenged and changed, but that this is harder to contemplate if you are working for somebody else and doing it to make a living.

In writing her reviews Virginia Stephen did not cultivate, even behind the mask of anonymity, a typical reviewer's voice, of authority, confidence and expertise. Her voice was, unlike her father's, not that of a patriarch. On the contrary, it was, she thought, too modest, suave and oblique (MB 129). She responded to the books she read not as a specialist but as a common reader. Her earliest reviews were rather laboured and she tended some-times to slip into an elevated Victorian diction, writing about 'exalted ends' and 'the sanctity of genius' and using such words as 'majesty' and 'noble' about prose she favoured. After some years, and particularly working for the *TLS*, she moved away from these uncertain beginnings and developed her own distinctively elegant, impressionistic and witty style. When writing about trivial books she could still be arch or supercilious, but as her essays on, for example, Gissing and Christina Rossetti show, she had learned, when her interest was engaged, to produce fine and mature work.

The essay which I most enjoy from her published output in these years is her marvellous essay on Sterne in the *TLS* in 1909 (E I 280). Her enthusiasm and excitement are obvious. She loved his oddity, his unconventionality ('one may believe that he delighted most in his wild researches into medicine, midwifery, and military engin-eering'). But most of all she loved Sterne's descriptions of the overwhelming exhilaration of writing. She recognised someone for whom writing was, as for herself, a passion, a way of being, almost a matter of being possessed. *Tristram Shandy* was, she noted, 'written at fever heat, "quaint demons grinning and clawing at his head," ideas striking him as he walked, and sending him back home at a run to secure them'. Perhaps her intensity in these passages comes from the fact that she is not only implicitly claiming kinship as a writer with Sterne, but that she is also writing against her father. His plodding judgmental prose and moralising criticism of Sterne she had read in the *Dictionary of National Biography*. Leslie Stephen made Sterne out to be a literary prostitute, with his eye too much on the market and the main chance. For his daughter, Sterne was above all someone who had experienced that very special rapture of discovering his own voice, and who could express the relief and joy of the moment when as if by magic all his experience is translated into words. With his books it is as if 'a wonderful conception, long imprisoned in the brain and delicately formed, seems to leap out, surprising and intoxicating the writer himself. He had found a key to the world. He thought he could go on like this . . . for ever, for a miracle had happened which turned all his experiences to words; to write about them was to be master of all that was in him and all that was to come'. Is she not intoxicated with this vision, with the desire that this should also happen to her? Perhaps her head had already sometimes spun in such a magic moment of illusory omnipotence, for she had by now begun to write some fiction and knew that that was above all what her life must be about.

Virginia Woolf published no fiction until 1915 but in these early years she had already begun to try her hand at short stories. In 1906 she wrote 'The Journal of Mistress Joan Martyn', an indication as much of her continuing interest in the history of women's lives as in fiction. Right from this and other early, unpublished stories her fiction was always formally experimental, as if she could not write without breaking the established formal conventions of narration and genre. This 'Journal' is an attempt to rediscover imaginatively the conditions of life of a country woman in the fifteenth century. The woman's journal is discovered by a modern woman historian. Virginia Stephen had found a way of experimenting with two quite different voices, both in the first person, within one work – that of a long dead sister and that of the modern historian of women, interested in the lives of women and more generally the lives of the obscure.[5] Some of her other early fictions were equally almost unclassifiable generically, so unconventional are they in form. 'A Dialogue upon Mount Pentelicus' (1906) is a mixture of essay, satire, travel diary and short story.[6] It tells of a comic encounter between myth-laden English public schoolboys and a monk on a mountain in Greece. 'Memoirs of a Novelist' (1909) is both a fictional biography and a meditation on biography. This was rejected by the *Cornhill* magazine and in fact Virginia

Woolf was to publish no stories until 1917, by which time she owned her own press and no longer had to suffer rejections by editors.

Even more unusual among her early experiments were a series of extravagant comic lives of her women friends. The only one of these that survives is 'Friendship's Gallery' of 1907, a joke biography of her friend Violet Dickinson. It is a fantasy, an affectionate tribute, and a celebration of women's friendships and superior natures: hence, in spirit and inspiration not unlike her later *Orlando*.[7] It narrates in wild comic vein Violet's coming-out party, describes a utopian community, a magical garden of women, and in a third section tells of the adventures of her friend transformed into a goddess on a visit to Japan. It is anarchic, ruled by the spirit of laughter and by a profound desire for the community of women. Virginia presented the work to Violet Dickinson, typed in violet ink and bound in violet leather. It was a fitting gift for Violet who, though in some ways prosaic had also, especially through her aristocratic acquaintance, a glittering fantastical side that appealed to Virginia's delight in wild story-telling.

So during these years when Virginia Stephen was learning to efficiently turn out sellable essays under the eyes of her editors, she was privately enjoying herself experimenting with any number of other kinds of writing – fiction, fantasy, biography, history. Her career, which was to be built on her astonishing formal inventiveness, was under way. One other genre is worth noting, for it was to be important in her life, and that is autobiography. In 1907–8 she wrote 'Reminiscences' (now published in MB). It is a memoir of the three most important women in her life, her mother, Stella Duckworth and her sister Vanessa. It was her first attempt to come to terms through writing with the great traumas of her youth. Perhaps because she knew that it would only be read by her very closest family, she allowed herself to enter areas where she risked dangerous self-exposure. In spite of this, it is as autobiography rather an immature piece of work. It largely sticks to conventional formalities and pieties. It is perhaps not surprising that this was the area in which she found it hardest to break with the conventions, which for this kind of writing aimed to arrive at some judicious verdict about a character, rather than to rediscover and expose the feelings of the child who experienced that person as a mother (though it is perhaps more revealing when it comes to her father). The eulogy for her mother consists of a list of prized qualities accompanied by suitably reverent authorial sentiment and illustrative anecdote. The language is Victorian ('the majesty of a nobly composed human being'). Oddly, I think a far more negative view of her mother is conveyed than in later portraits, as Mrs Ramsay or in 'Sketch of the Past'. She comes across as wilfully overcommitted, neurotically unable to make herself available in a relaxed, unhurried way to her children, over-anxious about wasting time, a person in whom a sense of duty has replaced spontaneous warmth. With the children in the schoolroom she is quick tempered, harsh in manner. We can detect, hidden away behind the official message of uncomplicated worship of a saintly woman, a powerful tide of hostility and resentment, though perhaps none of it is conscious. It is an anxious piece of writing.

These were difficult times for Virginia Stephen. In the years from 1907 to 1912 she was often more isolated and lonely than at any time in her life. Her relationship with Violet Dickinson began to cool. Most horribly, her much loved brother Thoby died of typhoid fever which he caught when they were all travelling together in Greece in 1906. In 1907 Vanessa, the person on whom Virginia was most emotionally dependent, married Clive Bell and moved into a separate apartment. It was as if every person she had ever loved had either died or abandoned her. Perhaps in desperation, she began a flirtation with Clive which caused her sister much pain. Later in her life nothing caused her such remorse as this episode. When Vanessa's first son Julian was born in 1908 she became even more distant from her sister. 'Reminiscences' was written almost as a declaration of love for Vanessa. Virginia wanted by almost any means to be included within the Bell family circle. 'Nessa has all that I should like to have, and you, besides your own charms and exquisite fine sweetnesses . . . have her. Thus I seem often to be only an erratic external force, capable of shocks, but without any lodging in your lives' (L I, May 1908). She took to going on holiday by herself for the first time. 'Kiss my old Tawny, on all her private places – kiss her eyes, and her neck socket', she wrote to Clive (L I, 19 September 1908). Between 1908 and her breakdown in 1913 her letters to Vanessa always address her as 'Beloved'. In the year after the Bells married she and Clive had a lively and loving correspondence. Clive's main gift to her, apart from being a means to a continuing closeness with her sister, was that he took her very seriously as a writer. She began in 1908 to write her first novel. It was called *Melymbrosia*. She sent pages of the work to Clive for his comment, which must have taken enormous trust. Never again in her life would she show work in progress to anybody.

These were the only years in her life when she did not live with someone she loved. She went without the daily unthinking loyalty and support that at other times she had from her family and later from her husband. Virginia and Adrian Stephen set up home together in Fitzroy Square. They were never close. The group of her brothers' friends from Cambridge who had, since 1904, taken to meeting together with the Stephen sisters in Bloomsbury, were of great but not intimate importance to Virginia in these years. Her descriptions of the evenings they spent together ('Old Bloomsbury' in MB) are hilarious. In her account of them these young men seem rather too self-satisfied. They would spend hour upon hour constructing great edifices of analytical thought on topics such as the good and the beautiful. There was a great deal of difficult silence. The one thing that mattered to Virginia was that here were a group of people who, unlike her Duckworth and Dickinson acquaintance, treated her and Vanessa primarily not as candidates for marriage but as people who might want to join in thinking about difficult topics. Among her other friends, Virginia remembered, 'we were not asked to use our brains much. Here we used nothing else' (MB 168). These young men were safe; they had no designs on the young women, and this, to the damaged and nervous young Virginia, was an enormous relief. In her life everything was still undecided. It was not settled in her mind what it would be possible for her to be. To mix with men such as Bell and Lytton Strachey, who took it for granted that a young woman could be a thinker, a writer or a painter, who would recognise and confirm for her that it was a real possibility and not a fantasy that she could be an author, must have helped her keep alive her determination through these lonely and uncertain years.

The Bloomsbury Group did not come alive for Virginia as an active influence on her work and thought until 1910 and beyond. I think it is a mistake to see in these years of friendship a route whereby Virginia Stephen was much influenced by the intellectual culture of Cambridge University with which she was now becoming acquainted at second hand. For those long and, for Virginia, impressive but unilluminating discussions about beauty and good were about the work of the man who most influenced and excited these impressionable young students, the philosopher G. E. Moore (1875–1958). Moore's status in the eyes of Clive Bell, Maynard Keynes and Leonard Woolf was extraordinary, almost celestial. For Virginia's work and thought he had, I believe, no importance whatsoever. There is a style of intellectual history which is based on the assumption that every body of work is to seen as rooted in some philosophy. In the case of Virginia Woolf, the roots are traced back to Moore, or to another Cambridge thinker, McTaggart, or to Bergson.[8] I do not myself think that there is any evidence that her work was significantly influenced by these thinkers. If she had any abiding philosophical ground it was in Plato, whose work she read when young and reread throughout her life.

Leonard's assessment of Moore was typical. Moore's book *Principia Ethica*, which was published in 1903,

> suddenly removed from our eyes an obscuring accumulation of scales, cobwebs, and curtains, revealing for the first time to us, so it seemed, the nature of truth and reality, of good and evil and character and conduct, substituting for the religious and philosophical nightmares, delusions, hallucinations, in which Jehova, Christ, and St. Paul, Plato, Kant and Hegel had entangled us, the fresh air and pure light of plain common-sense.[9]

Moore's influence, Leonard claimed, extended through him and through their reading of his book, to the Stephen sisters and many commentators have followed him in claiming to detect Moore's influence on Virginia's work. The sisters were, said Leonard,

> deeply affected by the astringent influence of Moore and the purification of that divinely cathartic question which echoed through the Cambridge Courts of my youth as it had 2,300 years before echoed through the streets of Socratic Athens: 'What do you mean by that?' Artistically the purification can, I think, be traced in the clarity, light, absence of humbug in Virginia's literary style . . . (LW 12)

However, one does not need to be a disciple of Moore to be free of humbug and the cobwebs of religious delusion. In Virginia Stephen's case she is more likely to have inherited such advantages from her father, who in these respects shared with Moore that Enlightenment style of secular, anti-metaphysical thinking. In fact, Virginia read Moore's book some years before she came to know Leonard Woolf well. He was away in Ceylon at the time and closer witnesses to her reactions to it were Clive and Vanessa Bell. We see in her letters to them and in her diaries that when she read Moore she was not particularly impressed.

Given his importance to her Cambridge friends and given the amount of time they spent making her mind spin with their Moorean constructions during those long difficult nights in Bloomsbury, it is an indication of just how unimpressed she was that she did not even bother to read his book until 1908. The stimulus then was her new intimacy with Clive Bell. She took *Principia Ethica* with her on her solitary holiday to read as bedtime reading. In letters she reported back to Clive: 'I am climbing Moore like some industrious insect, who is determined to build a nest on the top of a Cathedral spire. One sentence, a string of "desires", makes my head spin with the infinite meaning of words un-adorned; otherwise I have gone happily' (L I, 3 August 1908). It is worth taking a look at that 'string of "desires"' in the first chapter of the book, for they provide a clear taste of the flavour of Moore's thought:

> It may easily be thought, at first sight, that to be good may mean to be that which we desire to desire. Thus if we apply this definition to a particular instance and say 'When we think that A is good, we are thinking that A is one of the things which we desire to desire,' our proposition may seem quite plausible. But, if we . . . ask ourselves 'Is it good to desire to desire A?' it is apparent, on a little reflection, that this question is itself as intelligible, as the original question 'Is A good?' . . . But it is also apparent that the meaning of this second question cannot be correctly analysed into 'Is the desire to desire A one of the things which we desire to desire?': we have not before our minds anything so complicated as the question 'Do we desire to desire to desire to desire A?'.[10]

I do not believe that we can trace to this book any lucidity that we might discover in Virginia Woolf's own work. Over the next week she read on and reported to another Bloomsbury friend, Saxon Sydney-Turner: '10 pages nightly of Moore – many things

I don't understand'. So lost does she become that she doubts that she 'can even ask an intelligible question' (L I, 10 August, 14 August 1908). By the 19 August she is writing to Clive:

> I split my head over Moore every night, feeling ideas travelling to the remotest part of my brain, and setting up a feeble disturbance, hardly to be called thought. It is almost a physical feeling, as though some little coil of brain unvisited by any blood so far, and pale as wax, had got a little life into it at last; but had not strength to keep it.

Virginia's continuing scepticism about Moore's work is indicated in many places in her diaries and novels. In 1918, for example, she records a conversation with friends in which Moore was held up as comparable with Christ or Socrates. She was not convinced (D 1, 17 June 1918). Two years later, when Moore stayed with the Woolfs in London, she wrote, 'I dont see altogether why he was the dominator & dictator of youth. Perhaps Cambridge is too much of a cave' (D II, 23 June 1920). In *Jacob's Room* she made fun of Cambridge, and of the self-important young students and their enthusiasms. She felt affection for their boyish, innocent energy, not for their ideas. She stood somewhat aside from intellectual discussion and viewed it not as rational argument but as a slightly ludicrous tussle of competitive personalities. Maynard Keynes, when he came to look back on Bloomsbury in 1938, came to see those early philosophical discussions in much the same light:

> In practice, victory was with those who could speak with the greatest appearance of clear, undoubting conviction . . . [Moore] was a master of this method – *Do* you *really* think *that*, an expression of face as if to hear such a thing said reduced him to a state of wonder verging on imbecility, . . . *Oh*! he would say, goggling at you as if either you or he must be mad: and no reply was possible.[11]

On the most important matters, in their attitudes to language and meaning, G. E. Moore and Virginia Woolf could not have been further apart. Moore's thought was *premodernist*. He had faith in the capacity of careful reasoning and clear language to produce answers. The question for which he was famous, 'What exactly do you mean?', was designed to extract from his interlocutors precise definitions and clear, unequivocal meanings. The epigraph to *Principia Ethica*, which is a quotation from the eighteenth-century Bishop Butler, encapsulates the philosophical basis for this optimistic desire for complete clarity: 'Everything is what it is, and not another thing'.

For Virginia Woolf nothing could be further from the truth. She did not share Moore's confidence in clarity and common-sense. Everything, and every word, has many meanings, and Virginia Woolf's poetic prose is designed to explore and express this fact. Her work is based not on the clarity of saying exactly what one means but on the possibility of meanings proliferating beyond one's control, through ambiguity and metaphor. Her characters are always asking questions: 'What is life?', 'What is love?', but they never answer them. Their minds migrate restlessly from one unclear thought to another. They never settle. They never arrive, except at a vision which lies beyond language. Her whole work is a refutation of common-sense.

It was only when Bloomsbury, from 1910 onwards, found new members and new stimuli, that it came to offer to Virginia Stephen an intellectual diet that could nourish her own interests and beliefs.

3

1910–15: Moratorium and Crisis

'I can be m-m-myself', she stammered.' (VO 81)

On her death in 1909 Caroline Stephen left her niece a generous legacy. Virginia's capital was now and for the next few years enough for her to be able to live on the income. From 1910 onwards, for this reason but also later because of illness, her journalistic writing was reduced, eventually to zero. She had started to write a novel, *Melymbrosia*, in 1908. She now took this up full-time. It seemed in early 1912 to be almost finished. But then she began to rewrite it drastically. It became *The Voyage Out* and was eventually delivered to the publisher in 1913. Because of her mentally unbalanced state, publication was delayed until March 1915. It was not until 1916 that she started to write again for the *Times Literary Supplement*.[1]

Virginia Stephen's life took a decisive turn when in 1912 she married Leonard Woolf. But the pressures of her writing and her marriage took a terrible toll and she suffered repeated mental breakdowns. These were the worst years of her life. She was often in a nursing home and sometimes suicidal. It was only after the publication of her novel that she stabilised and settled finally into her career as a writer.

Her social life also eventually settled into a pattern of friendships with an expanded Bloomsbury Group that would be central to her for the rest of her life. But she and her new husband found themselves faced with repeated financial crises. It was not until 1918 that they succeeded in securing reasonable financial arrangements.

In summary, Virginia had launched herself upon her boldest project: 'I think a great deal of my future, and settle what book I am to write – how I shall re-form the novel and capture multitudes of things at present fugitive, enclose the whole, and shaped infinite strange shapes', she wrote to Clive Bell (19 September 1908). But the outcome was not yet certain. Each of the major dimensions of her life – her work, her desire to be married and have children, her financial affairs, her health, her relationship with the person who she loved above all others, her sister Vanessa – were thrown into terrible, potentially fatal crisis, one after another, over a period of years through which she had to struggle for survival. She suffered crises of confidence. She thought herself a failure as a writer and as a woman. 'I could not write, and all the devils came out – hairy black ones. To be 29 and unmarried – to be a failure – childless – insane too, no writer', she wrote to Vanessa in 1911 (L I, June 1911). In 1910 she was still, at the age of 28, asking what it was possible for her to be in her life. By the end of 1915 some of the answers had become clear: she was married, would never have children, she was a promising writer of fiction. She could survive.

MORATORIUM

In these years her life was in a period of 'moratorium'. This concept refers to a period of more or less deliberately protracted uncertainty in a young person's life, usually through adolescence though sometimes, as in Virginia Stephen's case, lasting much longer.[2] In the moratorium period a person fights to keep open possibilities for her life that she still needs to experiment with, to test. She contrives not to fall into one or other of the already accepted social scripts or life stories that seem to be the only available options open. She waits and waits, hoping to find a way to some as yet unknown alternative, some way of living a life that will allow her to hold on to something deeply desired. In Virginia Stephen's case, she needed time to find out whether her various needs were incompatible. She did want to marry and have children. She was lonely. She had experimented since 1907 with being on her own. She had developed the discipline to work on her journalism, to be independent. She knew that she valued autonomy very highly, and it meant even more to her when she started to write fiction. She had thought about but rejected her Aunt Caroline Stephen's life of dedicated solitude. She needed to be mothered, preferably by Vanessa, though that now seemed out of the question.

All this is stated very clearly by the fictional version of Virginia

Stephen, the character Camilla in Leonard Woolf's *The Wise Virgins*. In this passage, Camilla explains her conflicting needs to Harry, who wants to marry her:

> It's the romantic part of life that I want; it's the voyage out that seems to me to matter, the new and wonderful things. I can't, I won't look beyond that. I want them all. I want love, too, and I want freedom. I want children even. But I can't give myself; passion leaves me cold. You'll think I am asking for everything to be given and to give nothing. Perhaps that's true.
>
> And then there's so much in marriage from which I recoil. It seems to shut women up and out. I won't be tied by the pettinesses and the conventionalities of life. There must be some way out. One must live one's own life, as the novels say.[3]

It was also essential for her to keep alive her project of being a writer. It was not clear, in this transition period of history, whether or under what conditions, it would be possible for a woman to be both married and a mother, and yet to have a career as a writer. Her sister's case perhaps suggested that she should not give up hope, for Vanessa somehow contrived both to be a mother and to paint (though her marriage and love life were in disarray for years). In other words, Virginia did not know whether she was capable of writing novels, nor whether this could be combined, and in what sort of arrangement, with some kind of family life. Moreover, and this was certainly a very large uncertainty in her anxious thoughts, it was not clear that she could sustain a married life at all, for she had a dark secret; she regarded herself as sexually damaged beyond repair, as beyond any possibility of passionate sexual love with a man. Could she place herself outside society's ready-made narratives by marrying *on her own terms*?

When she agreed in 1912 to marry Leonard Woolf, she was taking an enormous risk. None of her questions were settled by her marriage. They were simply posed in a new and frightening context. She had to fight for what she felt to be necessary for her life. She tried to make clear to Leonard that she felt no sexual desire for him, but he hoped that that would change after they were married. He knew that she was determined to try to become a writer and that this might mean him making very big sacrifices. To marry her at all meant that he had to give up his career in the colonial civil service and to rebuild his life from the beginning. The outcome in all these respects was unknown. The anxiety was no doubt compounded by the fact that the novel that Virginia was writing was itself precisely about the drama of a young woman who, in order to secure her life against loneliness, allows herself to fall into the conventional social script of sexuality and marriage, with fatal consequences.

MONEY

When Leslie Stephen died he left his children financially secure. His estate was valued at £15 000, worth something like £500 000 at the present time. None of the four children had to work for a living immediately. Thoby and Adrian could take their time before settling on a career. Vanessa carried on with her training as a painter. Over the years they rented and furnished various apartments in Bloomsbury. However, travel and illness had caused considerable expense through 1904. When Virginia said that she wanted to write to earn money to pay for a few extras, we can take it that her need for money was not urgent. But if she was to aim to maintain her standard of life over the years, with servants, travel and comfortable central London apartments, then it would be necessary for her either to have a profession or to marry money. Her father's money was sufficient to finance the years of low-paid apprenticeship. She received for nine of her *Guardian* essays a sum of £3 9s. 0d. Andrew McNeillie calculates that her total earnings for the 26 000 words that she contributed to this paper were about £17 10s. 0d. (E I xviii)

After 1907, when Vanessa married, their situation changed, though this may not have directly affected Virginia. Clive Bell was from a wealthy family and was never in his life obliged to work for a living. £20 000 was made over to Clive on his marriage.[4] Virginia and Adrian Stephen then set up home together in a separate apartment. Her financial situation improved considerably in 1909 with Caroline Stephen's legacy. She left Virginia £2500, clearly intending to smooth her niece's path into a writing career; she left Vanessa and Adrian only £100 each. Virginia immediately reduced her journalistic work so that she could concentrate on her novel. The number of essays that she published dropped from 17 in 1909 to 4 in 1910, then to 2 in each of 1911 and 1912, 5 in 1913, and then none until 1916 when her crisis period was over (see Table 2.1).

From 1909 until she married she had a total capital of some £9000 producing an annual income of about £400. She also had a room of her own. The material necessities for her to be a writer were assured.

The situation changed and became financially more troubled when she married in 1912. Leonard Woolf also came from an upper-middle-class professional family, though it was culturally quite different from the Stephen family. His father was a successful barrister, but the family had, said Leonard, 'only recently struggled into [the upper-middle-class] from the stratum of Jewish shopkeepers'.[5] They were not rooted, as were the Stephens, in the worlds of literature and the old universities. There were nine children. The family's situation became economically precarious with the early death of the father. As a result, Leonard always felt himself to be an outsider. Unlike his friends, when he finished at Cambridge he needed to begin a career immediately. He spent six and a half years in the colonial civil service in Ceylon, and seemed to be destined for a secure future in that career when, in 1912 on leave in England, he decided to resign his position, hoping that Virginia Stephen would marry him. It was a brave decision. When they married he had savings of about £600 but no income. He took a temporary job, at 12 guineas a month, as Secretary to the second Post-Impressionist Exhibition at the Grafton Gallery in London. Leonard calculated that his savings would be enough to keep him going for about two years while he worked out a more permanent solution for the future. As a useful benchmark, a measure of the value of money at the time, we could note that his civil service salary had been £264 per annum, and on this Leonard calculated that one could 'live comfortably in London before the war' (LW 34).

The couple discussed their financial situation and decided, Virginia said, to 'take a small house and try to live cheaply, so as not to have to make money' (L I, June 1912). Virginia was thirty, Leonard thirty-two. Neither of them had yet established a psychologically or socially stable identity. They were quite old for such a degree of uncertainty, though no doubt this was made more tolerable by the fact that they were not forced to work immediately. They both had ambitions to write but neither had yet proved to themselves that they could build a literary career. Virginia had proved herself as a journalist, but Leonard raced ahead and was the first to publish a book. His novel about his life in Ceylon, *A Village in the Jungle*, was published in 1913. It was reprinted twice before the end of the year and again in 1925, but total sales amounted to only about 2000 copies. It earned over all those years only about £60 in royalties. In 1913 he also completed his second novel, *The Wise Virgins*, a fictional transfiguration of the Stephen sisters as perceived by a young Jewish suitor from a different cultural world. It was published in October 1914 and was a failure, earning no more than £20 in royalties. In these first few years of their marriage Leonard also successfully established himself as a journalist.

Virginia by contrast had sunk into failure. She had dropped her journalism. Her novel went through endless drafts but she could not bring herself to publish it. She was seriously ill for much of the time. With hindsight it is perhaps difficult for us to realise that her permanent failure was a very serious possibility. It seemed quite likely that she would never become an author. In fact, it was not at all clear that she would even survive. From our perspective, we cannot ignore the whole wonderful achievement of her subsequent writing. This is so outstanding that it obscures our view of the earlier, bleak landscape in which this desperate young woman, deranged with anxiety, was struggling so hard to write something that would not be ridiculed.

Virginia's illness not only threatened her career, it also upset their financial calculations. Being mad was very expensive. She was confined in a private nursing home in Twickenham in 1910, 1912, 1913 and 1915. When she was at home she still often needed expensive care. Full-time supervision was essential, especially after she attempted suicide in September 1913. It was then that Leonard, on doctors' advice, decided that they would never have children. 'In 1915, when Virginia's mental breakdown was at its worst, we had nurses – sometimes four – in the house for months and she was visited continually by Harley Street doctors. The doctors' and nurses' bills must have been more than £500 for the twelve months' (LW 62).[6] To get the measure of this we should note that these medical expenses alone accounted for more than Virginia's total income, and were twice what Leonard had been earning as an experienced colonial administrator. In other words, their financial situation had radically changed. In fact, it would not be inaccurate to say that Virginia's madness forced Leonard Woolf into employment.

Extra pressure came from their housing needs. With Virginia so often ill they could not remain in rooms. They needed a house and they needed servants and they needed to get out of central

London. They rented Hogarth House, in Richmond, at £50 a year. In addition, from 1912–19 Virginia also rented a farm house in Sussex, Asheham House. From 1916 Vanessa and her family would settle nearby at Charleston and the Woolfs and Bells remained anchored in this Sussex countryside for the rest of their lives. As for servants, they were very cheap, although they became harder to get as women were recruited as munitions workers during the war. Nelly the cook and Lottie the house-parlourmaid, both of whom were to appear a great deal over the years in Virginia Woolf's diaries, were the Woolf's two live-in servants. In 1917 their joint wages amounted to £76 1s 8d (LW 168). Vanessa and Clive had for their children a live-in nurse who in 1913 cost them £25 per annum. In other words, inequalities in income and differences in standard of living between working people and members of the upper-middle-class were very large indeed. The distance between them was also kept very great by their attitudes. 'The fact is the lower classes *are* detestable' said Virginia, irritated by Nelly's hypochondria (D II, 15 September 1920). Leonard, writing about Lily, a servant at Hogarth House in 1915, said 'Lily was one of those persons for whom I feel the same kind of affection as I do for cats and dogs' (LW 124).

They had aimed, when they married, to add some small earnings from writing to Virginia's unearned income, hoping that this would be enough to live on. But this proved impossible. Whereas their annual budget when they married was around £400, by 1919 it had doubled. Virginia's capital declined. In the worst year, 1915, when Leonard earned very little because he was nursing his wife and medical bills were at their peak, Virginia had to sell some of her jewelry and securities. Leonard, through his contact with Sydney Webb whom he met in 1913, managed to obtain work on the *New Statesman* and for the Fabian Society. But even by 1916, with Virginia recovered and back at her journalism, and Leonard earning £176 from his writing (including about £100 for his book *International Government*, which he wrote for the Fabians), their expenditure was still much greater than their income, as it was again in 1917. Virginia's capital was depleted. They had no hope at all of making from their novels the extra £400 a year that they needed. One of them would have to sacrifice his or her literary career. This, in effect, Leonard did. Their problems began to ease when he took regular work as editor of *The International Review*.

THE BLOOMSBURY GROUP

Sometime around 1910–12 the Bloomsbury circle of friends became the more significant Bloomsbury Group. In earlier years perhaps these young friends were still over-fond of their days at Cambridge and of concentrating narrowly on the thrills of love and beauty. They were, in Keynes's retrospective view of them, like 'water-spiders, gracefully skimming, as light and reasonable as air, the surface of the stream without any contact at all with the eddies and currents underneath'.[7] This view was shared by other, not unsympathetic associates, such as Gerald Brenan, with whom the Woolfs stayed in Spain in 1923. He captures something of their naivety, their optimistic trust in the power of civilised individuals to move history forward, away from superstition and illusion, towards enlightenment. 'Civilised, liberal, agnostic or atheist like their parents before them, they had always stood too far above the life of their day, had been too little exposed to its rough-and-tumble really to belong to it.'[8] They had, he claimed, too little patience with or understanding of the impulses that drive people to adopt less than civilised beliefs and attitudes.

If in the early years they were superficial individualists and aesthetes with no appreciation of the more destructive and uncontrollable forces at work in people's minds, there is no reason whatever to believe that Virginia Stephen or her sister shared these views. Virginia, says Roger Poole accurately, was not Bloomsbury's queen but its Antigone, undermining it from within.[9] She was well acquainted with both the destructive stupidity of nature, as manifested in the extreme vulnerability of the human body, and also with the alarming ways of the mind and its potential for derangement. In the early years, when the men would sit around endlessly going again and again over the most minute abstract points of intuitionist ethics, Virginia was, remembered her sister, 'apt to be very silent'.[10] Duncan Grant agrees that she was acutely shy, but also observed in her an 'inner fierceness of attitude'.[11] In spite of all the young men's advantages in education and experience of the world, she must have regarded herself as more tested by the traumas and shocks of life than they were. She had travelled further into the heart of darkness and it was this that she was privately exploring in her novel. The young men in *The Voyage Out* are witty, socially accomplished, well read and rather silly. It is a woman, Helen Ambrose, who has a glimpse of life which must have been nearer to the author's own: 'At her back was the awful waste of trees ringing with the cries of beasts; in front of her the enormous smooth-swirling water. All the disasters in her experience seemed to have come from civilised people forgetting how easily they may die'.[12] Compared with the young men, Virginia Stephen was relatively uneducated, and yet her 'inner fierceness of attitude' arose from her deeper acquaintance with tragedy and her commitment to less superficial values.

If the damning judgements of Keynes and Brenan seem fair when applied to the Bloomsbury friends up to 1910, they are harder to accept in relation to the more mature and expanding group from 1910 onwards. The group changed and drew in people of a wider and more appealing range of interests and values. There was E. M. Forster, also from Cambridge but not part of the Moore circle. He was to become a close, lifelong friend of Virginia Woolf. Then Leonard returned from his life of colonial administration to add a certain gritty realism to the group's discussions. Then there was Duncan Grant, a painter, the only member of the group with no university background. Probably the most influential newcomer was Roger Fry, who became for a while Vanessa's lover, who travelled with the Stephen sisters to Greece and Turkey in 1911 and who scandalised England with two exhibitions of Post-Impressionist painting, in 1910 and 1912.

The group was in effect a specialised segment of the upper-middle-class attacking the unsustainably archaic attitudes of their parents' generation.[13] They were all from professional families (except Bell whose wealthy family owned coal mines and lived in some style in the country). They were unified by their rejection of the culture of their parents' generation, an oppressively moralising culture, at the service of a confident imperial order. The group had no common programme. They wrote no manifesto. But they shared a sense of the need for renovation throughout domestic, intellectual, cultural and political life. In the early years at least many of them thought that the agent and hero of social progress was no longer the noble, dutiful, morally strenuous patriarch of Victorian ideology, but the 'civilised individual', aesthetically sensitive, with trained good taste, with a cultivated style of secular, sexually unconventional friendships, based on informality. Their overwhelming impulse was to break out of conventionality and to lead the way towards a more relaxed, less philistine and less cruel social order. This general sense of participation in a narrative of emancipation was of far greater importance than any shared philosophical basis for their work. They set out to demolish the Victorian family and the Victorian culture of muscular, imperial certainty and superstition. In their place they put pacifism and aestheticism. Above all, they rejected moralising in art and literature.

The Victorian family was a very large and patriarchal institution. The Strachey family had ten children; in the Stephen family there were eight from three marriages; the Woolfs had eight children. Their large households included many servants. The role of the wife and mother was as a manager of a considerable household economy and she had very little real prospect of any other life. Ruling over the whole institution was the Victorian father, with unquestioned power, not slow to impose things on his offspring. This whole pattern of family life changed totally in the next generation as did attitudes towards women and their lives, both private and public. They won the vote (Virginia Woolf did some small amount of work for Women's Suffrage in 1910). In all this the Bloomsbury Group were an important and scandalous vanguard. They flaunted their provocative sexual arrangements, some of which, especially those centred on Vanessa Bell, are still hard to contemplate tolerantly even today. For Virginia Woolf it was a matter of extreme importance to establish a domestic arrangement of some unconventionality (a non-sexual marriage with a mothering husband which could contain without rupture a lesbian love affair). This contribution of the Bloomsbury Group to the evolution of English social mores was of major importance to Virginia Woolf. It made possible a context in which she could pursue her career as a writer. Her work was intimately connected with the historical emergence of 'the new woman', a development which is depicted in *Night and Day*.

Though the young men and women of Bloomsbury may have been inexperienced and naive in the early years, they did later produce remarkable and culturally extremely important work in a very wide range of different fields. The Post-Impressionist Exhibitions were the first of their great successes. They provoked a storm by confronting English culture with the revolutionary new aesthetic of European art, based on a complete change in the conventions of painting. The representational image, with its Victorian narrative and moral content, was rejected. The picture surface was opened up to design and aesthetic effects that seemed quite mad to the conservative English audience. Fry championed Van Gogh, Matisse, above all Cézanne. A young generation of painters were suddenly liberated from old formal assumptions about painting. The Bloomsbury artists, Fry himself, Vanessa Bell and Duncan Grant, themselves began to produce post-impressionist work which, though largely derivative, had a certain vitality. It was colourful, witty, irreverent and provocative. Fry went on, from 1913 to 1919 to run the Omega workshops, an attempt to find a market for modern design in household objects, fabrics, furniture, ceramics and so on. When Virginia Woolf later remarked (in her essay 'Character in Fiction') that in 1910 human nature changed, she had in mind not only the end of the Edwardian era, but also the entry of modernism into Britain at the first Post-Impressionism Exhibition. Virginia Woolf's fiction, in her more formalist period through the 1920s, can be seen as Post-Impressionist in style and owes a great deal to the debates about art that were triggered by Roger Fry's exhibitions.

It was not only the painters and writers on art who provided a stimulating context for Virginia Woolf's early career. The other members of the group were also innovators who modernised thinking and practice in many fields – in psychoanalysis, biography, aesthetics, economics and politics. They picked up English culture and gave it such a shaking that nothing could ever be thought or seen in quite the same way again. Although it is easy with hindsight for us to see the limitations of the Group, its obsessions, its blindspots and its affectations, a fair assessment of its members has to recognise their contribution to the modernisation of English culture and its exposure to European artistic and intellectual innovations. Not the least of Bloomsbury's accomplishments was the introduction into England of the thought of Sigmund Freud. His work was published by the Woolfs at their Hogarth Press, translated by Lytton Strachey's brother James. Adrian Stephen and his wife Karin trained to be psychoanalysts. So the association of Bloomsbury with Freud was intimate, and this can stand as conclusive evidence that, even if in 1904–10 Bloomsbury people could do no more than skim surfaces and had no conception of the depths, in later years this was no longer true of at least some of them. In literature, psychoanalysis and politics they learned not to underestimate irrational drives and unconscious forces.

THE VOYAGE OUT

The Voyage Out was a hard-won book. It took six years to write and went through at least seven, and perhaps as many as eleven, drafts. It is a book about the effort by a young woman, Rachel Vinrace, to become a whole person in her own right, the very effort that Virginia Woolf was herself making at such terrible cost throughout these years. 'The vision of her own personality, of herself as a real everlasting thing, different from anything else, unmergeable, like the sea or the wind, flashed into Rachel's mind, and she became profoundly excited at the thought of living' (VO 81). What excites her is her right to her own life story, her own individual being. What frightens her are the forces which threaten to make her merge, to become swallowed up and engulfed in other people's identities. She struggles to draw boundaries, to negotiate safe distances, without becoming totally isolated. Virginia Woolf's aim in the book was, she said in a letter to Lytton Strachey in 1909, 'to give voice to some of the perplexities' of being a woman. In her own life she was trying to find a livable distance from her dead parents, from her sister and her sister's husband, and then from her own husband. In each case she would swing wildly from a furious, enraged rejection (in her bouts of madness it was common for her to rage against Vanessa and Leonard in the most hateful and violent language) and a desire for a kind of infantilised, loving but non-sexual intimacy. The novel charts these struggles, though often in ways which are so oblique that its meaning is quite obscure. As she wrote the final version of the novel, at many points she censored material which she felt had brought into the light too openly her most private thoughts and feelings. In early versions she had impulsively exposed some very disturbing emotions and in later versions she goes back over the ground covering her tracks. It was to be true of many of her novels, that she allowed herself in the earlier drafts to write in an unguarded way and to draw on feelings which she later judged that she must repress. So first drafts are often more revealing of her most private thoughts and feelings than are the published versions. She often censored her anger, the expression through her characters of her sexual fantasies, her obsessions and nightmares. This first novel suffers more than later works from this process.

Rachel Vinrace, whose mother had died, goes on a voyage to

South America with her father and her aunt Helen Ambrose. Once there she mixes with an English expatriate community in the local hotel. She meets a young aspiring writer, Terence Hewet. They take a trip together up river into the jungle and she agrees to marry him. In imagining the triangular relationships between Rachel, Helen and Terence, Virginia Woolf drew emotionally upon the drama of the tangled emotions between herself, Vanessa and Clive. On the voyage out Rachel is kissed by an older man, Richard Dalloway, and she is deeply disturbed and excited by this. The emotional storms which ensue, as with other incidents in the story, are extreme. They go far beyond what seems appropriate to the fictional episodes. It seems that the author was drawing on her own emotionally traumatising experiences but leaving the reader rather puzzled about just what could be going on. It is quite possible, for example, that this episode with Richard Dalloway, which awakens Rachel's sexual feelings but also a terrible wretchedness and fear, draws on Virginia Woolf's experience of being sexually interfered with by her step-brother. If this is so, then her severe anxiety about the book, her sense that it might be exposed too much, would be quite comprehensible, especially as it was to her tormentor Gerald Duckworth himself, who ran his own publishing company, that the book was sent for publication. Her anxieties were so extreme that publication of the book was delayed for two years. Her medical supervisor Jean Thomas (who became the model for Doris Kilman in *Mrs Dalloway*) wrote to Violet Dickinson, 'It is the novel which has broken her up. She finished it and got the proof back for correction . . . couldn't sleep & thought everyone would jeer at her' (14 September 1913).

Much of the writing in *The Voyage Out* is wonderful. The book does do what she set out in 1908 to achieve; it capture multitudes of fugitive things, and it shapes infinite strange shapes. But it has a disconcerting way of veering between different styles, or different registers. It swings from social satire to social realism, and settles often into a poetic, almost mythic style, in which the lives of the characters are drawn into some greater, symbolic design. Some of the social satire is very funny. She mocks the inane speech of the English upper classes, and the posturing of her Bloomsbury friends. The satire is so accomplished that we feel ready to place Virginia Woolf somewhere in the tradition of the English comic novel, along with Jane Austen and Dickens. Yet sometimes this impression is disturbed, when the tone changes from tolerant irony to an hysterical, misanthropic loathing of humanity. It is also disconcerting at times that the reader is left uncertain whether a scene is to be understood as satire or not. For example, what are we to make of the peculiar declaration of love between Terence and Rachel:

> She was walking fast, and holding herself more erect than usual. There was another pause.
>
> 'You like being with me?' Terence asked.
>
> 'Yes, with you,' she replied.
>
> He was silent for a moment. Silence seemed to have fallen upon the world.
>
> 'That is what I have felt ever since I knew you,' he replied. 'We are happy together.' He did not seem to be speaking, or she to be hearing.
>
> 'Very happy,' she answered.
>
> They continued to walk for some time in silence. Their steps unconsciously quickened.
>
> 'We love each other,' Terence said.
>
> 'We love each other,' she repeated. (VO 278)

This must be among the oddest declarations of love in literature. But is it satire? Declaration of love more usually triggers a copious discourse, an excess, in which, if we are to believe Roland Barthes, 'Language is a skin: I rub my language against the other. It is as if I had words instead of fingers, or fingers at the tip of my words. My language trembles with desire'. To speak amorously, he says, 'is to expend without an end in sight'.[14] But in *The Voyage Out*, speaking amorously is such a nerve-racking business that the lovers scarcely even manage to break the silence. They are very careful indeed to avoid copious expenditure. They are terrified of touching each other, even with words. When the great moment arrives, the moment of release when love, overcoming resistance, should flow forth, it is instead held back by a clever trick. Terence avoids making a declaration by making an observation instead. Not 'I love you' but 'We love each other', as though he had stumbled upon an odd fact which he wishes to make a note of. Instead of the first person singular, which would be too risky, he uses the plural, implicating Rachel in the emotion which he is unwilling to perceive simply as his own. Rachel herself avoids a declaration by simply echoing, repeating Terence's remark. Thus is love conducted among the tongue-tied upper classes. But the tone of the passage is unclear. Are we being asked to find this amusing, or has the author not realised just how very peculiar it is?

Here, as so often in the book, we suspect that there is much more going on than the surface story, a young woman's progress towards marriage, would lead us to expect. But we are never told just what else is at stake. Powerful, very disturbing forces lurk very near to the surface. Rachel tends to find herself engulfed in lurid dreams. It is clear that much stands in the way of Rachel's achieving a stable identity and that the outcome of her struggle is not a foregone conclusion.

The main problems with the novel centre on the tempests in Rachel's emotional life. The nightmares, the delirium and the anxieties, and eventually her fever and death, are all so extreme, so beyond what seems to be called for, that the reader has to speculate constantly about what hidden narrative could be behind all this. In the end, it turns out that it is impossible for Rachel to accomplish the voyage out, the journey into adulthood, that she had set out upon. She is shipwrecked upon the rocks of sexuality. She cannot solve the puzzle of how to combine marriage with independence. She cannot survive the 'perplexities of being a woman'. Her fatal incapacities seem to be her inability to inhabit her body sexually without disintegration, and the uncertain direction of her passion. That triangle of forces between Rachel, Terence and Helen is decidedly odd. They come together in a climactic scene, when the three of them join together in an intense, fantastical union. It is like a pleasurable hallucinatory wish-fulfillment. For one moment they seem to achieve a solution that reality would in fact never allow them. Helen throws Rachel to the ground and stuffs grass into her mouth and ears. They struggle and roll together until Rachel is dazed and semi-delirious. Terence and Helen now stand over her.

> Both were flushed, both laughing, and the lips were moving; they came together and kissed in the air above her. Broken fragments of speech came down to her on the ground. She thought she heard them speak of love and then of marriage. Raising herself and sitting up, she too realised Helen's soft body, the strong and hospitable arms, and happiness swelling and breaking in one vast wave. (VO 290)

Great emphasis is laid upon Rachel's extreme sexual ignorance and fear. She knows nothing about how children are born. She experiences every sexual encounter, even the most mild, as life-threatening. The earlier, unpublished versions are even more odd. In these, the physical contact of man with woman is shown to have for Rachel a nightmarish, repellent quality. For example, she and Terence come upon two other characters making love: notice how the lovers are metamorphosed into animals, Virginia Woolf's favorite form of rhetorical misanthropy.

They beheld a man and woman beneath them, pressed in each other's arms. They rolled slightly this way and that, as the embrace tightened and slackened. Then Susan pushed Arthur away, and they saw her head laid back upon the turf, the eyes shut, and a queer look of pallor upon it, as though she had suffered and must soon suffer again. She did not seem altogether conscious, which affected both Hewet and Rachel unpleasantly. When Arthur began butting her as a lamb butts a ewe, they turned away. Hewet looked, half shyly at Rachel, and saw that her cheeks were white.
    'Oh how I hate it – how I hate it!' she cried to him.
    'Yes' he said. 'It's odd how terrible that seems, until one gets used to it. But you know, you must get used to it, because if you don't you will exaggerate its importance.[15]

The basic question posed by the novel is this: 'How is it possible for a girl to become a woman, a mature, independent self?' The answer seems to be that this is not in fact possible, the obstacles are just too great. Rachel's death is a defeat. Helen, who mothers her and forms a dangerously close attachment to her, tries to convince her that men are not necessarily to be feared and despised, but these emotions win out. When Terence kisses her, during her final illness, she opens her eyes, 'But she only saw an old woman slicing a man's head off with a knife' (VO 346). Unable to survive such feelings, Rachel's only escape is in death.

Virginia Woolf, fighting this same battle while writing the book, very nearly suffered the same defeat. In February and March 1915, awaiting the publication of the book, she was more violently and dangerously deranged than ever before or since. 'She entered a state of garrulous mania, speaking ever more wildly, incoherently and incessantly, until she lapsed into gibberish and sank into a coma' (QB II 25). The book was published on 26 March to favourable reviews. She was 33.

It is a powerful, often beautifully written book, but in the end unsatisfactory. When she reread the book in preparation for a new edition, Woolf herself put her finger on its faults. It was, she said, 'a harliquinade' (D II, 4 February 1920), a patchwork of very good and very bad parts. She revised it considerably in 1919 for an American edition, tightening the narrative, cutting out extraneous matter, trying to excise those parts in which her own feelings obtruded too blatantly into the lives of the characters, where the novel had become what she would later condemn as a 'dumping-ground for the personal emotions' ('Women and Fiction', CE II 148). It is this revised and cut American edition that is still reprinted today.

4

1916–21: A Press of One's Own

'It amounts to a sense of freedom. I write what I like writing and there's an end on it.' (D II, 17 February 1922)

With the publication of her first novel behind her, Virginia Woolf regained her composure. She had found that a viable way of living was after all possible. She was to have a marriage, but it would be without sex. She would not have children. In spite of everything, she and Vanessa remained close. Above all, she had proved herself as a writer. Her career had begun. She was thirty-three and she still had a very long way to go before she would find her own distinctive way of writing. But the terrible experiences of the years 1910–15 were never to be repeated with anything like that ferocity.

Between 1916 and 1919 she was writing a new novel, a rather conventional, buttoned-up kind of novel, called *Night and Day*. She also went back to work for the *Times Literary Supplement*. But coexisting with these conventional activities was another and more important project. She was quietly struggling to find a certain kind of emancipation. For her life was still dominated by powerful men. Some were external (publishers and competitors) and some were ghosts. She felt that she was not yet free to write as she wished to write. A series of innovations in her life enabled her to find her way slowly, and at first quietly, towards independence. By far the most important of these was the Hogarth Press. The many, very significant ways that this affected her life are usually ignored. She began to write stories of a quite unprecedented kind. She became acquainted with other radical young writers, such as Katherine Mansfield and T. S. Eliot. She read *Ulysses* and tried to define the future direction of fiction. During all these years, it was as if there were two different Virginia Woolfs: the one pursued her steady, dutiful career while the other quietly, almost secretly, was preparing to be defiant, to write and publish in new ways, to speak out on her own terms at last. The other project which she began, in

1917, and which though she did not know it at the time would engage her to the end of her life, was her diary. She had begun diaries before, but had never kept them going. Now she began a diary that, with more or less minor interruptions, would eventually occupy some thirty manuscript volumes over a quarter of a century, and be judged by some to be her best book.

NIGHT AND DAY

Night and Day was written during the First World War. It was conceived in 1916 in Norfolk where Virginia was staying with Vanessa who had escaped to the countryside to find a refuge for her pacifist lover Duncan Grant. The story is set in the pre-war world and is about a cultural clash between different classes (this is her version of the different cultures of the Stephens and the Woolfs – Leonard had already written his account in *The Wise Virgins*). The main focus, however, is on the war between the sexes, between Katherine Hilbery, the new woman struggling to be born, and her suitors. The Hilbery family is wealthy and cultured, but she is emprisoned, allowed no expectations but domesticity and marriage. Ralph Denham needs to work for a living. His family has no money and no taste. Nonetheless, he is free in a way that she is not, for he can choose a career that will put his talents at the service of society and social progress. Each of them becomes entangled with a person whom they respect but do not love and each has to choose between comfortable marriage and passionate intimacy. This latter was always seen as dangerous by Virginia Woolf, for it involves one in giving up one's secrets, sharing one's most private thoughts with another. The novel is a comedy which enables love and intimacy to triumph without disaster.

Katherine's secret life is her passion for mathematics and astronomy. Not much of a risk in sharing that, one might have thought. Yet her hesitations make this Virginia Woolf's longest novel. Her night thoughts are for the stars. Her passion is Platonic. Can her passionate nights be contained between the days of a married life? What makes the novel readable, even intermittently delightful in spite of its overall tedium, is its mood of enchantment and magic. The lovers are plotted into and out of the required situations and relationships with virtuosity and charm in a way that is reminiscent of Mozart. Indeed, the music of Mozart is frequently heard in the background.[1]

In *The Voyage Out* self-exposure was perceived as a fearful, even fatal, mistake. But in *Night and Day*, the moments of sharing and mutual comprehension which are the climax of the novel, are portrayed as rapturous, like a magical duet staged in a conspicuously theatrical space. Katherine has to have her arm twisted before she will talk. 'I am a person who can't tell things', she pleads, worried that she will say something silly and be ridiculed.

> But he persuaded her into a broken statement, beautiful to him, charged with extreme excitement as she spoke of the dark red fire, and the smoke twined round it, making him feel that he had stepped over the threshold into the faintly lit vastness of another mind, stirring with shapes, so large, so dim, unveiling themselves only in flashes, and moving away again into the darkness, engulfed by it . . . they could pace slowly without interruption, arm in arm, raising their hands now and then to draw something upon the vast blue curtain of the sky. (ND 457)

In this conception to be intimate is to enter into someone else's shadow-filled Platonic cave. The other person's inner world is a mysterious, cavernous, half-lit place. This is a metaphor which is central to much of Virginia Woolf's later, mature fiction. Her whole effort as a writer in the twenties became to find ways of representing the inner worlds of her characters, of displaying the strange, streaming movement of images, ideas and sensations that flow there and that through subterranean tunnels connect up with each other in mysterious patterns of memory and meaning. Virginia Woolf had such a strong sense of the other person as a vast hidden space, a cavern, hard to penetrate, that we can understand how, for her, intimacy is always so hard-won. But these are strange metaphors for the culmination of a relationship in marriage. The climax has nothing to do with the more usual processes of negotiation and compromise, of comprehension won through talk. It is a strange, rapturous unveiling of a secret region. Perhaps it should be pointed out that this secret region and this penetration emphatically have nothing whatsoever to do with sex. Nothing could be further from the chaste Katherine's mind. Their intimacy gives rise to no physical excitement. Whenever in their relationship anything bearing on the physical or the bodily arises, Katherine's eyes turn unerringly to the stars. When they enter 'the enchanted region' (ND 459) their vision remains resolutely astronomical and Platonic.

Night and Day suffered from the fact that when it was published in 1919, its mood seemed quite inappropriate to the time. It represented a cheerful pre-war world. It portrayed the war between the sexes and the classes as a comedy, never spilling over into carnage, real or metaphorical. It was as if Virginia Woolf, having spent so much of the war years withdrawn into her own terrible, dark night of the soul, and having come through and rebuilt a stable, functioning personality for herself, was in no mood to respond to the broader historical catastrophe that had been going on all around. It was as if she had simply not heard the bad news. Her novel was written when she was convalescing. She was in bed. She could work for only an hour a day. She wanted to enjoy her sanity, not to have it disturbed by that deep fishing in the waters of the unconscious that she had undertaken in writing *The Voyage Out*. So she created an enchanting, basically benign world. The key metaphor is the reconstruction of the polished surface, the prosperous veneer of family life. The novel declares the triumph of civilisation. There is no place in it for its discontents. We can see this, for example, in the figure of the bullying old patriarch Mr Hilbery. He is fierce and insensitive, but his power seriously to damage his family is limited because underneath he has a warm Dickensian heart. Also in typical Dickensian style, he suffers what seems to the modern reader to be an excessive, incestuous love for his daughter. When her engagement to Ralph is announced the father reacts as if he has suffered a terrible loss. 'Had he loved her to see her swept away by this torrent, to have her taken from him by this uncontrollable force, to stand by helpless, ignored? Oh, how he loved her! How he loved her!' (ND 452). One is reminded of the grumpy old Leslie Stephen complaining about the loss of a daughter when Stella Duckworth became engaged to Jack Hills. Virginia, the author/daughter, comes up with the very same metaphor in the two cases (and as always, everything that is uncivilised in human behaviour is dealt with by making a person into an animal, in this case a lion). He 'strode out of the room, leaving in the minds of the women a sense, half of awe, half of amusement, at the extravagant, inconsiderate, uncivilised male, outraged somehow and gone bellowing to his lair with a roar which still sometimes reverberates in the most polished of drawing rooms'. But within no time at all the lamps are lit and shine upon the polished surfaces, wine is drunk, feelings are smoothed over, civilisation triumphs (ND 453).

The untroubled surface of civilisation wins out over the tantrums of the uncivilised male. In fact, the discontents have been so thoroughly repressed that they have entirely vanished from the scene. There is no moment in the book when we are given even a brief glimpse of the anguish of family life or of the shocking, murderous pit of violence and terror that lies underneath the veneer of civilisation, as we always are at some point in those works with which *Night and Day* tends to be compared, the novels of Jane Austen or Dickens or Mozart's operas. This is literature at its least dangerous, of a kind that Mr Hilbery himself would find satisfactory. 'The power of literature, which had temporarily deserted Mr Hilbery, now came back to him, pouring over the raw ugliness of human affairs its soothing balm, and providing a form into which such passions as he had felt so painfully the night before could be moulded so that they fell roundly from the tongue in shapely phrases, hurting nobody' (ND 452).

This is perhaps why the reaction to the novel was so muted. In the post-war world this serenity was the wrong mood. Her friends were polite about it but agreed that it had none of the brilliance of *The Voyage Out*. Katherine Mansfield loathed it. It was, she said privately 'a lie in the soul' (QB II 69). In a fine review in the *Athenaeum* (MM 79f) she put her finger very precisely on the problem, that in 1919 a novel which was basically a tribute to civilisation seemed like a relic from another era. It is, said Mansfield, as if we are sitting in a harbour and we look up and see a liner sail in. It is serene, aloof, majestic. It is unmarked by its voyage across the ocean. We know that there have been storms at sea, and yet there is a 'lack of any sign that she has made a perilous voyage'. It was an anachronism. 'We had not thought to look upon its like again' (MM 82).

Virginia Woolf herself looked back on the novel with mixed feelings. She knew why she needed to write it, the mystery was how anybody could have read it. 'I cant believe that any human being can get through Night and Day which I wrote chiefly in bed, half an hour at a time. But it taught me a great deal . . . like a minute Academy drawing: what to leave out: by putting it all in'

(L VI, 19 February 1938). But the spirit of dangerous literature had only temporarily deserted her and she was very soon to begin her own anti-war novel, *Jacob's Room*.

THE HOGARTH PRESS

Virginia Woolf wrote in her diary in 1925 that because of the Hogarth Press she was 'the only woman in England free to write what I like' (D III, 22 September 1925). The Press gave her both money and also freedom from interference. The story of the Press begins in 1917. Virginia was regarded as still vulnerable to break-down. She could only work for short periods and needed something to relax her and take her mind off her work. One day she and Leonard were walking through the Clerkenwell district of London, when they passed a shop displaying printing equipment in the window. 'We stared through the window . . . rather like two hungry children gazing at buns and cakes in a baker shop window', says Leonard (LW 169). They bought a press that was small enough to install on the dining room table, together with type and ancillary tools, and a sixteen-page booklet which explained in easy lessons how to use it all. It was carted to their home at Hogarth House in Richmond and it was from this that the Press took its name. Leonard Woolf typically recorded to the penny the details of their expenditure. They spent £38 8s 3d on the machine and type and the cost of materials for the first book they produced was £3 7s 0d. By the end of 1917 they had made an operating profit of £6 7s 0d, and this was put back into the business (LW 35). The Press thereafter was totally self-financing and indeed in later years made them a great deal of money.

Within a month they had mastered the machine so well that they decided to print a small booklet of their stories. It was a thirty-two page production called *Two Stories* and contained 'Three Jews' by Leonard and 'The Mark on the Wall' by Virginia . It was illustrated with four woodcuts by Dora Carrington, and they had to experiment with ink and pressure to get the printing right. They bound it themselves with paper covers. It sold for 1s 6d. They advertised by printing a circular which they sent to everyone they could think of and this produced orders for sixty copies and some subscribers for the series of such booklets which they were planning.

Virginia was involved in all the aspects of the work except for the accounts, for which Leonard had a passion. She wrote around commissioning work, she learned book-binding and she set type. For many years, even after they had hired staff, she continued to lend a hand with the physical work of printing, binding and mailing books. The Press gave her the material basis for her independence of spirit and also a strong sense of the production of books as a craft process. The work she learned to do was not unlike that which had been promoted by Roger Fry and Vanessa Bell at the Omega workshops. It was small craft production organised on a workshop basis. When the Press expanded and they moved into Tavistock Square, the Press lived in the basement. Virginia had her 'study' in the basement storeroom in which they warehoused their books. For the rest of her career every one of her works was published by the Hogarth Press. This liberated her from control by her step-brother and his company's readers and from the self-censorship and sense of intimidation that she felt as a result of the history of their relationship. 'Is the time coming', she asked herself, as she was preparing to go off to see Gerald Duckworth with the manuscript of *Night and Day*, 'when I can endure to read my own writing in print without blushing & shivering & wishing to take cover?' (D I, 27 March 1919). Even after the Woolfs themselves no longer did the printing, she was still never far from the workshop atmosphere of the Press. She had become in effect a self-employed artisan who specialised in the earliest steps in the production cycle, the writing of the pages. After *Night and Day* she had total control of her novel writing. She never again showed her work in progress to anyone. Even Leonard only saw it when it was finished. Her experience of the physical labour of book publishing gave her an unusually deep grasp of the material bases of culture which was very important to her understanding of the processes involved in the emancipation of women.

The most important consequence of the Press for Virginia Woolf was that it enabled her to begin writing in a non-commercial, experimental fashion, to make a break with the dutiful conventionality of *Night and Day*. One historian of small press publishing summarises its effect on Virginia Woolf thus: 'Self-publishing had not only been a therapeutic occupation; it had been her salvation as an artist – the means by which she had been freed to write in her own unorthodox way'.[2] Her very first Hogarth Press publication, 'The Mark on the Wall', was also her first experiment with first-person stream-of-thought narrative. She does not yet use a full blown stream of consciousness technique, but this story does represent a clear break with the more conventional third person narratives of her two early novels. Her sense of liberation was strong. She wrote it, she said, 'all in a flash', like a treat after she had done her duty in the conventional style, 'as if flying, after being kept stone-breaking for months' (L IV, 16 October 1930). Other stories followed, 'Kew Gardens' and 'An Unwritten Novel', each of them helping her to extend her techniques for capturing the flow of thoughts and impressions in consciousness. Writing them she 'trembled with excitement – & then Leonard came in & I drank my milk, concealed my excitement, & wrote I suppose another page of that interminable *Night and Day*' (ibid.). Writing these stories was a secret freedom and pleasure, whereas writing her novel was, like drinking milk which she hated, a duty which she owed to her husband. In 'The Mark on the Wall', which is a kind of reverie, more association of ideas than stream of consciousness, the 'speaker' contrasts the masculine point of view, which is associated with authority, conventions and mahogany sideboards, with the intoxication of illegitimate freedom (CSF 114). In writing these stories she felt that she was breaking the rules, so it is no wonder that it only became possible when she had not only a room but also a Press of her own.

Clive Bell and Lytton Strachey gave her courage to go on. They loved 'The Mark on the Wall'. It suggests the 'modern point of view', Strachey wrote to Leonard. It was a work of genius: 'How on earth does she make the English language float and float?' (QB II 43). 'Kew Gardens' was written in 1918 and published in May the next year. This time Vanessa provided two daring, impressionistic woodcuts, but she was very angry with the low quality of the printing. The Woolfs printed 170 copies on a new, larger press (the one which can still be seen in Vita Sackville-West's tower at Sissinghurst). This time they were bold enough to send a review copy to the *TLS*. It received a very favorable review and orders from booksellers flooded in. A second edition of 500 copies was printed for them by a commercial printer. They had already expanded beyond what they could produce themselves and had in effect become a profitable small press.

'An Unwritten Novel' was published first in the *London Mercury* in July 1920. Then in 1921 Virginia Woolf collected her stories together and they were published by Hogarth as *Monday or Tuesday*, again with woodcuts by Vanessa Bell. The printing of this volume was contracted out to a local jobbing printer and it proved a disaster. He used too much ink. The letters smudged. There was a terrible problem of show-through. The paper was horrible and there were many typographical errors. It was, said Leonard, 'one of the worst printed books ever published' (LW 174). He gives a wonderful description of the scene as he and the printer Mc-Dermott struggled with the cheap and nasty paper and the over-inked rollers to produce 1000 copies of his wife's book, until they 'sank down exhausted and speechless on the floor by the side of the machine, where we sat and silently drank beer until I was sufficiently revived to crawl battered and broken back to Hogarth House' (LW 174). With *Monday or Tuesday* Virginia Woolf began to establish herself with a small audience for avant-garde work as a serious figure on the literary scene. With writing like this, she must have thought, she was giving up any chance of commercial success. Yet she was beginning to see the possibility of writing in her own voice. She received a 'mildly unfavorable' review in the *Dial*, an American small literary magazine from which she had hoped for approval. But she was developing the courage not to mind this. 'It seems as if I succeed nowhere. Yet, I'm glad to find, I have acquired a little philosophy. It amounts to a sense of freedom. I like what I like writing & there's an end on it' (D II, 17 February 1922).

The Woolfs themselves printed by hand on their own presses thirty-four titles. They sought out short works by young writers that they could publish. In 1918 they published as Publication No. 2 of the Hogarth Press Katherine Mansfield's *Prelude*, which as Leonard later wrote was a very ambitious undertaking, for it was a sixty-eight page book. Virginia did all the type-setting and Leonard the machining of the 300-copy edition. In 1919 they published T. S. Eliot's *Poems* and in 1920 E. M. Forster's *Story of the Siren*. Each of these they printed and bound by hand themselves, Virginia becoming something of a specialist on patterned papers for covering boards and as end papers. In 1921 they published Roger Fry's *Twelve Original Woodcuts* and by now their printing standards had improved for these are rich black, clearly pulled prints.[3] In 1920 they had printed for them Gorky's *Reminiscences of Tolstoy*. In the first four years the Press made a net profit of £90 but this was without charging for rent or overheads and the Woolfs paid themselves nothing for their labours at printing and binding. Through the early twenties the Press began to take on more orthodox commercial methods and was soon established as a serious

publishing house, making an important contribution to the inno-
vative cultural trends of the time. They published Eliot's *The Waste
Land* in 1923, and in 1924 published Freud's *Collected Papers* and
started the Psychoanalytical Library. It was a suitable publishing
home for Virginia Woolf's own first modernist novel, *Jacob's Room*,
when it appeared in 1922.

MODERN WRITERS

Through her work at the Hogarth Press and as a result of her own
stories, Virginia Woolf began to contact writers who were trying in
a variety of ways to break free of the conventions of fiction and
poetry that had been dominant before the war. In 1919 she began
to write a series of essays, which I will discuss separately below, in
which she tried to define the characteristics and future lines of
development of 'modern fiction', seen in contrast with the rejected
old style of the 'Edwardians'. She read and reviewed the work of
Dorothy Richardson, praising but also worrying about the limitations of her rather shapeless first-person stream of consciousness
style (WW 188f). She became a competitive friend of Katherine
Mansfield, who was perhaps her closest rival. In her private
writings Virginia Woolf was sometimes extreme in her condemnation of Mansfield's work, though at other times she allowed
herself to estimate its merits more fairly. She herself wanted, like
Dorothy Richardson and Katherine Mansfield, to find a way of
conveying the stream of subjective experience. But she wanted to
find a way of representing the depths. She was not satisfied with
surface impressionism. She did not like the egoism of Dorothy
Richardson's first-person narration. She was looking for something more composed, less merely impressionistic, something that
conveyed a consistent pattern beneath the shifting surface. She felt
she could detect the lack of this in Katherine Mansfield's stories.
When she read 'Bliss' in the *English Review* in 1918, she threw it
down with disgust: 'Indeed I dont see how much faith in her as
woman or writer can survive that sort of story . . . her mind is very
thin soil, laid an inch or two deep upon very barren rock. For Bliss
is long enough to give her a chance of going deeper. Instead she is
content with superficial smartness' (D I, 7 August 1918). It is not
easy to distinguish here the genuine insight from her jealousy,
which she admitted that she felt for her rival. When Katherine

Mansfield died in 1923 Virginia Woolf wrote a long and detailed summary of their relationship in her diary (D II, 16 January 1923). Summoning her up by her usual method of thinking of her as an animal (her eyes were 'rather doglike, brown, very wide apart, with a steady slow rather faithful & sad expression. Her nose was sharp, & a little vulgar . . .') she notes her own confused and not particularly attractive feelings:

> . . . one feels – what? A shock of relief? – a rival the less? Then confusion at feeling so little – then, gradually, blankness & disappointment; then a depression which I could not rouse myself from all day. When I began to write, it seemed to me there was no point in writing. Katherine wont read it. Katherine's my rival no longer. More generously I felt, But though I can do this better than she could, where is she, who could do what I can't!. . . . I was jealous of her writing – the only writing I have ever been jealous of.

She gradually extended her network of acquaintances in the world of small press publishing of books and of magazines. In 1919 Katherine Mansfield's husband John Middleton Murry became editor of the *Athenaeum*, which merged with the *Nation* in 1921. He published the work of his wife and also of Forster and Eliot. Virginia Woolf contributed sixteen essays to his magazine in 1919–20. Another important publication was the *Criterion*, founded and edited by T. S. Eliot, which published two contributions by Virginia Woolf in 1923–24. Two other small literary magazines with which she had contact and which were of great importance in the history of literary modernism, were the American *Dial* and the *Egoist*. This latter was edited and paid for by Miss Harriet Weaver, now best known as the most generous and faithful of the contributors to the funds of the impoverished and spendthrift James Joyce. Miss Weaver printed Joyce's *Portrait of the Artist as a Young Man* in installments in *The Egoist*. When in 1917 she published *Portrait* as a book she had great difficulty in finding a printer who was willing to take the risk of prosecution under the obscenity laws. Eliot had become her assistant editor in 1917 and it was he who suggested to her that the Woolfs might be able to print and publish *Ulysses* in 1918. *The Dial*, an influential American magazine, publicised Virginia Woolf's work through reviews and in 1924 by an extremely positive article on her by Clive Bell. She began to publish articles with *The Dial* herself in 1923. Perhaps the most important connection with this magazine was that both the Hogarth Press and *The Dial* published Eliot's *The Waste Land*. *The Dial* gave Eliot the very substantial prize of two thousand dollars for the poem and published it in November 1922, one month after its appearance in England in the *Criterion*. It was a year later that Hogarth published it in book form in England, the poem being padded out to make it suitable for book publication by the addition of Eliot's notes. This provided it, he said, with a 'remarkable exposition of bogus scholarship'.[4]

Through all of these connections Virginia Woolf became a part of the extended network of radical, modernist writers and publishers. The little magazines were read only in very small circles and both they and their printers were oppressed and censored by the obscenity laws. Non-commercial small-press publishing played a vital role in the history of literary modernism. Writers were liberated from the pressures of the market for long enough to find their way and to reach a small but important audience. These were years when Virginia Woolf was herself nervously and uncertainly exploring the possibilities offered by her new-found freedom. She was experimenting with new formal techniques in her stories and in the novel *Jacob's Room* that she began to write in the Spring of 1920, while in her essays she was attempting to delineate through her reading of Lawrence and Joyce the shapes of modern fiction. She was beginning to find the courage to build her career and establish her identity as a writer on the difficult ground of experimentation and technical innovation. We could measure the growth of her independence by her willingness to admit herself into the company of literary outsiders. That the others *were* outsiders in their different ways there can be no doubt. Katherine Mansfield was a woman and a colonial from New Zealand, Joyce was lower-middle class, Irish and an exile, Eliot was an American who was laughed at by the snobbish English. Virginia Woolf was a woman and was moreover associated with the unconventionalities of Bloomsbury Group life-style. Yet she hesitated and felt anxious about her identification with these outsiders. She sneered and scoffed at Joyce and at the proletarian Lawrence. Relations among them all were not easy and Virginia Woolf's style was to combine the hostility that arose from rivalry or jealousy, with the aloofness and condescension of her superior class origins. She was liable to be brought down by the brilliance of the men. Even Leonard was a rival. Only later did she unambiguously and proudly claim the status of outsider.

It was through Hogarth Press work that Virginia Woolf came to meet T. S. Eliot. His *Prufrock and Other Observations* was published in 1917 by the Egoist Press. It was noticed by Clive Bell who took along a dozen copies to a gathering at Garsington, the house of Ottoline Morrell. Here Leonard obtained a copy and immediately contacted Eliot, offering to print and publish his next book of poems. The Hogarth Press had at the time only published one book, the Woolf's *Two Stories*. Virginia and Mr Eliot (he was only to become 'Tom' much later) first met in November 1918. Eliot was working at Lloyd's Bank and Virginia found him to be a model of rectitude, reserve and conventionality. 'But beneath the surface, it is fairly evident that he is very intellectual, intolerant, with strong views of his own, & a poetic creed. I'm sorry to say that this sets up Ezra Pound & Wyndham Lewis as great poets . . . He admires Mr Joyce immensely' (D I, 15 November 1918). They printed his *Poems* in 1919, printing the sixteen pages one sheet at a time, hand sewing them together and sticking a little label with the title and the author's name on the cover. It was, Virginia noted, the best printing job they had ever done and she was proud of it. They published it on the same day as *Kew Gardens* and Eliot immediately became a rival. She compared their sales and their reviews. 'I felt gorged & florid with my comparative success', she wrote after the *TLS* had been severe on Eliot (D I, 14 June 1919).

Relations between them gradually warmed and they were able to talk about literature and even to swap intimacies occasionally. They compared their methods of breaking free of literary conventionality. *Jacob's Room* was influenced by Eliot's work, especially 'The Love Song of J. Alfred Prufrock'.[5] Perhaps Eliot's work encouraged her to explore the particular kinds of difficulty that we find in *Jacob's Room*. The narrative is fragmented, the scenes are discontinuous, the images are condensed. The reader has to struggle for an interpretation. She was in the early stages of the composition of *Jacob's Room* when she discussed with Eliot the discontinuity in his poems. 'I taxed him with wilfully concealing his transitions. He said that explanation is unnecessary. If you put it in, you dilute the facts. You should feel these without explanation' (D II, 20 September 1920). Both Eliot and Woolf composed starting from certain intensely imagined *scenes*.

Her contact with the modernist men was simultaneously encouraging and threatening. It gave her something to measure her work against and at the same time made her feel that she was failing to come up to their standards. We can see this, for example, in her diary for October 1920. She was at this time about half-way through the first draft of *Jacob's Room* and writing with pleasure. Suddenly the writing stops and her confidence collapses. Eliot had come to stay. As they all talked together, Virginia found herself out of her depth, though apparently Leonard was comfortable with the conversation. 'I kept myself successfully from being submerged, tho' feeling the waters rise once or twice. I mean by this that he completely neglected my claims to be a writer, & had I been meek, I suppose I should have gone under – felt him and his views dominant and subversive' (D II, 20 September 1920). They talked about *Ulysses*. 'This, so far as he has seen it, is extremely brilliant, he says. Perhaps we shall try to publish it.' Eliot also praised Pound and Wyndham Lewis. All this left Virginia Woolf feeling anxious and uncertain about her own capacity. At this time the only experimental work she had completed were a few small stories. She had as yet no substantial work to put into the balance. She was knocked off her stride by the conversation, feeling that even Leonard showed up better than she did. Her writing came to a halt.

> Eliot coming on the heel of a long stretch of writing fiction (2 months without a break) made me listless; cast shade upon me; & the mind when engaged upon fiction wants all its boldness & self-confidence. He said nothing – but I reflected how what I'm doing is probably being better done by Mr Joyce. Then I began to wonder what it is that I'm doing: to suspect . . . that I have not thought my plan out plainly enough – so to dwindle, niggle, hesitate – which means that one's lost. . . . An odd thing the human mind! so capricious, faithless, infinitely shying at shadows. Perhaps at the bottom of my mind, I feel that I'm distanced by L[eonard] in every respect. (D II, 26 Sept 1920)

On this very same day she fought back her fears of being beaten by the men by writing a 'counterblast' to Arnold Bennett's recently published book *Our Women*, which had argued that 'intellectually and creatively man is the superior of woman' (cited D II p. 69). She felt that she was under attack from all sides.

Virginia Woolf and Eliot gradually established less nervous, frosty relations. They had a great deal in common, including mental breakdowns and a propensity towards visionary experience, though their views on religion remained totally different. Their anxious competitiveness gradually transformed into mutual respect. Within two years she was calling him 'Tom' and cooperating in the setting up of an Eliot Fellowship Fund, an attempt to collect enough money together to allow Eliot to leave his job at the bank. They aimed to find £500 per annum, the very sum which Virginia Woolf some years later made into a symbol for a woman's independence.

As for Joyce, her views remained ambiguous. The Hogarth Press did not publish *Ulysses*. There was never any question of their printing a work of that size themselves and they found it impossible to get any other printer to touch it, just as Miss Weaver herself had. It was first published in book form in Paris in 1922. Virginia Woolf read early chapters when they were published in instalments in *The Little Review* from 1918 to 1920 and made notes which, though full of puzzlement, were more positive than her later, better known remarks in her diary.[6] She glanced at the manuscript which Miss Weaver brought them in the Spring of 1918. Miss Weaver, now forty-two years old, feminist, communist and editor of the avant-garde review the *Egoist*, turned out to be amazingly proper, modest, full of decorum. Virginia was astonished. 'How did she ever come in contact with Joyce and the rest? Why does their filth seek exit from her mouth?' (D II, 18 April 1918). When the book was eventually published in 1922 she read it through completely this time and her reactions were far more negative. She found it good as far as the Hades section, but from then on she was 'puzzled, bored, irritated, & disillusioned as by a queasy undergraduate scratching his pimples. And Tom [Eliot], great Tom, thinks this on a par with War & Peace! An illiterate, underbred book it seems to me: the book of a self-taught working man, & we all know how distressing they are, how egotistic, insistent, raw, striking, & ultimately nauseating' (D II, 16 August 1922). There are many more comments in the same vein (see especially D II, 6 September 1922). Perhaps nothing could better illustrate the immense importance to Virginia Woolf of having a publishing press of her own, of never having to submit her work to the judgement of others, than the treatment that Joyce received at the hands of printers and publishers. Not that there was any question, of course, of her ever writing a book which would risk being prosecuted for obscenity. But Joyce suffered censorship on political grounds, with *Dubliners*, and for the unconventionality of his style, as well as for the masturbation of Leopold Bloom in *Ulysses*. *Portrait of the Artist as a Young Man* was censored by the printer when it was published in the *Egoist*; without informing Joyce he omitted whole sentences which he found unacceptable. In an effort to have a non-expurgated version published, the book was submitted in 1915 to Duckworth in London. After long delays it was rejected, in fact by their reader Edward Garnett, a man with Bloomsbury connections and the very reader who had two years earlier praised and accepted for Duckworth, *The Voyage Out*, thus initiating Virginia Woolf's career as a novelist. Garnett's report on *Portrait*[7] commented negatively on its unconventionality and its unfinished, fragmentary style. One wonders whether he would ever have accepted *Jacob's Room* without demanding changes. Through her Press, Virginia Woolf had escaped the possibility of such interference by Duckworth or anyone else for ever.

5

1922–24: Her Own Voice

'Orphans is what I say we are – we Georgians.'
(L II, 21 May 1922)

It has been pointed out that by 1918, in spite of the fact that she had published more than a quarter of a million words of reviews and essays, Virginia Woolf was known only for two works, *The Voyage Out* and the story 'The Mark on the Wall' (E III xi). With very few exceptions all her other writing had been anonymous. *Night and Day* did not do much for her reputation, but the volume of eight stories and other short pieces, *Monday or Tuesday*, was well received when it was published in 1921. Reviews highlighted the originality of these pieces, and noted that they were mostly attempts to capture the activity of minds thinking. But the word most frequently used was 'beauty'. 'No one who values beauty in words should miss "The Haunted House"', said the *Daily News*. 'It is a new thing, made up of a new way of using words and a new way of suggesting emotions' (*Woman's Leader*). The novelty of what she was attempting was pointed out by everyone, and the analogy with the revolution in painting was clear. 'And how amazingly it is rendered! No one interested in the expression of modern thought through modern art should miss these consummate renderings . . . her pictures do not seem made with words, but with the very stuff of our mental processes', said the reviewer in the *Observer*.

Over the next few years Virginia Woolf herself returned again and again to the attempt to formulate just what it was she was trying to do in her fiction. The analogy with painting was always, and often misleadingly, near the surface. These efforts resulted in a series of articles, starting with 'Modern Novels' in 1919 and culminating with the publication of a Hogarth Press pamphlet, *Mr Bennett and Mrs Brown* in 1924. These essays established her reputation as a formidably intelligent and original polemicist and defender of modern writing. At the same time she was writing her first novel in a modernist style, *Jacob's Room*, and it was published in

1922. As a result of these works, she had become by the age of forty-two a well-known and respected, though not popular or best-selling, figure on the literary scene. Her anonymity as an essayist diminished. She wrote more signed essays for the *TLS*, and began to write much more for other publications and other audiences. She published her first feminist polemic, in the *New Statesman*, in 1920. She began her career of publication in the USA where *The Voyage Out* was published in 1920 and a little later her articles began to appear in the *New York Post Literary Review*, *New York Herald Tribune*, the *New Republic* and *Dial*. In terms of earnings, however, she was not yet a success.

CAREER AND MARRIAGE

In 1919 the Woolfs bought Monks House in the village of Rodmell, Sussex and in 1924 they bought the lease of 52 Tavistock Square in London. Here they lived on the upper floors and installed the Hogarth Press in the basement. They lived in these two homes until the Tavistock Square house was destroyed by German bombs in 1940. After Virginia's recovery in 1916 the couple's marriage stabilised and their relationship became increasingly warm and affectionate. The rules were established. There were to be no children. Leonard had given up writing novels and had settled into a life of professional journalism. For some years only his earnings enabled Virginia to write. She was docile and submissive to his instructions on matters to do with her health. They enjoyed each other and shared not only the Hogarth Press but also travel and politics. Their marriage became the bedrock of her life.

In 1920 Virginia could still feel professionally competitive with Leonard: 'I'm distanced by Leonard in every respect' (D II, 26 September 1920). They had each published two novels and were established reviewers. But Leonard was by now a paid editor of the *International Review* at £250 per annum. In 1924 he obtained the post of Literary Editor of the *Nation*. His earnings were much more substantial than hers. In 1919 he earned a total of £578, (including £262 freelance fees for journalism and £66 book royalties). Their joint expenditure was around £800 a year. In the same year Virginia earned only £153, all of it from journalism. Leonard calculated that in the twelve years 1909 to 1921 Virginia's earnings from her books totalled only £205. By 1924 she had become a success in terms of literary reputation and no longer needed to feel that Leonard might overshadow her. But it was not until 1926, when she was forty-four years old, that her earnings reached that level of £500 a year which she calculated could support an independent writer's life (LW 291f). 1926 was the first year in which she earned more than Leonard. Thereafter she achieved this in every year of her life. Leonard wrote, 'If she had had to earn her living during those years [before 1922], it is highly improbable that she would ever have written a novel' (LW 197). It is worth comparing her situation with that of Eliot, who was working in a bank (friends, including Virginia, tried to organise an Eliot Fund of £500 pa so that he could give up work) and Joyce, who was scraping a living as a language teacher and by soliciting donations from friends, family and admirers.

Because of her subsequent celebrity as a novelist, it is easy to forget that through her thirties Virginia Woolf was still working primarily as a journalist. In 1918 she still found reviewing exciting. It gave her a sense of importance. When she was staying in the country at Asheham, special arrangements had to be made to get books to her from the *TLS* for her urgent attention. 'When I have to review at command of a telegram, & Mr Geal [a workman living in a cottage nearby] has to ride off in a shower to fetch the book at Glynde, & comes and taps at the window about ten at night to receive his shilling & hand in the parcel, I feel pressed & important & even excited a little' (D I, 23 September 1918). Within a few years her attitude changed as she published her fiction and became better known. She could allow herself to feel some resentment at the loss of time which reviewing came to represent. This was an unannounced but significant change. The pattern of her work as an essayist and reviewer, which can be seen in Table 5.1, is very interesting, and helps one to appreciate the conditions of work of an aspiring professional writer trying to build a career in those years.

The amount of time that she put into journalism began to fall off from 1920 when she began writing *Jacob's Room* and *Mrs Dalloway*. She often discussed whether she could give up writing for money altogether. Leonard's earnings enabled her to decrease it. It was an important act of self-assertion when she decided drastically to reduce the amount that she was writing for the *TLS* and also to upgrade its character, for now she began to write longer, signed articles rather than anonymous reviews. These more ambitious

TABLE 5.1   *Essays and Earnings, 1916–24*

Year	Number of essays	Earnings	Notes
1916	16	not known	15 for TLS, 1 for *The Times*
1917	35	£95	all for TLS
1918	44	£104	all for TLS
1919	45	£153	33 for TLS
1920	31	£234	18 for TLS, 6 for *New Statesman*
1921	14	£47	10 for TLS, 4 for *New Statesman*
1922	5	£69	4 for TLS, 2 for *New Statesman*
1923	11	£158	2 for TLS, 8 for *Nation*
1924	42	£128	4 for TLS, 33 for *Nation*

Sources: *The Essays of Virginia Woolf*, ed. Andrew McNeillie: vols. I–III; Leonard Woolf *Autobiography*, vol. 2.

articles were to become the basis of her collection *The Common Reader* in 1925. She began to reject books offered for review by both the *TLS* and the *Athenaeum*. She had found the courage to liberate herself from a tiresome duty. 'To have broken free at the age of 38 seems a great piece of good fortune – coming at the nick of time, & due of course to L. without whose journalism I couldn't quit mine . . . Now, of course, I can scarcely believe that I ever wrote reviews weekly; & literary papers have lost all interest for me' (D II, 15 September 1920).

In 1923–24 she began to work instead for the *Nation* (Leonard was the Literary Editor) writing very short pieces on a variety of topics, including theatre reviews. She also began to write for and earn money from American magazines. At the end of 1921 her relations with the *TLS* had undergone a further deterioration, though this turned out to be temporary. She was reminded of how much she was, as a professional reviewer, under the authority of an editor, and she had a dispute with Bruce Richmond who, she felt, was interfering with her work. In an article on Henry James she had used the word 'lewd' and Richmond would not accept it. Virginia was annoyed and struggled to decide whether to stop working for him or to pander. 'No more reviewing for me, now that Richmond re-writes my sentences to suit the mealy mouths of Belgravia (an exaggeration, I admit) & it is odd how stiffly one sets pen to paper when one is uncertain of editorial approval' (D II, 3 January 1922). This little dispute with Richmond was just one example of how in her mind her fortunes as a modern writer were somehow connected with her struggle as a woman to emancipate herself from the constraints of patriarchal authority. Far more important was her battle with Arnold Bennett.

MODERN FICTION

Open many a book on Virginia Woolf and you will find a discussion of her 'method' and of her views about the aims of the modern novel, that relies heavily upon a series of quotations from her article 'Modern Fiction'. The very same passages are always quoted. They are often taken to be Woolf's clearest definition of what she was attempting to do in her work. They tell us that on any ordinary day a myriad of impressions falls upon the ordinary mind and that the task of fiction is to record these impressions as they fall, in the order in which they fall. We are also told that life is not a series of gig lamps symmetrically arranged, but a luminous halo. After seventy years of repetition, these passages have become apparently immovably fixed as the main reference points for the exposition of Woolf's work. However, I believe that her essay, and the logic of her argument, have been misunderstood. Her irresistably attractive metaphors, the myriad of impressions and the shower of atoms, the semi-transparent envelope and the luminous halo, have charmed a thousand critics, all looking for a vocabulary in which to discuss her rather baffling work. But do these metaphors help us to understand her work? I believe not. Moreover, it is not clear in 'Modern Novels' (the first version of 'Modern Fiction') that she intended that they should even be applied to her own fiction. Not only has the argument of 'Modern Novels' been misunderstood, but so also has its place in Woolf's development as a writer. It has been inappropriately elevated to the status of her major statement of method and purpose. It is more accurate to see it, I believe, as a confused and uncertain attempt by Virginia Woolf to define her own purposes by charting her dissatisfaction with some other modern novelists, and it was written years before she developed her own characteristic fictional methods.

In the early 1920s the word that critics grasped hold of, in an effort to categorise Virginia Woolf's fiction and thereby to make it seem more approachable, was 'impressionist'. The passages and metaphors which they found in 'Modern Fiction' seemed to validate this way of understanding her work. They suggested that she saw the task of fiction as the transcription of the flow of impressions upon consciousness, as capturing, in another popular phrase of the time, the 'stream of consciousness'. Yet as I read it, the argument of 'Modern Fiction' (and of other essays from this period) repudiates that definition of the proper object of fiction. That object is rather the 'dark region of psychology', which is a different matter entirely.

'Modern Novels' was published unsigned in the *TLS* in April 1919. A revised version, 'Modern Fiction', was included in *The Common Reader* in 1925. It is worth remembering that in 1919 Virginia Woolf had just finished *Night and Day*, which is very much not a modernist novel. Her only attempts to write in a radically new style were two stories, 'The Mark on the Wall' and 'Kew Gardens'. At this date she was unsure about the future directions of her work. She had not yet started writing *Jacob's Room*. We can best understand her article as her tentative exploration of the way that her fiction should develop. It was not based on any clear idea that she yet had of her own future work but on her confusion and puzzlement on reading those early chapters of *Ulysses*, which had appeared in installments in 1918. In this and other essays written in these years, she was attempting to clear the ground, to make some space for herself to work in. This was essentially a negative exercise, a series of refusals. It did not result in a programme or a clear statement of positive ideas. 'We can't see the whole terrain of literature from a lofty pinnacle – we're on the flat, in the crowd, half blind with dust, in the thick of the battle' (E III 31). She was trying to make choices without being able to scan the literary landscape from a vantage point on high. In this article she did not succeed in finding a usable positive solution to her problem. She did not define the way forward. Certainly nothing in the article even remotely prepares one for the audacity and novelty of her writing in *Jacob's Room* let alone its astonishing successor *Mrs Dalloway*.

In 'Modern Novels', and the rewritten version, Virginia Woolf was at war with herself. She was tempted by several different pictures of human experience, different ways of thinking about what life is, and seduced by a variety of metaphors. But she was also dissatisfied with the kinds of writing that these seem to elicit, both her own and others'. She was confused. It was a confusion and an anxious self-contesting of her own thoughts that she could not resolve by any amount of essay writing. It was only in writing the novels themselves that she discovered the way forward. In 1919 her greatest dissatisfaction was with her own work, both with the conventional *Night and Day* and with the experimental first person impressionist reveries of her stories. It has not been sufficiently remarked that she never ever returned, in any of the novels which she was to write, to this first person stream-of-thinking technique of her early stories. They were experimental and as far as their author was concerned the experiment was a definitive failure. She rejected it once and for all. The conventions of fiction, including those that she had herself employed to that date in 1919, were at odds with the vision of life that she wished to express.

The 1925 version of her essay, 'Modern Fiction', is the one which most people read today. Even more than its predecessor it seems to be fuelled not only by the impulse to clarify for herself a way forward across the uncharted terrain of modern fiction, but by a fury against the male giants of the previous generation, the Edwardian patriarchs. Her emphasis had changed. Instead of merely agonising about the conventions of fiction, she now personified these as a 'powerful and unscrupulous tyrant' who enslaves the writer. Her problem is not only to discover which way to proceed, but to emancipate herself from the forces of convention that held her back, forces of coercion that are undoubtedly imagined by Virginia Woolf in feminist terms. (I will discuss later the specific context for her anger in 1924, which was an argument about a book by Arnold Bennett called *Our Women*.)

If we read her polemic against the Edwardian novelists with an open mind, I think we soon come to realise that her arguments against them are really not very convincing. No doubt they work well as ground clearing, as a way of liberating their author from the expectations of conventional narrative methods. Her polemic enables her to work up a good measure of scorn and anger. However, this does not mean that she succeeds in stating clearly just what it is that is objectionable about their work. Her argument is that in the Edwardian novel 'life' escapes, 'life itself' is not captured by their methods. But is this to say any more than that she just is not very interested in the kinds of lives that they were writing about with their provincialism, their villas and their holidays in Brighton. She dislikes Wells's characters because of their 'inferior natures'. Her argument is pure snobbery.

The word she uses to sum up her objections is 'materialist'. It is a difficult word, loaded with value judgements. Trying to clarify it in 'Modern Fiction' she says, 'they write of unimportant things; . . . they spend immense skill and immense industry making the trivial and the transitory appear the true and the enduring'. But what are these allegedly trivial things? They are the externals of people's lives, the clothes they wear, the houses they live in, the work they do, the constraints that social relations place upon their lives. The materialists focus upon these things and as a result something that seems to Virginia Woolf to be vastly more important, more 'spiritual', 'life itself', escapes. Again, in this argument Virginia Woolf was trying to clear the ground for her own agenda. She has a strong sense of something that seems to her to be of the utmost importance in life, and it is something that the conventions of the novel will not allow her to open up in her writing. She has a vision but cannot find a way of translating it into verbal form. In words like 'spiritualist' and 'life' she is trying to label for herself the nature of this vision. But in trying to clear the way for her own writing she relies on a series of dichotomies that are highly questionable. She does not provide us with convincing reasons for accepting her implied value judgements, that the material aspects of life, the constraints of social order, the requirements of work, cooperation with others in social projects, the disciplines of the reality principle, are trivial and transitory, whereas the spiritual, the contemplative, the world of secret, intimate, private meanings, are enduring and true. In her more convincing later argument, in *A Room of One's Own*, she had come to accept the importance of the material life. It is central in the story of the defeat of Judith Shakespeare. In this early article, she is making some progress in her own struggle to clear away the dust and get a view of the options open to her as a writer. But this progress is not achieved by a successful articulation of a convincing polarity between the trivial/material and the enduring/spiritual aspects of life. These quasi-philosophical categories function here as alibis for choices that are really being made on other grounds.

With hindsight we can see what her choice is; it is to try to find ways of representing the inner worlds of her characters. Each person has an inner world of images, memories, meanings, private feelings, secret thoughts, unconscious desires. We can see how Virginia Woolf attempted to represent this world in *The Voyage Out*, in Rachel's nightmares and delirious fantasies. Her inner world, of which we catch only these distorted glimpses, is frightening, even maddening, and she cannot share it with Terence and so must die. We can recognise in *Night and Day* that intimacy, two people coming to share something of their private worlds, is represented as crossing over the threshold into the vast, deep cavern of secret meanings. Virginia Woolf saw people as having a dual existence, an outer, public life of conventional activity and talk, and an inner, private life of secret meanings. This is the dichotomy which the quite different distinction between the 'materialist' and the 'spiritualist' is supposed to capture.

She felt trapped into overemphasising the former by the prevailing conventions of fiction. Her own choice, even obsession, as an author, through the twenties, was to find better, richer, more flexible ways of opening up and displaying her characters' inner worlds in language, something which in her first two novels she had hardly begun to do. But in 1919, when she was writing 'Modern Novels', she still had no idea at all how to achieve this. Moreover, in her later novels, there is always an active questioning of the relations between these two realms, the inner and the outer. This finds expression in an unresolved contest between spiritual or mystical and materialist visions. Her mature fiction is not based on the simple one-sided scorn that we find in this early essay.

It is at this point in her argument that Virginia Woolf spells out what she takes 'life', and hence the proper subject of fiction, to be.

> Examine for a moment an ordinary mind on an ordinary day. The mind receives a myriad impressions – trivial, fantastic, evanescent, or engraved with the sharpness of steel. From all sides they come, an incessant shower of innumerable atoms: and as they fall, as they shape themselves into the life of Monday or Tuesday, the accent falls differently from of old. ('Modern Fiction', CE II 106)

The reference to Monday or Tuesday was added to the revised version of the essay presumably as a nod towards her collection *Monday or Tuesday* which had appeared in 1921 and much of which is indeed written as a kind of impressionistic capturing of streams of atoms falling upon fictional minds. If life is like this, she argues, then we have no need of the old conventions of plot, tragedy, love interest and so on, that have sustained the traditional novel.

Life is not a series of gig-lamps symmetrically arranged; life is a luminous halo, a semi-transparent envelope surrounding us from the beginning of consciousness to the end. Is it not the task of the novelist to convey this varying, this unknown and uncircumscribed spirit, whatever aberration or complexity it may display, with as little mixture of the alien and external as possible?

Is life a shower of atoms falling upon the mind? A luminous halo? Is the mind a passive receiver, a receptacle for this rain of impressions from elsewhere? Are the contents of the mind, the thoughts and feelings, the moral choices and the fleeting desires, the sensations and aspirations, necessarily so disordered, so uncircumscribed? Are these illuminating metaphors? Do they help to identify a 'proper stuff of fiction' or some new conventions for writing fiction that will replace the tired old conventions of plot and life story? In the earlier version of the article the structure of Virginia Woolf's argument is clearer. One possibility for fiction, she seems to say, is this: 'Let us record the atoms as they fall upon the mind'. Then fiction will not shape or organise, highlight or select. It will simply record the passively received impressions. It is clear, in 'Modern Novels', that she is only stating this option in order to reject it. She is not giving us her own strategy as a writer, though this is what she is usually taken to be doing. In fact the metaphors are given not because Virginia Woolf thinks they are clear signposts to the tasks of modern fiction, but as a means of 'hazarding' a guess as to the intentions of other young writers:

In some such fashion as this do we seek to define the element which distinguishes the work of several young writers, among whom Mr James Joyce is the most notable . . . Any one who has read *The Portrait of the Artist as a Young Man* or what promises to be a far more interesting work, *Ulysses*, . . . will have hazarded some theory of this nature as to Mr Joyce's intention. ('Modern Novels', E III 33–4)

What then is her assessment of this definition of 'life itself' and of the method of fiction based upon it?

Faced, as in the cemetery scene ['Hades' in *Ulysses*] by so much that, in its restless scintillations, in its irrelevance, its flashes of deep significance succeeded by incoherent inanities, seems to be life itself, we have to fumble rather awkwardly if we want to say what else we wish; and for what reason a work of such originality yet fails to compare . . . with [Conrad's] 'Youth' or *Jude the Obscure*. (E III 34)

She is arguing that the passive recording method that she takes Joyce to be using, while bringing us closer to life itself than the materialism of the Edwardians, nevertheless fails to capture that vision which she herself is after. It fails because, she says in 'Modern Fiction', in writing such as that in *Ulysses*, we feel trapped within a self which 'never embraces or creates what is outside itself and beyond' (CE II 108). For she wants to look inside, into the private cavern of the characters' minds, in order to discover what is outside, not in the material world of society and active physical life, but 'beyond'. (As in *Night and Day*, when admitted into the secrecy of Katherine's mind, what we discover there is precisely a vision of this 'beyond', a vision of the heavens.) Her argument is that passive impressionism is not enough, because it fails to focus on and emphasise those visionary aspects of experience that were, for Virginia Woolf, so much more important than the transitory and trivial details of material life. She is not interested in the stream of consciousness for its own sake, and certainly not when it carries along the kinds of indecent detritus that it does in *Ulysses*. It only concerns her when it sweeps us 'beyond' what are for her the trivial details of the material life.

We should not be surprised to find her expressing dissatisfaction with the impressionistic method in these essays, for she had already identified this as the source of her dissatisfaction with the work of Dorothy Richardson (see her review of *The Tunnel*, E III 10, also written in 1919). Richardson had the courage to give up conventional narrative forms. Her novel has no story and no characters in the traditional sense, only the consciousness of the central mind of Miriam Henderson. The reader, Woolf says, is invited to register 'one after another, and one on top of another, words, cries, shouts, notes of a violin, fragments of lectures, *to follow these impressions as they flicker through Miriam's mind*, waking incongruously other thoughts, and plaiting incessantly the many-coloured and innumerable threads of life' (emphasis added).

Nothing could be closer to the kind of fiction identified in the celebrated passages in 'Modern Fiction', for here we have precisely the record of an ordinary mind on an ordinary day, with its incessant shower of atoms, its myriad of impressions, and so on, all of which are, according to so many critics, the proper stuff of fiction as identified by Virginia Woolf. But this is not so, for once again, just as in 'Modern Fiction', she says that this style of fiction is superficial and unsatisfactory. She rejects it. For what does this method give us but a surface? It gives us the sensations, the impressions, the ideas and emotions, but it sheds no light on 'the hidden depths'. 'We find ourselves in the dentist's room, in the street, in the lodging house bedroom frequently and convincingly; but never, or only for a tantalising second, in the reality which underlies these appearances.' These hidden depths and this underlying reality will receive many contradictory interpretations in Virginia Woolf's own work. The one thing that she surely makes quite clear is that for her the proper stuff of fiction is not a record of impressions as they fall or of atoms as they strike the mind.

In 'Modern Novels' the target that the moderns should aim to represent is identified as the 'dark region of psychology' ('the dark places of psychology' as she puts it in 'Modern Fiction'). Unfortunately, she gives little indication here just what she has in mind. It is interesting though that in trying to convey what she means she turns not to Joyce nor to Dorothy Richardson but to Chekhov. In seeking out her affiliation, the family of writers that she feels that she belongs to, she rejects both the tyrannical conventions of the Edwardians and what she takes to be the triviality and 'trickery', of the modern British writers. She turns instead to the Russians. She loves what is 'vague and inconclusive' in Chekhov's stories. In a statement that tells us far more about the general pattern of her feeling than the celebrated myriad of impressions, she says:

> The conclusions of the Russian mind, thus comprehensive and compassionate, are inevitably, perhaps, of the utmost sadness. More accurately indeed we might speak of the inconclusiveness of the Russian mind. It is the sense that there is no answer, that if honestly examined life presents question after question which must be left to sound on and on after the story is over in hopeless interrogation that fills us with a deep, and finally it may be with a resentful, despair.

Life, it turns out, is not a luminous halo, but an endless interrogation.

One way of confirming this reading of Virginia Woolf's argument in 'Modern Novels' is by noting that in her essays from these years there is one author who more than any other confirmed her vision of the proper stuff of fiction, who helped her to define it as both the dark region of psychology and that which is 'beyond', that is, as both hidden depths and transcendent reality, and this was Dostoevsky. A stream of translations of his work appeared in these years and there were regularly reviewed by Virginia Woolf. She herself added to this stream in 1922 when the Hogarth Press published his *Stavrogin's Confession* (three unpublished chapters of *The Possessed*), translated by S. S. Koteliansky and Virginia Woolf. Perhaps particularly significant is this passage from her 1917 essay 'More Dostoevsky':

> . . . if we try to construct our mental processes later, we find that the links between one thought and another are submerged. The chain is sunk out of sight and only the leading points emerge to mark the course. Alone among writers Dostoevsky has the power of reconstructing these most swift and complicated states of mind, of rethinking the whole train of thought in all its speed, now as it flashes into light, now as it lapses into darkness; for he is able to follow not only the vivid streak of achieved thought, but to suggest the dim and populous underworld of the mind's consciousness where desires and impulses are moving blindly beneath the sod. (E II 83)

These metaphors for mental process and for literary creation are quite different from and proved far more fruitful for Virginia Woolf than those so often quoted from 'Modern Fiction', the recording of a shower of atoms and the luminous halo. Here writing is conceived as like drawing a map of a submerged mental landscape. It involves not passively recording experience but learning how to sink down into layers of experience which are beneath consciousness, where meanings never verbally articulated are structured like underwater valleys and mountains. We sometimes become aware of this landscape of subconscious thought and feeling in moments of especially complex meaning, in which connections are glimpsed between the recent feeling and the most distant memory, between some fragment of an idea and the whole context of mental landscape from which it draws its significance. These moments are called 'moments of vision' (the title of a poem by Hardy published in 1917) and Virginia Woolf returns to them over and over again (see E II, essays on Conrad, Dostoevsky, Chekhov and Sassoon). She praises Conrad's gift of expounding moments of vision, when the submerged landscape of a mind is suddenly and briefly illuminated so that the valleys and the peaks stand out clearly and we can grasp their shape. She says of Sassoon, 'As it is the poet's gift to give expression to the moments of insight and experience that comes to him now and then, so in following him we have to sketch for ourselves a map of those submerged lands which lie between one pinnacle and the next'. It was in these essays and with these metaphors, dating from 1917–18, that Virginia Woolf anticipated her own method of composition and her own insight into mental process, as these were to be exemplified in the discovery of the technique of 'tunnelling' in *Mrs Dalloway* in 1924.

ONLY DISCONNECT: JACOB'S ROOM

Early in 1920, searching for a new form for a new novel, Virginia Woolf speculated about writing a book with 'no scaffolding; scarcely a brick to be seen' (that is, no plot and no framework of 'reality' in the Edwardian sense). She thought that she would use the reverie form of her stories and extend it over 200 pages, 'mark on the wall, K[ew]. G[ardens]. & unwritten novel taking hands & dancing in unity' (D II, 26 January 1920). However, what is remarkable about the new novel *Jacob's Room* is just how unlike anything she had written before it turned out to be. There are some passages of reverie, of stream of consciousness, but they are not by any means the most original or strange features of the novel. For when she actually wrote the book, she did not put into effect a programme that she had worked out in advance in her essay on modern novels, nor extend to novel length a method she had practised in short pieces in *Monday or Tuesday*. Jacob's Room is not a development of previous discoveries at all. It is an amazing leap into drastically new formal territory. As Virginia Woolf composed the novel she made choices, and as she made choices the novel evolved in form. It was not until late in the history of its composition, in the final drafts, that she found ways of building the novel that at last seemed right to her.[1]

Always in Virginia Woolf's work, the choices she made about technique, about the details of a novel's construction, were not determined by an abstract interest in formal innovation for its own sake. She searched out her methods and made her choices because she was struggling to put into words a vision that she had of something that seemed to her to be important. Her innovations in formal technique were always purposive, they were 'statements about what life is'.[2] Sometimes, as in this case, she did not narrow down her focus onto the central vision of the novel until after she had worked through a whole first draft.

Looking back we can see among her earlier discussions and reflections on literature, some that stand out as especially relevant to the way that this new novel developed. Especially important was her interest in the *difficulty* of Eliot's poetry, which arose from its discontinuity. Hence the significance of her conversation with him about his transitions, his unwillingness to spell out the narrative and psychological connections that hold his scenes together. We can see above all the significance of her praise for Chekhov's inconsequential stories, his willingness to repress the desire to explain and to judge. For *Jacob's Room*, in its final version, is a collage of discontinuous scenes; it is a 'disconnected rhapsody' (D II, 23 June 1922). It is, in the metaphor from her essay on Dostoevsky, a survey of pinnacles appearing above the water, with only hints and suggestions as to the submerged hills and caverns in the depths below that may connect them together into a continuous landscape. What has no bearing whatsoever on this novel is the theory that she had considered and rejected in 'Modern Novels', that the proper stuff of fiction is the recording of a stream of atoms falling upon the mind, for Jacob, the central character of the book, is perceived by the narrator primarily from the outside. The impressions in his mind are not recorded, for they can only be a matter of speculation to the narrator. Virginia Woolf had rejected, and never again returned to, a first-person stream of consciousness technique.

At first glance the novel seems to tell the life story of Jacob Flanders. It opens with Jacob as a boy on holiday with his mother, and follows him through to his life as a student at Cambridge and then afterwards tells of his adventures in London and on holiday in Greece. At the end we learn that he has been killed in the Great War. Yet the novel refuses to shape up as a traditional *bildungsroman*. It does not make the kinds of connections that we expect a biography to make. Above all it is inconclusive in the sense that the events and episodes of Jacob's life do not lead anywhere. His death is a brutal interruption of his growth, not its final culmination. The war does not give meaning and value to his life, but simply stops it senselessly. It is an anti-war book, and it is bitter and angry not only about war itself but also about the values, historical myths and social illusions that gave rise to the war. The formal strangeness of the book is an oblique expression of the author's response to the personal and historical experience of that generation of young people who felt themselves to have been cut off from the past, to be orphans as she put it, disconnected from the traditions, meanings and values of their parents' generation as a result of the First World War. Because it is anti-war, it is an anti-biography, and anti-*bildungsroman*, an anti-epic. It is the story of a Ulysses who never comes home, woven by a Penelope who loathes the war he has gone off to and the myths that made it possible. She cannot weave a continuous tapestry out of Jacob's life, but can only assemble bits and pieces, like his mother surveying the disordered clutter and confusion of Jacob's room, in the final pages of the novel. The narrator can only imagine episodes, speculate about motives, assemble memories, in a collage of disconnected scenes. This narrator, who is a woman some ten years older than Jacob, is the other central character in the novel. It is the only one of Virginia Woolf's novels in which she uses a personal narrator, who uses the first person, who addresses the reader in the second person, and whose commentary about the impossibility of knowing anyone else provides a rationale for the novel's unfamiliar form.

'Only connect', the epigraph to Forster's *Howards End* (1910), had been offered by Forster as a way of defeating the forces of disconnection that threaten modern society. Life can be made whole and intelligible if we connect to the past through a sense of place, of having roots both in a locality and in the generations, if we connect with one another by imaginative sympathy, and if we connect within ourselves the romantic passion and the prosaic demands of reality. All of these forms of life-giving connection are denied by *Jacob's Room*. The basic form of narrative connection, said Forster, is 'The king died, and then the queen died of grief'. Narrative gives us both a sequence of events and also a connecting thread between them. By contrast, the basic narrative form in *Jacob's Room* is: 'Jacob Flanders, therefore, went up to Cambridge in October, 1906' (JR

27). The sentence stands alone on the page surrounded by large white spaces, isolated from any narrative thread that would allow us to make sense of that 'therefore'. It is a connective which fails to connect.[3] In fact, Jacob's going up to Cambridge seems to be the result of a series of accidents. The significance of the date is not contained in the 'therefore' but in the surrounding historical time frame which readers are familiar with but which played no part in Jacob's going to Cambridge: we know that this date places Jacob historically in the years just before the First World War. Another example is: 'So Clara left him' (JR 86). This is also surrounded by white spaces separating it from the scenes which come before and after. The 'so', another narrative connective, is again unable to function because we do not know why Clara left Jacob. We know that there has seemed to be the possibility of love and marriage between the two of them. It is not clear just why this possibility is never realised. Sometimes it seems to be the result of accidents, at other times there is a hint of some desire or aspiration in Jacob, never articulated for he is a tongue-tied young man, and which he could never satisfy with Clara. Perhaps for this reason (for this connection is a guess) he seeks out sexual adventures in London.

Virginia Woolf's use of those white spaces on the page is a brilliant invention, perhaps importing into the novel devices of layout that had intrigued her when she was laying out Eliot's poetry on the page for the Hogarth Press. The gaps hold scenes in a state of disconnection, so that the reader is provided with a sequence of separated scenes rather than a narrative. They are an immediately visible sign of Virginia Woolf's choice of a collage framework for the novel. It is as if the narrator cannot find sufficient momentum to keep going, but starts and stops. The effect has been likened to freeze frames in a film, stopping the flow of narrative and holding the viewer's attention temporarily onto one moment. But just as with a visual collage so also here, the destruction of a normal narrative or visual framework not only disconnects but also allows and encourages other, less expected, forms of connection to come into focus. For the book is not just a jumble of random elements. It has a strong sense of composition. Each element, because the connections with its surrounding narrative are loosened, can take on new meaning by finding a different, broader context. For example, at the very beginning of the book we find twice on one page, and both times surrounded by the white spaces; 'Ja-cob! Ja-cob! Archer shouted' (JR 6). When this is

repeated a third time, the narrator adds, 'The voice had an extraordinary sadness. Pure from all body, pure from all passion, going
out into the world, solitary, unanswered, breaking against rocks –
so it sounded' (JR 6). The narrator has taken a minor narrative
fragment and by disconnecting it and repeating it, has given it an
intense expressive charge, a pure elegiac sadness, which es-
tablishes a tone, a mood which settles over the whole book.

Throughout the book there are elements which are lifted out of
their immediate context and given a richer significance, transformed from simple narrative details into poetic images, by virtue
of repetition. There is hardly a single page on which one does not
find some signifier of mortality, a gravestone, a lamentation, a
skull. This assembly of fragments returns us again and again to the
theme of mourning, to the atmosphere of bereavement, and it is
this, 'the effect of the black' (JR 7), rather than narrative and
character, which unifies the book.[4]

Narrative disconnection means that there is no story, in this case
no life story or biography. The narrator explains that though 'the
streets of London have their map, . . . our passions are uncharted'
(JR 92); '. . . there has never been any explanation of the ebb and
flow in our veins – of happiness and unhappiness' (JR 134). Since
we have no map of the submerged landscape of our minds, our
actions can seem wild. We leap from one thing to another without
obvious reason. When a life reaches a turning point, how can we
know why one direction rather than another is taken. There are
'chasms in the continuity of our ways' (JR 93). Narrative and
character are both conventions which have enabled writers to
disguise these chasms. But they no longer offer a viable form of
writing. For as Virginia Woolf put it a year later, when preparing to
defend her fiction against Arnold Bennett's criticism, 'character is
dissipated into shreds now' (D II, 19 June 1923), and she again
cited Dostoevsky as her inspiration.

The particular reasons why the narrator can only speculate about
Jacob's character are not only that he died young, before he had
settled into a stable life, but also because he was a man whereas
she is a woman. She experienced him as distant, as silent. He
withdraws and excludes. He sits in his room reading Plato oblivi-
ous of the woman pounding on a door down the street begging to
be let in. There are many places where we feel the narrator's
subtle, scarcely hidden resentment and anger at Jacob's dealings
with women. He thinks them stupid, a distraction, and yet he

desires them. Moreover, Jacob was an inheritor, whereas women are left outside looking in, trying to glimpse what it is like to belong, to be privileged with traditions and education. As an inheritor Jacob is both victim and perpetrator; he enjoys privilege and is promised power, yet he is also deformed by the foolish self-satisfaction of his social position and his inability to understand women. The narrator's attitude is a mixture of sympathy and resentment. Jacob and his friends themselves feel that what they have inherited is 'civilisation', that keyword in Cambridge–Bloomsbury circles, that designates the assumed superiority of culture, of knowledge, of educated taste, that the young men thought connected them to the civilisation and art of the past, all the way back to the Greeks. A historical narrative of the continuity of civilisation, linking Athens and Cambridge, gives the young men their sense of self-satisfaction and mastery (JR 42), the self-confidence with which they move into positions of power. Civilisation is built on our 'astonishing gift for illusion' (JR 133).

Jacob knew no more Greek than served him to stumble through a play. Of ancient history he knew nothing. However, as he tramped into London it seemed to him that they were making the flagstones ring on the road to the Acropolis, and that if Socrates saw them coming he would bestir himself and say 'my fine fellows', for the whole sentiment of Athens was entirely after his heart. (JR 74)

This historical myth affects the way the men think about their women ('Wild and frail and beautiful she looked, and thus the women of the Greeks were, thought Jacob' JR 75). Women are not innocent, for they too take part in sustaining these illusions. Women fantasise about the men as Greek warriors. The narrator makes fun of these myths and illusions, these ways of making up stories and heroes, and contrives to bring Greece and the Greeks into her scenes in many unexpected ways. The tendency to transform lives into epics and young Londoners into Greek heroes, was not simply a joke or a private foolishness, but a dangerous lie. In 1914, as the young men marched to the trenches they had no idea of what they were doing, and the copies of Homer which they carried in their pockets helped to blind them to the fact that in the mud of Flanders they would be transformed not into heroic Greek sculptures but into corpses.

In writing about the life and death of Jacob Flanders, Virginia Woolf was partly drawing on her relationship with her brother Thoby, and the history of puzzled love and resentment that she had felt for that silent, awkward man. But she was also remembering her friend Rupert Brooke who had been turned into a national hero after his death in the war. There was no more extreme example of mythologising Hellenism than the case of Rupert Brooke. He had stayed with the Stephen family on holiday at St Ives when they were children. They met again when he was a student at Cambridge and for a time they were close friends. She knew what most of those who were acquainted only with his legend did not, that he had had an affair with Virginia's friend Ka Cox in 1912 and had had a nervous breakdown. She visited him in Granchester in 1911 and, incredible as it seems in her case, they swam together naked in the river. He was famous for his good looks. He was a minor poet. He died in April 1915 in the Aegean while serving in the British Navy. Because of his volume of sentimental poems about war he was instantly turned into a hero, a noble warrior in the Greek mould. In fact he died not in action but of blood poisoning.

As Richard Jenkyns says, ' . . . the fragments that Brooke scribbled on his fatal voyage show how he saw the war in Homeric terms'.[5] This Brooke shared with any number of his fellow officers, for many of them consciously turned to images and sentiments from the *Illiad* to make sense of their experience. 'They say Achilles in the darkness stirred . . ./ And Priam and his fifty sons/ wake all amazed, and hear the guns,/ And shake for Troy again' jotted Brooke in his notebook. Perhaps there was more excuse for this fantastic anachronism in Brooke's case than in that of the soldiers in Northern Europe, for at least Brooke was in the Aegean and sailing towards Gallipoli, which faces the site of Troy across the Dardenelles. En route he wrote that he would 'recite Sappho and Homer. And the winds of history will follow me all the way'.[6] He wrote in a letter, 'I've been looking at maps. Do you think that *perhaps* the fort on the Asiatic corner will want quelling, and we'll land and come at it from behind and they'll make a sortie and meet us on the plains of Troy?'[7] Brooke was buried in an olive grove on the island of Skyros, the island on which Achilles hid, disguised as a girl. A friend who attended his funeral wrote back home, 'One was transported back a couple of thousand years and felt the old Greek divinities stirring from their long sleep'.[8] But burying the dead as if they were heroes of ancient Greece was precisely what

Virginia Woolf found so objectionable. Making Greek warriors out
of dead Englishmen seemed to her deeply offensive and absurd.

In 1918 she was sent for review a copy of *The Collected Poems of
Rupert Brooke: with a Memoir* by Edward Marsh. She found Marsh's
memoir so dreadful that she hesitated to review the book. For
Marsh was contributing to that fantastic and false version of
Brooke that had become an accepted public myth.[9] She found this
distortion of the truth of that 'volatile, irreverent, and extremely
vivacious spirit' intolerable (E II 203). Marsh's book was she
thought a 'disgraceful sloppy sentimental rhapsody, leaving Rupert rather tarnished.' For in fact he was jealous, moody, ill-
balanced, 'all of which I knew, but can hardly say in writing' (D I,
23 July 1918). Those who knew Brooke should, she thought, 'put
their view on record and relieve his ghost of an unmerited and
undesired burden of adulation'.[10] The conventions of reviewing
did not allow her to be very open about her feelings. In another
essay (E II 278) she was able to say, in words that are relevant to
our understanding of her project in *Jacob's Room*, 'To have seen a
little of him . . . was to have seen enough to be made sceptical of
the possibility of any biography of a man dying, as he died, at the
age of twenty-eight'. His legend fixes him forever in a particular
shape, entombs him in an inconguously static and finished character, whereas in life he was fond of 'amusing disguises, experiments
in living'. We can recognise the fluidity, the unfinished quality, of
Jacob Flanders in these thoughts.

For Virginia Woolf the questions raised by Marsh's book were of
more general significance than just the case of Rupert Brooke. For
it raised the question, 'Can biography tell the truth?' Not only are
there public conventions of dishonesty which prevent certain
aspects of a person's life and personality from being truthfully
discussed, but there are the conventions of biographic form itself.
Biography turns a person's life into a story. *Jacob's Room* was
written as an anti-biography which dispensed with the life-story
convention in order, paradoxically, to de-fictionalise the lives of
young men whose deaths had been falsified by the myths of
official culture. In the novel, Jacob himself writes an essay on the
topic 'Does history consist of the biographies of great men?', a
reminder of the conventions of biographic writing practised by
Leslie Stephen. Virginia Woolf's experimenting with new ways of
writing novels was a response to broader issues than just those
raised by Marsh's book ('One of the most repulsive biographies I

have ever read' L II, no. 959) and these were to involve her in a long and heated battle on the question of 'character in fiction' with her arch-enemy. Arnold Bennett.

CHARACTER IN FICTION

Jacob's Room was a decisive turning point in Virginia Woolf's career. In this book she had broken through into ways of thinking and writing that initiated the most productive and creative decade of her life. 'There's no doubt in my mind that I have found out how to begin (at 40) to say something in my own voice' (D II, 26 July 1922).

The novel gained her a reputation of being a difficult writer. The gap had opened up between those like herself, Eliot and Joyce, who wrote esoteric works for a small elite audience and those like Bennett who wrote serious fiction for a mass market. The very appearance of the book, with its 'crocus-yellow cloth boards; cream printed paper label . . . and cream dust jacket printed in cinnamon and black, designed by Vanessa Bell',[11] announced its allegiance to the Post-Impressionist aesthetic. It was marked out as avant-garde and this created resistance among the booksellers, several of whom laughed at it (LW 241). It is clear looking at the reviews that critics did not know in quite what terms to discuss this strange book. They were inclined to be respectful but struggled to understand the significance of Woolf's way of writing The book was quickly labelled by many reviewers as an 'impressionist' work. It was even seen as belonging to an impressionist school of fiction, of which Dorothy Richardson was taken to be the founder. This provided a line of criticism, that the book was too fluid and lacked 'constructive solidity', as J. Middleton Murry's review put it (MM 109). This criticism came to centre on the question of character. Did her strange style represent a failure to create characters whom readers could come to care about and understand? Her favorite response was a letter from E. M. Forster: 'I like *Jacob's Room* and am sure it is good. You have clean cut away the difficulties that so bother me and that I feared in *Night and Day* were gaining on you – all those Blue books of the interior and exterior of life of the various characters'. The terms in which he criticises *Night and Day* are interesting for they are the very terms in which Virginia Woolf herself in her polemic with Bennett would attack the Edwardians. The problem, Forster goes on, is to detach character from all this external detail without losing the reader's interest in the characters. 'You keep this interest in Jacob. This I find a tremendous achievement – the greatest in the book and the making of the book. I don't yet understand how, with your method you managed it.'[12]

It was this problem of character that Arnold Bennett commented on when he made a passing observation about the book in an essay 'Is the Novel Decaying?' in *Cassell's Weekly* in March 1923:

> I have seldom read a cleverer book than Virginia Woolf's *Jacob's Room*, a novel which has made a great stir in a small world. It is packed and bursting with originality, and it is exquisitely written. But the characters do not vitally survive in the mind because the author has been obsessed by details of originality and cleverness. I regard this book as characteristic of the new novelists who have recently gained the attention of the alert and the curious, and I admit that for myself I cannot yet descry any coming big novelists.

Virginia Woolf's response to this fairly mild criticism was a series of hard-hitting essays. They were signed, unlike her earlier 'Modern Novels', which had been published anonymously in the *TLS*. She was no longer unsure of her ground and did not hesitate publicly to set out her arguments against Bennett with as much noise as she could make. No doubt this was partly a result of the increased confidence that came from having found her own voice at last. But it was also because her feminist anger had become directly involved, in 1920, with the publication of Bennett's *Our Women*.

Bennett argued that 'intellectually and creatively man is the superior of woman'. He was supported by Desmond MacCarthy, a member of the Bloomsbury Group, in his column in the *New Statesman*. Virginia Woolf wrote in reply her first public feminist argument, in a letter to the *New Statesman* published under the title 'The Intellectual Status of Women' and in another letter which was published two weeks later (D II, Appendix III). We can see from these letters that Virginia Woolf already thought in terms of a women's literary tradition, of which she herself was the inheritor. She drew strength from her affiliation to this tradition and could see that women had in the past been obstructed in numerous ways in their desire to write. Writing can only take place in suitable social and cultural conditions and it has been the absence of these and not some supposed innate inferiority which has held women back. Only with the utmost freedom of action and experience, always denied women, can literature flourish. MacCarthy must have shocked Woolf with his obtuseness, his refusal to concede that women had been obstructed by confinement, constraint, exclusion and prohibition, and this must have helped to sharpen her feeling of resentment against the male inheritors as she was writing *Jacob's Room*. Clearly exasperated, she reminded MacCarthy, and indirectly Bennett, that 'women from the earliest times to the present day have brought forth the entire population of the universe' and that this has cost them time and strength. Women, she concluded, must overcome their fear of ridicule and condescension and express their difference from men openly.

This determination not to be put down by men, not to fear dispute with them, is the background to her hostility to Bennett when it flared up again in 1923.[13] The emphasis in 'Modern Novels' had been on 'life' or 'reality' and on these matters she was still not sure of her position. Now her attention switches to 'character'. On this she felt more confident. While preparing a response to Bennett's attack on *Jacob's Room* she noted in her diary:

> People, like Arnold Bennett, say I cant create, or didn't in J's R, characters that survive. My answer is – but I leave that to the Nation: its only the old argument that character is dissipated into shreds now: the old post-Dostoevsky argument. I daresay its true, however, that I haven't that 'reality' gift. I insubstantise, wilfully to some extent, distrusting reality – its cheapness. But to get further. Have I the power of conveying the true reality? (D II, 19 June 1923)

As in 'Modern Novels', Dostoevsky is the ancestor she calls upon. Character is in shreds because it is, as conventionally constructed in the novel, a matter of isolated peaks above the surface of the water. The conventions do not allow us to get at the submerged hidden landscape, the dark regions. But 'reality', that is more difficult. She distrusts what is called 'reality' in conventional writing, the externals of material and social life. But the 'true reality', what is that? She has become convinced that there is some other ambition for fiction, to add to the exploration of the dark places of psychology, and that is to convey the 'true reality'. It is a theme to which we will return.

Virginia Woolf's article 'Mr Bennett and Mrs Brown' was published in three places in November and December of 1923, in the
Nation and Athenaeum in London and in the *New York Evening Post*
and the Boston *Living Age* in the USA (and is printed in E III 384).
In spite of its title, in this version of the article the figure of Mrs
Brown appears only in a short flourish at the end. Dostoevsky on
the other hand plays a very large part in the argument. *Crime and
Punishment* and *The Idiot* had destroyed belief in the Victorian
literary conventions for creating character. His fictional people do
not have those features or traits that make character. Instead, 'we
go down into them as we descend into some enormous cavern.
Lights swing about; we hear the boom of the sea; it is all dark,
terrible, and uncharted'. These are the dark places of psychology,
and writers must learn to explore in these regions rather than to
remain with the superficial psychology of traits and motives. The
Edwardians have failed the challenge. What is at stake is not
merely literary fashion or style, but differences of view about what
a person is, why a human being behaves so unpredictably one way
rather than another. Writers of the younger generation are attempting to find ways of representing people that are true to their
deep complexity, and it is this that is the motive for what is strange
and difficult in their methods. This is a fine statement of Virginia
Woolf's case. It is confident, sharply focused, and clear in argument. It is an illuminating statement of her intentions in *Mrs
Dalloway* as well as *Jacob's Room*. She has not only a clear sense of
her own purposes but also of the mission of her generation, of the
historic importance of what they were jointly trying to do. She was
speaking for a group of writers, Eliot, Joyce, Strachey and herself,
who were only just breaking out of the tiny world of small press,
non-commercial publishing and the esoteric magazines. She had
found her identity in denying her fathers, in affiliation with the
Russians, and in solidarity with her colleagues in the Georgian
avant-garde.

In the Spring of 1942 Virginia Woolf returned to the debate with
Bennett when she was invited to speak to a women's society, The
Heretics, at Cambridge University. For this occasion, perhaps
because it involved an audience of women, her argument was
given a feminist slant which it did not have before, and the
marginal Mrs Brown was promoted to a far more central role. How
Woolf must have enjoyed delivering such blows as this: 'It seems
to me that to go to these men [the Edwardian novelists] and ask

them to teach you how to write a novel . . . is precisely like going
to a bootmaker and asking him to teach you how to make a watch'.
This talk has none of the ladylike politeness of her *TLS* articles. It
was called 'Character in Fiction', and it was published in Eliot's
Criterion (and how in E III). In October 1924 a revised version was
published as a short book by the Hogarth Press, and later reprinted
in the *New York Herald Tribune*. Unfortunately, this heavily revised
piece was given the title 'Mr Bennett and Mrs Brown', and it is easy
to confuse it with the shorter and substantially different essay of
the previous year. The attack on the Edwardian patriarchs had
now appeared five times as journal articles, once as a lecture and
once as a hardcover Hogarth book, with a fine drawing by Vanessa
Bell on the cover and clearly promoted as something more substantial than ephemeral journalism. The later version is said by Quentin Bell to be her 'manifesto' (QB II 104). It could be seen as the
culmination of that long process of her search for independence
which began in 1917 with the printing of 'The Mark on the Wall'.
She was now a public figure with a public voice.

Unfortunately, this most publicised version of 'Mr Bennett and
Mrs Brown' does not have either the conceptual clarity nor the
polemical force of its shorter predecessor. It centres on the celebrated overhead conversation in a railway carriage between Mrs
Brown and her male tormentor who is called Mr Smith. Virginia
Woolf no longer argues her point about 'character' but dramatises
it in this fictional scene. Her argument is that there is a connection
between the literary conventions for constructing character in fiction
and patriarchal conventions for exercising power over people in
society. They are both tyrannies. They both involve imposing
categories on people rather than listening to them and appreciating
their uniqueness and oddity. These are themes which she developed with great intensity in *Mrs Dalloway*, in the confrontations
between the deranged Septimus Warren Smith and his doctors.
The Edwardians, she claims, would be so interested in Mrs
Brown's material circumstances – her house, her father and his
social position, the system of property, and so on – that they
would pay no attention to the woman herself. We cannot know
Mrs Brown inwardly even by listening carefully to what she says,
for her words are separated by silences and in the silences we are
reminded of her unknown inner world. The novelist must make a
person up by creating an inner context for the fragments of speech
and gesture which we can observe but not understand.

Leaving aside the question of the fairness of Woolf's assessment of the Edwardians, we must ask whether this article tells us anything positive about her own solutions to the problems that she raises, about how to renovate the conventions for creating character. In one intriguing remark we are given a glimpse of a possible way forward. Understanding a person, she seems to be saying, is not providing external explanations of that person's motives or behaviour. It is rather to know what it is like to be that person, what it is like to view the world as if through her eyes. What we need is not explanation, and emphatically not judgement, but views through the character's eyes, of 'religion, of landscape, of love, of the immortality of the soul, of man's relation to the world' (E III 509). In spite of remarks such as this, however, I do not think that this article points a clear way forward. It does not have the lucidity or force of vision of a manifesto. The pointers in her earlier work which were so suggestive, the metaphors of self and life which she had mined from Dostoevsky and Chekhov, the dark regions of psychology, the submerged landscape of the mind, the moments of vision, the inconsequential story, these have all disappeared. The very strange thing is that Dostoevsky and Chekhov, who had been the central figures in her argument all the time between 'Modern Novels' in 1919 to the 1923 'Mr Bennett and Mrs Brown', have now in 1924 suddenly vanished completely from her argument.

The problem may be that she was writing at a moment when she had two rather different conceptions of how to move forward in her mind, conceptions associated with the very different novels, *Jacob's Room* and *Mrs Dalloway*. She had been attacked over the lack of character in *Jacob's Room*. Her emphasis in that novel was on the impossibility of knowing people. The novel, with its discontinuities and its silences, was written as a record of the narrator's failure to know Jacob. The fictional scene in the railway carriage has the same structure. The narrator overhears Mrs Brown talking but has no way of getting to know her. The only way of knowing someone seems paradoxically to be by making them up. In her new novel, *Mrs Dalloway*, this is just what Virginia Woolf succeeded in doing. She discovered new techniques for rendering the inner worlds of her characters. The emphasis was no longer on Jacob's silence but on Clarissa Dalloway's interior sounds and images. *Jacob's Room* was a critique of the category of character, whereas *Mrs Dalloway* reconstructed it according to new rules.

Jacob's Room emphasised the Dostoevskian dispersal of character viewed from the outside; *Mrs Dalloway* shows how this character, still dispersed, wild, unpredictable, may nonetheless be displayed from the inside in words. Unfortunately, there is no account of this discovery of new ways of creating character in 'Mr Bennett and Mrs Brown', perhaps because Woolf was so diverted by her excitement at the attack on Arnold Bennett. Her emphasis and, it seems, her thrill, is all on breaking of old conventions, the 'smashing and crashing', the 'falling and destruction', and not at all on the new edifice that will rise up in their place. This is why this essay, celebrated though it became and much quoted though it still is, seems so oddly beside the point.

6

1925–27: Modernist Fictions

'Have I the power of conveying the true reality?' (D II, 19 June 1923)

In the decade from 1922 to 1931, Virginia Woolf was astonishingly productive. She published five major novels, a collection of essays and a path-breaking work about women and fiction. By the end of the decade she was successful and famous. But perhaps the most astonishing thing about her work in these ten years is that every one of her books differed in the most basic ways from each of the others. It was not a matter of her hitting upon a successful and fruitful 'method' and staying with it. Each work was a new experiment, innovatory in form, fundamentally changing the rules of the fictional game. The other feature of the decade's production as far as the fiction is concerned, is that it is all, in spite of the differences and constant invention, within a modernist aesthetic. 'Modernism' has so many different varieties that it might be as well to spell out briefly the meaning of the term in this case. Virginia Woolf's modernism, in this decade, has much in common with the modernist 'formalism' of the Bloomsbury painters. Its main features are these. First, a self-consciousness about the categories and conventions of art. She could not write fiction without being aware of the artificial, conventional nature of the rules by which fiction is constructed – rules of character, plot and narration. Her writing forced this conventionality upon the reader's attention. Just as with cubism in painting, we can no longer take the space of the made-up scene for granted. Secondly, these conventions are radically changed. The stable, unified character and the meaningful coordinations of plot are abandoned. There is a third feature, and it is one which suggests the analogy with Post-Impressionism in painting. It is her emphasis on the unity of composition or design. However, Virginia Woolf was not interested in design for its own sake. There were always reasons for her formal inventions, for they always sprang from her attempts to display aspects of reality that otherwise remained hidden and ignored. Her purpose was always to bring things into the light, not to construct formal designs as an end in themselves. These aspects of Woolf's modernist fictions are enough to show just how much it misses her point to discuss her work mainly in terms of the effort to capture the 'stream of consciousness'. Although she was highly conscious of the fact that art is fabrication, a kind of making, and thought of herself, in her basement in Tavistock Square among the packages and the printing press, as a craft worker in her workshop, for her *vision* always ruled over *design*. Her craving for unity or aesthetic harmony, can be seen as an anxious desire to be in complete control of her material, or perhaps as the result of her typically Bloomsbury conviction that aesthetic form is significant, and that what it signifies is 'true reality', something that transcends human life. After *The Waves* in 1931, the last work of this period, she began to take yet again a radically new direction.

THE PERISHABLE HOURS OF LIFE

Whenever she read, Virginia Woolf made notes. More than sixty reading notebooks survive, in which she carefully recorded, tabulated and copied as she read. The contents of these notebooks are described and discussed by Brenda Silver in *Virginia Woolf's Reading Notebooks* (referred to here as RN). From these books we can sometimes follow her mind at work in great detail. Some time in the period 1922–24 she read Book VII of Wordsworth's *Prelude*, and she copied out these lines:

The matter that detains us now may seem,
To many, neither dignified enough
Nor arduous, yet will not be scorned by them,
Who, looking inward, have observed the ties
That bind the perishable hours of life
Each to the other, & the curious props
By which the world of memory & thought
Exists and is sustained.

Underneath she commented, 'Good quotation for one of my books' (RN 30). The book which she set about writing was called *The Hours* (only when it neared completion, in the summer of 1924, did the title become *Mrs Dalloway*). The matter of it certainly seemed neither dignified nor arduous, being a day in the life of a society hostess as she prepares for a party. Virginia Woolf worried that it would seem too trivial, and yet, as she argued in her essays and as Wordsworth confirmed for her, we can, by looking at the apparently trivial in a new way, hope to bring things of great importance to light. Wordsworth's lines very accurately identify what it was that Virginia Woolf fixed her attention upon at this time as 'the proper stuff of fiction', namely 'the curious props by which the world of memory and thought exists and is sustained'. For our experience is not merely of a shower of impressions, but at each moment is interconnected through memory into a hidden landscape. Meaning pours into each moment through channels (or props) that tie it to the past. At the same time that she wanted in her novel to promote these ties to a principle of unity, she wanted to portray disunity or dispersal of 'character' and comic disconnection of plot.

The new novel in fact started life in 1922 as a series of short stories, to be called 'At Home: or The Party'. One of them, 'Mrs Dalloway in Bond Street', was published in *Dial* in July 1923. She was interested in what she later called 'party consciousness', the way we have of secreting around ourselves a protective screen in the form of a public self which we use for this particular kind of display and amusement. This is an aspect of that dispersal of the self that she had noted from her reading of Dostoevsky. We have not one self but many, and they are activated for different occasions, as responses to different threats or opportunities. 'But my present reflection is that people have any number of states of consciousness (second selves is what I mean) & I should like to investigate the party consciousness, the frock consciousness &c.' For example, she was fascinated by clothes and fashion, by which 'people secrete an envelope which connects them & protects them from others . . .' (D III, 27 April 1925).

By October the project had expanded into a book. Although we can often follow in her diary the choices she made as a novel developed, the problems that arose and their solutions, this is the only one of her novels for which she wrote and published a sketch of the process of its composition. She wrote an 'Introduction' for an American edition (the Modern Library Series edition of 1928), in which she explained that in the original conception, Mrs Dalloway 'was to kill herself, or perhaps merely to die at the end of the party'. The whole idea of the novel changed radically when she decided to introduce another main character, Septimus Warren Smith, who was to be a young man who had become insane after his experiences in the war and who would be the one to kill himself at the end of the book. The book was now to be thought of as 'a study of insanity & suicide; the world seen by the sane & the insane side by side' (D II, 14 October 1922). She tried to imagine a structure that could contain this new notion, and jotted in her notebook: 'Suppose it to be connected in this way: sanity and insanity, Mrs D seeing the truth, S. seeing the insane truth . . . The pace is to be given by the gradual increase of S's insanity on the one side; by the approach of the party on the other . . .'[1] By June 1923 her conception of the novel had become even more complex, for she was now thinking in terms of adding to that central contrast of the two main characters a critical view of society: 'In this book I have almost too many ideas. I want to give life & death, sanity & insanity; I want to criticise the social system, & to show it at work, at its most intense' (D II, 19 June 1923). The social system works intensely in the novel in any number of ways, most dramatically through the power that doctors exercise over Septimus, driving him to his death, but also in that every one of the characters struggles to maintain an identity while being subject to a complex field of social and cultural forces, which hold them in place in society. As Virginia Woolf invented more characters, Peter Walsh (Clarissa's ex-lover), Elizabeth (her daughter), Elizabeth's unappealing friend Miss Kilman, the arrogant doctor Sir William Bradshaw, and so on, the portrayal of a society which works powerfully on people, squeezing them into the required shapes, training their emotions, punishing their misdemeanours, and eliminating the failures, those who cannot conform to the required conventions of selfhood, becomes more and more complex and intense.

Later in that summer of 1923 Virginia Woolf made her crucial discovery, of how to represent the inner worlds of her characters, how to depict 'the ties that bind the perishable hours of life'. 'I should say a good deal about The Hours, & my discovery; how I dig out beautiful caves behind my characters; I think that gives exactly what I want; humanity, humour, depth. The idea is that the caves shall connect, & each comes to daylight at the present moment' (D II, 30 August 1923). In October she recorded that she was finding her way of writing so satisfying that she felt that she could put everything she had ever thought into it, and that this has come about not as the result of her writing according to a preconceived plan, but because she had stumbled, after much misery and frustration, upon a discovery. 'Of course, I've only been feeling my way into it – up till last August anyhow. It took me a year's groping to discover what I call my tunnelling process, by which I tell the past by instalments, as I have need of it. This is my prime discovery so far. . . .' It proves, she says, that writing fiction creatively cannot be a conscious process. 'One feels about in a state of misery – indeed I made up my mind one night to abandon the book – & then one touches the hidden spring' (D II, 15 October 1923). So excited was she by this discovery, and so confident that it allowed her access through writing to hidden complexities of the personality that had hitherto been unexplored, that she remained buoyant and confident about this book in a way that was not at all characteristic. She wrote with a sense of ease and fluency and she suffered none of those prepublication anxieties, that with some other novels, were severe enough to be disabling . 'I may have found my mine this time I think. I may get all my gold out . . . And my vein of gold lies so deep, in such bent channels. To get it I must forge ahead, stoop & grope. But it is gold of a kind I think' (D II, 9 February 1924). She finished writing *Mrs Dalloway* on 17 October 1924. She revised it that December and it was published on 14 May 1925. So great was her self-assurance (and this showed in the aggression of her polemical writing in 1924, as I've noted above) that, waiting for the publication of *Mrs Dalloway*, she wrote in her diary:

I have at last, bored down into my oil well, & can't scribble fast enough to bring it all to the surface. I have now at least 6 stories welling up in me, & feel, at last, that I can coin all my thoughts into words . . . I have never felt this rush & urgency before. I believe I can write much more quickly: if writing it is – this dash at the paper of a phrase, & then the typing & retyping – trying it over, the actual writing being now like the sweep of a brush; I fill it up afterwards . . . Oddly, for all my vanity, I have not until now had much faith in my novels, or thought them my own expression. (D III, 20 April 1925)

For the six stories she had returned to the conception with which *Mrs Dalloway* had started, of a series of stories about the 'party consciousness', about the 'selves' which we secrete around us like protective envelopes to prevent traumatic contact and exposure. In fact most of these stories were not published until after her death.[2]

This history of the composition of *Mrs Dalloway* confirms that Virginia Woolf's detailed objectives and her literary methods of achieving them were unknown to her as she started to write the book. Although in her essays she had attempted to clear the ground by articulating her dissatisfaction with the prevailing traditions of the novel, she had not, in those essays, formed a clear idea for herself of what to do. Hints from Dostoevsky and Chekhov came closest to providing her with metaphors for self in terms of which she could begin to work. Once engaged in composition, however, she allowed an intuitive process to take over. She was no longer in control. That this was so she confirmed in her 'Introduction' of 1928, in which she argued that novels are not rooted in a preconceived plan or method but in hidden parts of their author's own life. 'Books are the flowers or fruit stuck here and there on a tree which has its roots deep down in the earth of our earliest life, of our first experiences.' She denies the idea, which reviewers and early readers may have resorted to in order to explain the difficulty of her work, that the novel was born of a 'method'.

> The author, it was said, dissatisfied with the form of fiction then in vogue, was determined to beg, borrow, steal or even create another of her own. But, as far as it is possible to be honest about the mysterious process of the mind, the facts are otherwise. Dissatisfied the writer may have been; but her dissatisfaction was primarily with nature for giving an idea, without providing a house for it to live in . . . The novel was the obvious lodging, but the novel it seemed was built on the wrong plan. Thus rebuked the idea started as the oyster starts or the snail to secrete a house for itself. And this it did without any conscious direction. . . . the book grew day by day, week by week, without any plan at all, except that which was dictated each morning in the act of writing. (Introduction to *Mrs Dalloway*)

It is possible to work the other way round, she says, 'But in the present case it was necessary to write the book first and to invent a theory afterwards'. It is worth emphasising this because it confirms my view that one should not read her essays as 'manifestos' or as having successfully defined a way forward for her writing.

For many readers, the most puzzling aspect of *Mrs Dalloway* is that it tells two unconnected stories. These interweave with each other but they never mesh in the ways we expect. It is as if characters from two different stories have become jumbled up by mistake. The narration jumps backwards and forwards between the story of Clarissa's party and the story of Septimus's death. Though they take place in the same world of London on one day in June 1923, the two stories never fuse. She invents a plot that instead of manoeuvering the characters into a single story, keeps them moving around London, their paths crisscrossing the city and moving unknowingly past each other in the streets, on buses, looking at each other in the park, without ever linking up. She concocts a series of coincidences that never create connection. The narration is constantly side-tracked as it jumps from one character to another for no better reason than that they are passing by each other in the street. Only in the very last scene, when Clarissa overhears a guest at her party talking about Septimus's death, does she even become aware of this young man's existence. Virginia Woolf worried about whether the book would seem for this reason to be disjointed, 'because of the mad scenes not connecting with the Dalloway scenes' (D II, 13 December 1924). Leonard Woolf agreed that *Mrs Dalloway* was 'difficult owing to the lack of connection, visible, between the two themes' (D III, 6 January 1925). So strong are our expectations of connection that the temptation was not so much to dismiss the book as disconnected as to speculate on the missing, *invisible* connection, that the author was perversely witholding from our view. Forster said that we are inevitably tempted to speculate on whether 'the societified lady and the obscure maniac are in a sense the same person'.[3] We can speculate about how Woolf came to make such an unusual choice of structure for the novel, and our guess, not for the first time in the story of her career, settles on the figure of James Joyce.

Ulysses was published in book form in Paris in 1922 and Virginia Woolf read through the whole of the novel that year, perhaps for the first time (in 1918 she may only have read the first half dozen chapters). She recorded her reactions in detail in her diary and spoke about the book often with T. S. Eliot, as we have seen above. It is quite possible that *Ulysses* was the original inspiration for her choice of the basic framework for the novel, which is that it records one day in the life of the inhabitants of a city, just as *Ulysses* records life in Dublin on 16 June 1904. Moreover, there is one particular

episode of *Ulysses* which narrates unconnected movements of
separate characters around the streets of the city, in such a way
that the narration jumps confusingly and constantly between the
different stories of these simultaneous itineraries, and that is the
episode known as 'The Wandering Rocks'.[4] This, at the beginning,
describes the progress around Dublin of Father Conmee, the Jesuit
rector of Clongowes College, and at the end of a viceregal caval-
cade carrying the Earl of Dudley, most elevated representative in
Ireland of the British King. These two figures, high authorities of
the two occupying powers in Ireland, Roman Church and British
State, remind one of the mystery figure in a car who rolls through
Bond Street and on to Buckingham Palace in *Mrs Dalloway*, church
and state being in this novel also represented as oppressive powers,
forces of order and discipline ('the spirit of religion' is blind
sentimentality, 'her eyes bandaged tight and her lips gaping wide'
MD 17). The worship of the state is the sickly emotion of patriot-
ism, which reduces the cold little Mr Bowley to tears (MD 23).
Virginia Woolf found it impossible to tolerate Joyce's 'indecency',
but in imitating a structural principle of *Ulysses* she paid a tribute to
him and allowed herself to recognise, beneath his repellent surface, a shared modernist attitude.

We can also recognise some structure of feeling shared with
Eliot, another poet of the modern city, whose characters' speech is,
like that of Clarissa and Septimus, also punctuated by fragments of
Shakespeare. The words of the enchanted Ferdinand in *The Tempest* ('This music crept by me upon the waters' and so on) appear
unexpectedly in *The Waste Land*, and words from the dirge to
Imogen in *Cymbeline* ('Fear no more, says the heart in the body;
fear no more' MD 154) appear in the deranged musings of Septimus Warren Smith. In both cases, the quotation of Shakespearean
tags is a tranquillising move played by desperate souls in the
'Unreal City' of modern London. Eliot read *The Waste Land* aloud to
Virginia Woolf: 'He sang it & chanted it rhythmed it. It has great
beauty & force of phrase: symmetry; & tensity. What connects it
together, I'm not so sure' (D II, 23 June 1922). The following year,
when she was in the middle of writing *Mrs Dalloway*, she set the
type for *The Waste Land* herself for the Hogarth Press edition of
Eliot's poem. Of course, their attitudes to the modernity of the city,
the impermanence, the speed and the anonymity, the fragmenta-
tion of experience, were quite different. For Virginia Woolf, the
city was not a metaphor of modern alienation but of the excitement

of impermanence. She loved walking and window shopping, and was fascinated by the glitter and gaudiness of it all. She found the crowds flowing through the streets exhilarating, a river of life rather than the bleak procession of dead souls as in Eliot's vision. Rather than a heap of broken images, she views the plunder and commerce sucked in from the whole world to the heart of Empire with an almost post-modern sense of fun. Of Oxford Street shops she wrote that they

> crush together in one wild confusion the styles of Greece, Egypt, Italy, America; and boldly attempt an air of lavishness, opulence, in their effort to persuade the multitude that here unending beauty, ever fresh, ever new, very cheap and within the reach of everybody, bubbles up every day of the week from an inexhaustible well. The mere thought of age, of solidity, of lasting for ever is abhorrent to Oxford Street.[5]

But in spite of their differences of class, of mood, of fastidiousness or vulgarity, this is probably the point at which the modernisms of Eliot, Joyce and Woolf come into closest contact. By a wonderful coincidence, simultaneously meaningless and yet obscurely thrilling, and of exactly the sort that both *Ulysses* and *Mrs Dalloway* are built upon, in August and September of 1922 Joyce and his wife Nora visited London and Sussex on one of their very rare visits. Staying at the Euston Hotel, on the northern boundary of Bloomsbury, and wandering the streets visiting dentists and eye doctors and spending Harriet Weaver's money lavishly, the Joyces' itineraries must have taken them through Tavistock Square. It is pleasing to think of the collisions that were narrowly avoided in the streets of Bloomsbury that summer, between the two, utterly unlike, wandering rocks of modernism.

DOWN A DARK PASSAGE

In *Mrs Dalloway* Virginia Woolf had found a way forward for her writing. Her discovery of how to narrate the inner worlds of characters, and to dispense with the usual trappings of plot, had opened up a line of research which she could pursue much further. In the same diary entry in which she recorded the completion of *Mrs Dalloway* on 17 October 1924, she dismissed the charge which

John Middleton Murry had brought against her, that her method had led her into an impasse, for she knew that her discoveries had opened up for her a way of writing that had an unlimited potential: 'The only difficulty is to hold myself from writing others. . . . My cul-de-sac, as they called it, stretches so far, & shows such vistas. I see already The Old Man'. This is the first glimpse of what was to become *To the Lighthouse*. By May of 1925, when *Mrs Dalloway* was published, she was straining to finish with journalism and to get on with her new novel: 'This is going to be fairly short: to have father's character done complete in it; & mothers; and St Ives; & childhood; & all the usual things I try to put in – life, death &c. But the centre is father's character, sitting in a boat, reciting We perished, each alone, while he crushes a dying mackerel' (D III, 14 May 1925). Two months earlier she had sketched in a small note-book, under the heading *To the Lighthouse*, her ideas for the new book.[6] It was to be in the form of 'two blocks joined by a corridor'. She drew a diagram.

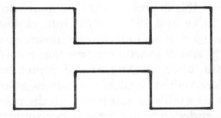

This is a powerfully suggestive figure. It holds together in one image many of the main themes of the book – the relation between husband and wife, the tunnel which connects the present moment with powerful scenes from the past, the relationship of a child with its mother in being born into a separate space. It is even an image of the birth of a work of art; when Lily Briscoe the painter is struck for a moment by panic, 'the demons set on her who often brought her to the verge of tears and made this passage from conception to work as dreadful as any down a dark passage for a child' (TL 23). Above all it recalls the stunning scene of Mr Ramsay stumbling along a dark passage one morning, his arms stretched out empty, for his wife had died suddenly in the night. The diagram seems to contain in one abstract geometry so many of the archetypal ideas, the varieties of connection and separation, that the novel was to explore.

She began writing the book in August 1925 but her progress was interrupted by ill-health and she had to start again in January the next year. She wrote through 1926, with one major interruption in July when she had a 'nervous breakdown in miniature', and the book was finished in January 1927. She showed it to Leonard who pronounced it a masterpiece, and she went back to a final revision of the book between January and March 1927. It is worth noting an oddity about this book which is that to this day the British and the American editions are significantly different. The book was published simultaneously by Hogarth in Britain and Harcourt Brace in the USA. Woolf revised the novel at the proof stage, making different revisions to the two different sets of proofs.[7] It was published on 5 May 1927.

In letters and diary she noted that she had never written so fast and so easily, that her imagination had never been so profuse. On the other hand, her nervous state was extremely fragile. She was sometimes severely depressed, sometimes very agitated and once, when she finished the first draft of the book in September 1926, nearer to suicide than at any time since 1913 (D IV, 17 October 1934). In this book she was dealing with deeply disturbing, though also deeply satisfying, autobiographical material, recovering her childhood ambivalence toward her parents, and mourning the mother by whom she had been obsessed all her adult life. While writing the novel she studied again the photographs of her mother taken by her great-aunt Julia Margaret Cameron, and put together a book of these photographs, which was published in 1926 by the Hogarth Press as *Victorian Photographs of Famous Men and Fair Women*. Julia Cameron, who took up photography at fifty, and who was a wonder of Victorian eccentricity and unconventionality, is now recognised as an important artist in that medium. Several plates of Mrs Herbert Duckworth (as Virginia's mother then was) were included in the book and Roger Fry and Virginia Woolf each contributed an introduction. In her effort to think her way back to her mother Virginia not only studied these photographs but was herself photographed in May 1926 wearing her mother's dress.[8] This must have been an eerie experience, an impersonation that she could never hope to bring off successfully. The resulting picture makes Virginia look so thin as to be almost insubstantial. Perhaps this strengthened her tendency to think of herself as someone who could not become a mother, who could never be 'a real woman', and encouraged her to write her self-portrait in the novel as Lily Briscoe, the artist who rejects physical love and marriage. Twelve years later, in 'A Sketch of the Past', she wrote about the composition of *To the Lighthouse*:

> Until I was in the forties . . . the presence of my mother ob-sessed me. I could hear her voice, see her, imagine what she would do or say as I went about my day's doings. She was one of the invisible presences who after all play so important a part in every life . . . It is perfectly true that she obsessed me, in spite of the fact that she died when I was thirteen, until I was forty-four. Then one day walking round Tavistock Square I made up, as I sometimes make up my books, *To the Lighthouse*; in a great, apparently involuntary, rush. One thing burst into another. Blowing bubbles out of a pipe gives the feeling of the rapid crowd of ideas and scenes which blew out of my mind, so that my lips seemed syllabling of their own accord as I walked . . . I wrote the book very quickly; and when it was written, I ceased to be obsessed by my mother. I no longer hear her voice; I do not see her.
>
> I suppose that I did for myself what psychoanalysts do for their patients. I expressed some very long felt and deeply felt emotion. And in expressing it I explained it and then laid it to rest. (MB 81)

So writing this book, perhaps more than any other, involved Virginia Woolf in sinking back into her past and rediscovering feelings of the most painful kind. This recovery of her lost time was not, however, the only emotionally demanding aspect of the work. She wanted her writing to have a value over and above its mem-orialising of her dead parents, its value as elegy. She craved for a greater significance for her art, a significance which would centre on the nature of time and reality. She invented the character of Lily Briscoe not only as a surrogate daughter for Mrs Ramsay but as someone through whom she could give voice to her desire for transcendence, her more visionary nature. During 1926 she was at times almost unbalanced by her desire to capture her vision. In the unguarded first draft versions of Lily Briscoe and 'Time Passes' that she wrote between January and September 1926, she allowed herself to express the most mystical, visionary side of herself. This she then restrained or censored in the published versions of the book. So important and revealing is this year of her life, so eventful and turbulent, that it is worth telling the story in some detail. It provides a broad context which will help to highlight the forces at work in the writing of *To the Lighthouse*. It is important not to confine discussion of *To the Lighthouse* to its relation to Virginia Woolf's childhood and family life.

In December 1925 her life took a decisive turn when she started a love affair with Vita Sackville-West. A friendship had developed between them and it now turned into something far more intense when Virginia went to stay at Long Barn, Vita's home, for three days. The small amount of sexual activity which their relationship gave rise to seems to have occurred at this time. They began writing frequent, intimate and passionate love letters to each other. On 20 January 1926 Vita left on a journey to Teheran, to join her husband, the diplomat Harold Nicolson. The journey took her six weeks and as she travelled she wrote long, intense letters to Virginia.[9] The relationship provided the emotional context in which Virginia sketched her self-portrait as Lily Briscoe in her novel. She saw Vita as being what she herself had never been, 'a real woman' (D III, 21 December 1925). She had children, she was a competent, glamorous, eye-catching person, who knew how to wear clothes and jewelry and to be commanding and at ease in company. She was colourful and adventurous. She was everything that Lily Briscoe is not, for Lily is plain, dried up, retiring, unambitious, fearful of and inexperienced in love. Of course, this would only express one aspect of Virginia's feelings in the matter, for Vita did make her feel loved and admired. Virginia swung between two extremes; she could feel that she was a failure, having never been a real woman, or she could more defiantly feel that secretly, under her odd, unglamorous exterior, she hid a soul capable of a visionary eroticism, moved by the desire to get outside herself, to make contact with something 'beyond', something which could only be captured through art. This side of herself is revealed in moments of vision or revelation, when she experienced a rapturous sense of contact with 'reality'.

I have some restless searcher in me. Why is there not a discovery in life? Something one can lay hands on & say 'This is it?' My depression is a harassed feeling – I'm looking; but that's not it – thats not it. What is it? And shall I die before I find it? Then (as I was walking through Russell Sqre last night) I see the mountains in the sky: the great clouds; & the moon which is risen over

Persia; I have a great & astonishing sense of something there, which is 'it' – It is not exactly beauty that I mean. It is that the thing is in itself enough: satisfactory: achieved. A sense of my own strangeness, walking on the earth is there too: of the infinite oddity of the human position. . . . I do fairly frequently come upon this 'it'; & then feel quite at rest. (D III, 27 February 1926)

We find here a combination of elements that Virginia Woolf had already portrayed in Clarissa Dalloway's experience of rapture, or of religious feeling, as she called it. There is a sense of meaning withheld, then this is followed by a sense of revelation, and finally there is satisfaction, the feeling that 'it is enough'. The questioning mind is stilled not by an answer but by a sense, looking towards the sky, of 'the thing itself', which is, as she explained elsewhere, whatever remains when we are not there.

Both Mrs Ramsay and Lily Briscoe in *To the Lighthouse* have experiences of this kind, with this same movement from frustration, through rapture, to satisfaction. Mrs Ramsay, sitting by herself in the early evening, feels all the demands of her family fall away and she sinks into a reverie. She watches the strokes of the lighthouse and allows her mind to be lifted up and carried along on their rhythm: ' . . . there curled up off the floor of the mind, rose from the lake of one's being, a mist, a bride to meet her lover' (TL 62). It is as if the beam could take her out of herself, or connect her across space with something else. The idea of a physical union, of overcoming separation, is typically both erotic (a bride) and yet suggestive of disembodied ecstasy (a mist) at one and the same time.

. . . she looked at the steady light, the pitiless, the remorseless, which was so much her, yet so little her, which had her at its beck and call (she woke in the night and saw it bent across their bed, stroking the floor), but for all that she thought, watching it with fascination, hypnotised, as if it were stroking with its silver fingers some sealed vessel in her brain whose bursting would flood her with delight, she had known happiness, exquisite happiness, intense happiness, and it silvered the rough waves a little more brightly, . . . and it rolled in waves of pure lemon which curved and swelled and broke upon the beach and the ecstasy burst in her eyes and waves of pure delight raced over the floor of her mind and she felt, It is enough! It is enough! (TL 62)

This kind of experience is for Mrs Ramsay given an overwhelmingly sexual connotation, whereas Lily, as we shall see, is determined to keep the meaning spiritual and aesthetic.

Lily Briscoe did not figure in Virginia Woolf's early plans for her new novel. Once the first draft was under way, however, Lily was quickly introduced. She rapidly developed into a vehicle for some of her author's more inadmissable feelings and attitudes. As so often, in the drafts of her novels Virginia Woolf allowed herself to write without restraint about certain parts of herself that in her life (and in the published versions of the books) were kept hidden. It is as if she used the writing as a way of experimenting with feelings that in part appealed to her but which she could not normally allow herself to admit. In the case of Lily Briscoe in her draft versions, perhaps the most interesting example of this is that she is allowed to express bitterness and anger against Mrs Ramsay, her surrogate mother, feelings which are not admitted into the published novel. In the third part, at the height of her grief for Mrs Ramsay, Lily feels demoralised and degraded by her pain, and she finds herself feeling bitterness and resentment. Her author struggles to define her emotions: 'It was not love [either]; for her feeling towards Mrs Ramsay [meanwhile] was [almost] [hatred] – bitter . . .' (TL/MS 303; the words in brackets are struck through in the manuscript).

More developed than this, however, are Lily's feelings and attitudes about art, politics and sexuality. She is used as a way of exploring those attitudes which most separate Virginia Woolf from her husband and her lover. In the imaginary debate that the character personifies, she is neither a 'real woman' (because she rejects sex and marriage) nor a 'political animal' (because she gives higher priority to art and the mystic vision which it expresses than to social life). As Lily struggles with her painting she argues in her head with Mrs Ramsay, who had believed both in marriage and in charity, attending to people's needs. Whereas Mrs Ramsay's instinct was to go to the aid of suffering humanity, Lily's was to paint. Both are efforts that we make to 'reduce chaos to order', but Lily defiantly asserts that of the two, painting is the higher, more important activity. If she could solve the problem posed by her painting 'she would have done more to help the dying woman . . . than by giving her food and clothing, shelter and sympathy' (TL/MS 279–80). Lily here spells out a belief in the saving powers of art as an expression of our higher, spiritual nature, that Virginia Woolf with part of herself must have wanted to believe. It is worth quoting at length.

> There is something better than helping dying women. Some-
> thing heaven be praised, beyond human relations altogether, . . .
> all this talk of . . . one loving another . . ., all this little trivial
> baseness about which we made so incessant a to do of marrying
> & giving in marriage . . . is irrelevant beside it. *Yet so terrible a
> doctrine could not be confessed* . . . Mrs Ramsay would never have
> spoken to her again. Pictures are more important than people.
> [emphasis added]

Virginia Woolf used her draft character as a mouthpiece for doctrines which she could never openly confess, either in print or to Leonard or Vita, but which she at least liked to imagine being able to believe. What is involved here are Platonic beliefs about time and the soul. Physical love is, as in Plato's *Symposium*, an analogy or reminder to the soul of a higher kind of love, and a higher kind of uniting, a mystic union of soul and space. Lily has a vision of this 'everlasting and undeniable relationship'.

> She was cut loose from the ties of life; she enjoyed that intensity
> and freedom of life which, for a few seconds after the death of
> the body, one imagines the souls of the dead to enjoy: one
> imagines that they have gathered themselves together, . . . com-
> plete and forcible with the force of an organism which is now at
> last able to unite all its powers.
> It was attended, too, with an emotion, which could be com-
> pared only with the gratification of bodily human love. So,
> unhesitatingly, without fear or reserve, at some moment of
> culmination when all separation is over, . . . bodies unite; the
> human love has its gratification. But that, even, was less com-
> plete than this; for who could deny it? Even while the arms are
> locked, . . . a cloud moves across the sky; & each lover knows,
> but cannot confess, his knowledge of the transience of love. . . .
> But here, since the lover was the formidable enemy – space –

their union, could it be achieved, was immortal. No cloud moved, in that landscape; no death came between them. It was an awful marriage; forever. (TL/MS 280)

That art is in some manner an overcoming of time is a common-place. What is unusual is the extent to which in drafts and diary Virginia Woolf attempted to spell this out into a system of beliefs ('My theory being that the actual event practically does not exist – nor time either', she noted in her diary later in the year (D III, 23 November 1926), thinking ahead to a future novel. In the equivalent published passages of *To the Lighthouse* the questions are never answered in this way, but are rewarded instead with the by now familiar 'revelations' – no great revelations, no theory or meaning, only moments of illumination.

What is the meaning of life? That was all – a simple question; one that tended to close in on one with years. The great revelation had never come. The great revelation perhaps never did come. Instead there were little daily miracles, illuminations, matches struck unexpectedly in the dark. . . . Mrs Ramsay saying 'Life stand still here'; Mrs Ramsay making of the moment something permanent (as in another sphere Lily herself tried to make of the moment something permanent) – this was of the nature of a revelation. In the midst of chaos there was shape. (TL 150)

Lily in the drafts takes a position, is committed to a belief, an answer to the question about the meaning of life. Virginia Woolf herself had no stable belief. She could appreciate the temptation to settle, the desire for the comfort of a fixed position, but the truth of her experience was of a constant movement between different positions, a never-ending restless search among the different possibilities. Her most enduring belief is that stated in 'Modern Fiction', that 'if honestly examined life presents question after question which must be left to sound on and on after the story is over in hopeless interrogation'. It is a mark of her integrity that her experiments in position taking in the drafts of *To the Lighthouse* were deleted from the published novel.

For whatever reason, Virginia Woolf was more preoccupied with speculations about time, reality and art, of a semi-religious character, in this year than at any other time of her life. Perhaps this was because of her strong sense of her mother's presence and her effort to recover the lost time of her childhood through writing *To the Lighthouse*. Or perhaps it was somehow to do with the troubled intensity of her relationship with Vita, which raised for her disturbing questions about the body (sexuality, marriage, children). In either case, we can see that during 1926 her values and attitudes were tested, severely and often, more than at any other time since her marriage. She was forced over and over again to think hard about the meaning of her life. Everything that mattered to her was in question – art, religion, marriage, motherhood, sexuality, fame and politics. Her questioning moved around among all these aspects of her life endlessly and inconclusively. But in 1926 she came closer than ever before or after to putting an end to the restless motions of her desire, by settling for an identity, grounded in the fictional self-portrait of Lily Briscoe. In creating Lily she was attempting to give birth to herself as a mystical, virginal artist whose mind, through her art, rises above the ephemera of bodily, time-bound life.

Questions of values and priorities were posed dramatically in May of 1926 by the eruption of the General Strike. The strike arose when miners' wages were cut and other workers came out in support. It provoked very strong feelings indeed, on both sides of the argument. The strike was called on 2 May and formally ended ten days later. Leonard's reaction was an unambiguous and militant outrage. 'If ever there has been right on the side of the workers in an industrial dispute, it was on the side of the miners in the years after the war; if ever a strike and a general strike were justified, it was in 1926. . . . I was entirely on the side of the workers.' Many, however, saw the strike as a threat to civilisation. Arnold Bennett thought it was a political crime. Galsworthy refused to sign a petition which Leonard helped to circulate when the strike collapsed, demanding no victimisation. Virginia Woolf was of course on the side of the workers; she went round on her bicycle with Leonard's petition, and she acted as a courier, carrying documents to the House of Commons. She wrote lengthy impressions of the results of the strike in her diary, more than in relation to any other political event in her life before the Second World War. But her heart was not really in it. She could not share Leonard's sense of commitment. Arguing about the strike, she wrote, was not 'nearly as exciting as writing To the Lighthouse or about de Q[uincey]' (D III, 11 May 1926). 'I suppose all pages devoted to the Strike will be skipped, when I read over this book.

Oh that dull old chapter, I shall say. Excitements about what are called real things are always unutterably transitory' (13 May). Her mind was really elsewhere; in fact at the very time that the strike was throwing life in London into chaos, with armoured cars ferrying stores of frozen meat along Oxford Street, the city on the verge of riot, and the business of the Hogarth Press at a standstill, Virginia Woolf was writing 'Time Passes', the most impersonal, abstract piece of writing that she ever attempted. In the perspective of the flight of inhuman time and nature's complete indifference to all things human, which is the perspective of 'Time Passes', the strike like all other mundane affairs must have seemed a very trivial episode. This was indeed Virginia's attitude. She wrote to her sister, 'Roger [Fry] . . . agrees with me in thinking it all unutterably boring and quite unimportant and yet very upsetting' (L III, 12 May 1926). She had a serious argument with Leonard about it. 'And L. & I quarrelled last night. I dislike the tub thumper in him; he the irrational Xtian in me' (D III, 9 May 1926). She could never trust the 'preaching voice' in politics; it involved such self-assertiveness, definite position-taking and the rhetoric of persuasion. It is a voice which she avoids even in her most polemical works. Equally interesting here, though, is Leonard's perception of his wife as religious, as an irrational Christian, for it confirms (though no doubt with the exaggeration of argument, for there is no evidence that she was ever tempted by Christianity) that at this time religious, or at least metaphysical, speculation was the main tendency and direction of her thinking. She always thought about social conflict as arising from childish tantrums or masculine aggressions. Amazingly, she noted during the strike: 'What one prays for is God: the King or God; some impartial person to say kiss and be friends – as apparently we all desire' (6 May). One can see why Leonard was furious with her. Is this the context for Lily Briscoe's doctrine that could not be confessed, that art is more important than helping people?[10]

Curiously, although it was to the flight of time and to God that her thoughts turned at this time, she did also allow herself to attend to more trivial things. She had become friends with Dorothy Todd, the editor of *Vogue*, and on the very day that she noted her desire for God or King to settle the childish disputes of the men, she wrote in her diary: 'And I am involved in dress buying with Todd; I tremble & shiver all over at the appalling magnitude of the task I have undertaken – to go to a dress-maker recommended by

Todd, even, she suggested, but here my blood ran cold, with Todd. Perhaps this excites me more feverishly than the Strike' (6 May). The strength of her feelings here remind us not so much of her relative lack of interest in politics at this time but of just how uncomfortable she was with her own appearance, and how that was such a contrast with the confident, glamorous Vita.

This was the context in which she wrote the first draft of 'Time Passes', between 30 April and 25 May 1926. In the autumn she began a second draft of *To the Lighthouse* and then, for the only time in her career, she produced a version of a part of her work-in-progress, this 'Time Passes' section of her novel, to be published separately, in advance of the novel itself. It was translated into French by Charles Mauron and appeared in the journal *Commerce* as 'Le Temps passe' in January 1927.[11] Comparison of this version with that published in the novel shows that some of the latter's most effective aspects were not devised and added until the very last moment. In the published novel this middle section is integrated into the novel as a whole by having the characters fade out slowly in the first two, and reappear again in the last two chapters. Most importantly and dramatically, the announcements of the deaths of Mrs Ramsay and two of her children are placed, within square brackets, in the middle of this section, making them appear as shocking but minor interruptions to the flight of time and the ongoing processes of nature. The effect on the reader is startling, since the deaths are so unexpected, and since they are narrated from a point of view, an 'eyeless', impersonal point of view, from which they have no more significance than the fall of a leaf or any other natural event. The overwhelming impression of the section as a whole is of the indifference and destructiveness of nature, and the transitoriness of all things human.

In her diary two years later Virginia Woolf wrote, 'Now is life very solid or very shifting? I am haunted by the two contradictions. This has gone on for ever; will last for ever; goes down to the bottom of the world – this moment I stand on. Also it is transitory, flying, diaphanous. I shall pass like a cloud on the waves' (D III, 4 January 1929). She could not decide whether human beings are somehow continuous, all part of one lasting pattern, or fleeting, transitory things. As I have argued above, in most of her published work she is concerned not to answer the question, not to settle on one or the other of these alternatives, but to show the restlessness of the mind uncertainly moving between them. In 'Time Passes' there are various strange glimpses of mystics and poets who walk on the beach, attempting unsuccessfully to settle the question of time. The remarkable thing about 'Le Temps passe' (and about the earlier drafts of 'Time Passes') is that in them she does seem to propose an answer to the question, to present a vision of timeless reality hidden behind the appearance of the flight of time. Standing alone, without the characters from the novel and without the intrusive reminders of death, this piece reads as a prose poem, the general drift of which seems to be quite the opposite of the *To the Lighthouse* version. In an opening chapter, deleted from the novel, we are plunged into a world of nameless sleepers, who are joined at night by mysterious, ghostly figures ('comforters', 'sharers', 'confidantes') who take the sleepers by the hand and lead them to a vision of reality on the beach. This night knowledge is of completeness, perfection, union. It is as if Virginia Woolf were drawing on her sense of her dead mother's presence as a proof that our daytime reality is an illusion, that haunting confirms the unreality of time, that time is just a corridor of individuality between two spaces of union.

It is not clear why Virginia Woolf published 'Le Temps passe' nor why she subtly altered its emphasis. It is possible that she felt safe having it published in French, where such mystical prose poems are a more familiar genre. Possibly it was a result of her associations this year with her Bloomsbury friends, including Charles Mauron.[12] Since she was writing the portrait of a painter, she may have gone back to her friends' writings on art in an effort to think about what it is to see with the eye of an artist. She may have reread Clive Bell's *Art*, in which he asserts that the 'significant form' captured in painting is 'form behind which we catch a sense of ultimate reality'.[13] She may have attempted to make a connection between this 'form' and her own meaning of 'revelation' or 'vision'. In a letter which she was later to quote in his biography, Roger Fry said that 'the contemplation of form is a peculiarly important spiritual exercise' and that 'the emotions resulting from the contemplation of form were . . . more profound and more significant spiritually than any of the emotions which had to do with life' (RF 230). We do know that at the time she was writing *To the Lighthouse* Virginia Woolf read an essay by Charles Mauron which was then published by the Hogarth Press in 1927 as *The Nature of Beauty in Art and Literature* (translated and with a preface by Roger Fry). Mauron was a friend of Fry and he took as his problem in this essay the elucidation of the significance of Fry's formalist aesthetics for literature. He was at that time translating into French Forster's *A Passage to India*, another novel which flirts ambiguously with the mystical. Virginia Woolf wrote an appreciative letter to Mauron in October 1926 after reading his essay. It was Mauron who translated 'Le Temps passe' and arranged for it to be published in France. Mauron's ideas about literature, like Fry's about art, are based on a dichotomy between art and life, the former dealing with ultimate reality and the latter being merely trivial and transitory. It is in this period, between 1924 and 1931 (from *Mrs Dalloway* to *The Waves*) that Virginia Woolf was most influenced by these ideas and values, by 'formalist modernism', treating art and literature with a rather exaggerated solemnity, searching for a mystical or spiritual vision of 'ultimate reality', and at times downgrading 'life', which is to say everything having to do with the body, material reality and social existence.

The summer and autumn of 1926 were difficult months for Virginia Woolf. At the end of July she went with Leonard to Rodmell, to escape from London so that she could finish *To the Lighthouse*. There is a gap in her diary until the beginning of September, filled with jottings, including a description of 'a whole nervous breakdown in miniature'. On 5 September she recorded in her diary that she was on the verge of finishing her novel, trying to devise some way of composing the end. On the same day she noted that she had been 'knocked off her perch for a moment' by a visit to Tilton and Charleston (the homes of the Keynes and the Bells). She felt that she had missed out on family life and that it was her own fault: 'a little more self control on my part, & we might have had a boy of 12, a girl of 10'. She was thinking back to the time of her marriage and her serious breakdowns and the decision that they would not have children. As she finished *To the Lighthouse* she was plunged into a very severe depression, which she recorded in some detail in her diary through September. Though it can hardly be a coincidence that this happened as she was ending her novel, the problem does not seem to have been any anxiety about its reception (it was only the first draft that she had written; publication was still a very long way off). Rather, she seemed to concentrate on her failure to have become a mother, a fate which she had imagined in the novel for Lily Briscoe, and in her life was reminded of constantly by both Vanessa and Vita. If through Lily she was experimenting with a self-image as the artist who has sacrificed sex, marriage and children, but who in compensation can through her work capture a vision which holds together life and reality, she was in fact finding this assumed identity distressing. She was grieving not only for her own mother, but for the mother in herself.

Woke up perhaps at 3. Oh its beginning its coming – the horror – physically like a painful wave swelling about the heart – tossing me up. I'm unhappy unhappy! Down – God, I wish I were dead. Pause. But why am I feeling this? Let me watch the wave rise. I watch. Vanessa. Children. Failure. Yes; I detect that. Failure failure. (the wave rises). Oh they laughed at my taste in green paint! Wave crashes. I wish I were dead! I've only a few years to live I hope. I cant face this horror any more – (this is the wave spreading out over me). (D III, 15 September 1926)

There is another lengthy description of her depression on 28 September. Vanessa and Vita had visited. Vita's book *The Land* was published this month and although Virginia did not much like it its success may have caused her some misery. 'One is in truth rather an elderly dowdy fussy ugly incompetent woman vain, chattering & futile.'

The questions of sexual love and motherhood, around which *To the Lighthouse* revolves, preoccupy not only Lily Briscoe but also Mrs Ramsay, her daughters, and Minta Doyle. All of these characters are used as ways of imaginatively treating the questions 'What does a woman want?' and 'Should they want to be wives and mothers?' These questions were still tormenting the author in February 1927 when she finished the final draft of her novel. In a letter to Ethel Sands she wrote about Vanessa's children, 'They are such an immense source of pleasure to me . . . I'm always angry with myself for not having forced Leonard to take the risk in spite of doctors; he was afraid for me and wouldn't; but if I'd had rather more self-control no doubt it would have been all right' (L III, 9 February 1927). By the end of the year, however, the agony seems to have gone out of the issue for her. The wounds which she had reopened in writing *To the Lighthouse* had healed. In December she went to a party at her sister's house and again enjoyed the children.

And yet oddly enough I scarcely want children of my own now.

This insatiable desire to write something before I die, this ravaging sense of the shortness & feverishness of life, make me cling, like a man on a rock, to my one anchor. I don't like the physicalness of having children of one's own . . . I can dramatise myself as parent, it is true. And perhaps I have killed the feeling instinctively; as perhaps nature does. (D III, 20 December 1927)

As always with Virginia Woolf, the story of her literary career and the story of her identity, its formation, realignment, disintegration and restabilisation, are intimately connected. In writing *To the Lighthouse* she had let go of parts of herself that she had clung onto for a very long time, her obsession with her own mother and her own desire to be a mother. Her conception of herself as a writer was solidified, and this new, more compact self-image immediately inspired a new project. She replaced her self-portrait as Lily Briscoe, tormented daughter and dried up old maid, with that of a mystical, visionary, solitary woman writer, the central figure in a new book, which she called *The Moths*. The destructive, potentially suicidal instability which she experienced in September of this extraordinary year, 1926, had its creative side.

Even in the middle of her worst depression Virginia Woolf observed that it had a positive aspect, that it was a process of stripping away all sorts of superficial activity which allowed her to sink down to more profound layers of herself. 'These 9 weeks give one a plunge into deep waters; which is a little alarming but full of interest. All the rest of the year one's curbing and controlling this odd immeasurable soul. When it expands, though one is frightened & bored & gloomy, it is as I say to myself, awfully queer. . . . One goes down into the well & nothing protects one from the assault of truth' (D III, 28 September 1926). Two days later she recorded in her diary an experience which seemed to her in retrospect to be a decisive turning point.

I wished to add some remarks to this, on the mystical side of this solitude; how it is not oneself but something in the universe that one's left with. It is this that is frightening & exciting in the midst of my profound gloom, depression, boredom, whatever it is: One sees a fin passing far out. What image can I reach to convey what I mean? Really there is none I think. The interesting thing is that in all my feeling & thinking I have never come up against this before. Life is, soberly & accurately, the oddest affair; has in it the essence of reality.

She suspected that this strange experience might be the first stirrings of another book, and confirmed this two years later when she jotted in the margin of her diary next to this entry, 'Perhaps *The Waves* or moths'. She returned to this vision of a fin passing far out across a waste of waters several times, both in her diary and in *The Waves* itself. She was convinced that through or underneath the depression some important movement was taking place, one which would both give her an impersonal, mystical glimpse of the universe itself and also consolidate in her a change of identity. After this her life would not be the same. In *The Waves* and her diary (see 4 September 1927) the moment is given as an example of something which official or traditional biography could never record, a change or turning point in a life of the greatest significance and yet so subtle, so inward, as to be quite invisible (as it would be for us were it not for her diary and her novels).

It is as if, as she redrafted *To the Lighthouse* and toned down the more mystic aspects in both Lily and 'Time Passes', she simultaneously invented a new vehicle for that confirmed part of herself, the solitary visionary woman. By the end of October she was noting, 'I begin to think . . . of a solitary woman musing[?] a book of ideas about life . . . It is a dramatisation of my mood at Rodmell. It is to be an endeavour at something mystic, spiritual; the thing that exists when we aren't there'. A month later (D III, 23 November 1926) she returned to this thought: 'Yet I am now & then haunted by some semi mystic very profound life of a woman, which shall all be told on one occasion; & time shall be utterly obliterated; future shall somehow blossom out of the past. One incident – say the fall of a flower – might contain it. My theory being that the actual event practically does not exist – nor time either'. As it turned out, these thoughts were to mature slowly for three years before she first began to draft her new novel in 1929.

When *To the Lighthouse* was published in May 1927 it was reviewed very favorably, and was proclaimed by many to be her best novel. Even Arnold Bennett came close to admiring it, in his column in the *Evening Standard*: 'I have read a bunch of novels. I must say, despite my notorious grave reservations concerning Virginia Woolf, that the most original of the bunch is *To the Lighthouse* . . . Her character drawing has improved. Mrs Ramsay almost amounts to a complete person'. Her friends liked the book, though some were not convinced by the 'Time Passes' section. Roger Fry thought that this piece was not of her best vintage. 'She is so splendid as soon as character is involved . . . but when she tries to give her impression of inanimate objects, she exaggerates, she underlines, she poeticizes.'[14]

By 1927, after the publication of *To the Lighthouse*, Virginia Woolf was a famous if still not very popular author. *To the Lighthouse* sold under 4000 copies in the first year, substantially more than any of her earlier books but still a long way short of best-seller sales. She was accepted as a major figure on the literary scene and her reputation was by now international. At the end of 1926 she was invited by the *New York Herald Tribune* to visit New York. She was offered her expenses plus a fee in exchange for four articles. She took the offer seriously before turning it down. In France her reputation grew, partly with the help of T. S. Eliot who praised her highly in an article on contemporary English fiction in the influential *Nouvelle Revue Française* in 1927. In contrast to D. H. Lawrence, he announced, 'she prefers civilisation to barbarity' (MM 192). In 1928 she was awarded the Femina–Vie Heureuse Prize of £40 for *To the Lighthouse*. There was a presentation, which she hated, and her photograph appeared in *The Times*. Fame was, she said, becoming 'vulgar & a nuisance' (D III, 4 May 1928). French translations of her work began to appear – that of *Mrs Dalloway* came out in 1929 (MM 32f) and her work has been highly regarded in France ever since. When books about her began to be written, one of the first was in French, *Le roman psychologique de Virginia Woolf* by Floris Delattre (1932). She began to appear on academic courses, even as far afield as Japan (MM 24).

No doubt more people read her articles than bought her difficult novels and her fame grew when she started to write for such magazines as *Vogue*. Her friend Dorothy Todd was given the sack in 1926 for trying to introduce serious 'highbrow' authors to her readers. Virginia Woolf had appeared in *Vogue's* 'We Nominate for the Hall of Fame' feature as early as 1924. She was photographed by *Vogue's* photographer Maurice Beck, and photographs of her appeared on several occasions in the magazine. Although Leonard Woolf later asserted that his wife could not bear to be looked at or to be photographed, she does seem in the twenties to have enjoyed performing various selves for the camera. In *Vogue* she is a glamorous lady, someone with whom to have polite but intelligent conversation over tea.[15] This is Virginia Woolf's 'society' persona, with no threatening Bloomsbury unconventionality on view, and none of that extreme vulnerability of the famous early Beresford photographs, taken when she was only twenty years old and probably now the best known images of her. In 1927 she was photographed by Man Ray. This was a significant recognition of her status by this time, for Man Ray specialised in photographing the great figures of modern culture, including Joyce, Eliot, Gertrude Stein and Ernest Hemingway. For these photographs she had her hair cut short. She explained to Vita in February that she had had it shingled late one evening after having drunk rather a lot. Until this time she had always worn it very long and pinned up. It was a significant gesture. Virginia Woolf was more than commonly aware of the gap between the secret inner self and those selves that are presented to the world through one's appearance. She seemed at this time to enjoy the self-impersonation involved in photographic sessions, when she was allowed to make herself up for the camera rather than having the camera attempting to pry into her secret, intimate life. On this occasion she was at the very height of her passionate affair with Vita and was beginning to write *Orlando*. For that book she persuaded Vita to pose to be photographed as the sexually ambiguous Orlando. For Man Ray she allowed herself to impersonate a rather mannish character, with short hair and severe face. She is, in another of these photographs, a daring, painted modern woman, and in another of ambiguous sex. John Lehmann suggestively prints together on one page of his book on Virginia Woolf two photographs together, one of Vita as Orlando and one Man Ray photo of Virginia looking rather like Aubrey Beardsley.[16] Man Ray chose to emphasise her boney nose and full chin as if determined to make of her something more angular, less dreamily 'beautiful' than she was reputed to be. He persuaded her to put on lipstick by telling her that it was necessary for technical reasons and would not show up in the photographs, and was amused when at the end of the session she forget about it and went off down the street with it still on.[17]

There is a completely different view of Virginia Woolf's appearance at this time in drawings by Richard Kennedy, in which we see her neither in society nor as Vita's lover but at work.[18] She wears work clothes, rolls her own cigarettes and, most interestingly, she wears spectacles; these never appear in any of her photographs! She sits surrounded by bales of books in the Press stockroom. She still worked for the Press; she set type, read manuscripts, attended to jacket designs and packed up parcels of books. Kennedy's book gives an interesting picture not just of Virginia Woolf but also of the Press in 1928. It was by now a sizeable operation, employing various kinds of workers in its basement premises. Managers had come and gone, mostly finding it very hard to establish amicable relations with Leonard. The Press was a significant intellectual presence in English culture, but financially it was not very profitable until the publication of such best-sellers as Virginia Woolf's *Orlando* (1928) and Vita Sackville-West's *The Edwardians* (1930) and *All Passion Spent* (1931). This latter sold 30 000 copies in six months and in a year made a profit for the Hogarth Press of nearly £2000. The Woolf's financial situation had already eased enough by 1926 for them to have WCs and a bathroom installed at Monks House. In July 1927 they bought their first car, a second hand Singer, in which they went in March 1928 touring in Europe. According to Leonard, no other addition ever so changed their lives (LW 318).

7

1928–31: Androgyny and the End of the Novel

'I feel more & more sure that I will never write a novel again.'
(D III, 18 March 1928)

THE DUAL VISION

Having rejected the 'materialism' of the Edwardian novel, what had Virginia Woolf put in its place? Her novels turned away from those aspects of life and personality which had seemed to most previous writers to be of greatest importance. Forster, for example, for all his appreciation of her novels, was unsure about her ability to portray character.[1] In Forster's novels the focus is on moral development and moral agency, all those aspects of personality that are involved in learning how to behave, to deliberate and choose, to conduct oneself wisely among other people. His characters are in the midst of practical life. These aspects of personality are more or less entirely absent from Virginia Woolf's fiction. She represents people as held in place by the invisible forces of social life (patriarchal family, gender roles, empire, militaristic culture, and so on). She does not emphasise moments of moral enlightenment or decisive choice, and the way that these develop character. Instead she turns her attention in two different directions, towards the unconscious and towards the transcendent. Through her fiction the world is viewed with this 'dual vision' (a phrase that Woolf used in characterising the work of Proust).

Firstly, she seeks out a layer of mental activity and meaning that is below consciousness. As we follow the stream of consciousness of Mrs Ramsay or Lily Briscoe, we are quickly swept towards areas of their mental lives of which they themselves are not fully aware. We are drawn deep into their inner worlds. Her prose is like a beam shining into a cavern, and it reveals strange, haunting images – silvery fingers caressing some vessel in Mrs Ramsay's brain, a metallic beak thrusting repeatedly into her breast, water, stretched like silk across the bay, which is suddenly violently torn apart by a knife. Into these images, like images in dreams, are condensed many strands of feeling, many thoughts and wishes. Their associations lead one in many surprising and unpredicted directions.

Secondly, her gaze is turned away from the characters and towards something impersonal. Most obviously, but not only, in 'Time Passes', she has her eye upon time itself. Her prose carries us to a point of view from which we can see human beings and their activities and emotions not from a human perspective but from far away, merged into an inhuman panorama of 'reality'. It is as if she wants to contain within one statement two quite contradictory values, two ways of seeing things which could not be further apart. At one and the same time, she thinks, the pulse of human life and its deepest, most secret creations matter more than anything, and yet, also, they matter no more than a leaf falling or a cloud passing in the sky. She enables us to see close up and in great detail the experience of men and women, dense with meanings and values, constantly surging forward with desire and fear. At the same time we are encouraged to see that those lives are lived on a surface, that there is beneath it some other reality, something that has nothing to do with the trivial dramas of personality.

In thinking about her art and trying to explain what she aimed to do, Virginia Woolf in these years no longer talked about 'myriads of impressions' falling upon the mind. The word which she most often used now was 'poetry'. She aimed to write prose fiction which drew upon the resources of poetry in order to express her dual vision. Most importantly, she wrote not to a plot but to a rhythm (D III, 2 September 1930). She used musical effects of metre and repetition. The word that seems to identify most accurately what is special about her works is that they are *composed*. Attempting to clarify her position Virginia Woolf wrote several important essays between 1926 and 1929, and they are far more significant for an understanding of her work than the more widely quoted essays, 'Modern Fiction' and 'Mr Bennett and Mrs Brown'. In the later essays her emphasis has shifted away from psychological realism and towards a definition of poetic fiction.

In 1926 she wrote 'Impassioned Prose', an essay on De Quincey, whose work confirmed her belief that there was a need for some other form of writing than that prose which represents the personal voice of characters or the details of their daily experiences. De Quincey was obsessed with the kinds of memory which hint at the unreality of time. These show us how our experience in the present is informed by a pressure from events in the distant past, which seem to be perfectly preserved somewhere in our deepest memory but which, so strong is our attachment to time, are hard to recapture. As Virginia Woolf was obsessed and haunted by her mother, so De Quincey was haunted by his long dead sister. His attempts to portray how his experience, in dreams or in opium visions, was still pregnant with images and memories deriving from that time long ago led him to experiment with poetic prose, in which narrative gives way to imagery, rhythm and incantation.

In February 1927, while waiting for *To the Lighthouse* to be published, Virginia Woolf returned to a major project for a book about fiction; 'I've suddenly become absorbed in a book about reading novels, and can't stop making up phrases' she wrote to Vita (L III, 5 February 1927). She first mentioned this project in 1925 but had made no progress on it and may have been stimulated to return to it by E. M. Forster's *Aspects of the Novel* which was published in 1927. Forster's correspondence with Virginia Woolf was very active in the mid-twenties and he wrote to her about his book, asking for her advice. She reviewed it politely in October 1927, though she was not in fact convinced that Forster's rather bland and commonsensical ideas were very helpful. The two of them were friendly and respectful but had a guarded, unconvinced attitude to each other's work. She also re-read all of Forster's novels in 1927 for an article ('The Novels of E. M. Forster') for the *Atlantic Monthly*. Her own projected book on fiction was announced as 'in preparation' in Hogarth Press publicity material in 1927, but she put it aside while she was writing *Orlando*. It was never completed as a book, but appeared as three articles in the New York *Bookman* in 1929 under the title 'Phases of Fiction'.

In these articles she discussed a large number of novels. There is a great deal of interest in seeing what kinds of questions about fiction, its varieties and possible futures, she was interested in asking, both here and in the other major articles about the novel which she wrote at this time, 'The Narrow Bridge of Art' (1927) and 'Women and Fiction', which was first delivered as a lecture in October 1928. Both 'Phases' and 'The Narrow Bridge' climax with the same passage from *Tristram Shandy*. She uses this as a way of conveying her conception of the dual vision of the novel. In this passage, as in all great fiction, we hear the voices of the characters and get close up to the detail of their lives. But at a certain moment the prose suddenly achieves a different perspective and we pass beyond a concern for personality and into a position above the world of the fiction, so that we 'look out at life in general'. In *Tristram Shandy* this is accomplished by a sudden intrusion by the voice of the author:

> I will not argue the matter; Time wastes too fast: every letter I trace tells me with what rapidity Life follows my pen; the days and hours of it more precious, – my dear Jenny – than the rubies about thy neck, are flying over our heads like light clouds of a windy day, never to return more; everything presses on – whilst thou art twisting that lock; – see! it grows gray; and every time I kiss thy hand to bid adieu, and every absence which follows it, are preludes to that eternal separation which we are shortly to make. – Heaven have mercy upon us both!
> CHAP. IX
> Now, for what the world thinks of that ejaculation – I would not give a groat. (cited in CE II 227)

What appeals to Virginia Woolf here is the way that Sterne moves between the voice of the story-teller or narrator and that of the soliloquist. There is a change of perspective from the details of fictional lives to the context of all lives, time and mortality. It is a movement which she herself manages to achieve by her own means in both *To the Lighthouse* and *The Waves*. 'Phases of Fiction' makes clear the degree of awareness with which she chose her modernist devices or 'methods' in the novels of this period.

She discovered in Proust the very same combination of detailed individual lives and transcendent perspectives (and it is here that she introduces the idea of the 'dual vision'). She argues that Proust, more than anyone else, reveals in the most minute details of what is involved in even so simple an act as a kiss. Thousands of incongruous elements of mental life are there. It is not just that myriads of impressions follow one another in a stream, but that there are contained in each single moment a huge number and complex compound of meanings deriving from deep as well as superficial sources, and these must be meticulously unravelled and displayed in an impersonal, impartial narration, without the intrusion of the judgements and emotions of the author. But over and above that there is the voice of the poet. The point of view shifts from that of the characters, immersed in the bustle of life, to some point above all the individual lives,

> as if the mind . . . suddenly rose in the air and from a station high up gave us a different view of the same object in terms of metaphor. This dual vision makes the great characters in Proust and the whole world from which they spring more like a globe, of which one side is always hidden, than a scene laid flat before us, the whole of which we can take in at one glance. (CE II 85)

This is a perfect description of what she herself attempted in *The Waves*.

If one wanted to identify one single article which more than any other sums up the deeper purposes of Virginia Woolf's art and how they led her to adopt her particular stylistic means, it would have to be 'The Narrow Bridge of Art', of which the revealing original title was 'Poetry, Fiction and the Future'. Again her theme is her dissatisfaction with both 'the sociological novel' and with that psychological realism which focuses on 'character'. Something of the utmost importance is left out. What is left out are the impersonal emotions that are expressed in poetry,

> . . . those monstrous, hybrid, unmanageable emotions. That the age of the earth is 3,000,000,000 years; that human life lasts but a second; that the capacity of the human mind is nevertheless boundless; that life is infinitely beautiful yet repulsive; that one's fellow creatures are adorable but disgusting; that science and religion have between them destroyed belief . . . (CE II 219)

Whereas in previous ages there were readily available conventional means for the expression of these impersonal emotions (and she refers to Elizabethan drama as an example), in our modern age, with our sceptical modern minds, there is no direct route to them. We have no language that we can trust, no conventions of expression that we can rely on. So we have to create our own modern forms of art, suitable for the modern age, and for the novel this means finding ways of combining the ordinariness of prose with the exultation of poetry. 'Prose will be used for purposes for which it has never been used before.' It will aim at that dual vision which allows it both to scrutinise parts of the mind hitherto left unexplored and yet also to give the mind's 'soliloquy in solitude'. This modern form of prose 'will show itself capable of rising high from the ground, not in one dart, but in sweeps and circles, and of keeping at the same time in touch with the amusements and idiosyncracies of human character in daily life' (CE II 228). This article can stand as Virginia Woolf's modernist manifesto.

NO MORE NOVELS

Virginia Woolf had suggested that *To the Lighthouse* was not a novel but an elegy. In subsequent years she became more and more determined to distance herself from the conventions of the novel and her work up to 1931 shows the astonishing inventiveness with which she came up with one idea after another for different anti-novels. 'I doubt that I shall ever write another novel after O[rlando]. I shall invent a new name for them' (D III, 18 February 1928). Each book involved not merely the imaginative creation of new content but a reinvention of the form. It was as if the success of *Mrs Dalloway* and *To the Lighthouse* gave her the freedom and the confidence to experiment, to devise, to play, never settling on any one discovery and building an oeuvre upon it, as someone less determined and more easily satisfied might have done. At the age of forty-five she was determined to keep moving, to sustain an amazing and apparently permanent revolution in literary form.

This is particularly astonishing when one considers that in *To the Lighthouse* she had in many readers' eyes perfected her new, modernist narrative method. At last, after so many years of inde-fatigable experimentation, from *Monday or Tuesday* through *Jacob's Room* and *Mrs Dalloway*, she had arrived at an unequivocal success. In *To the Lighthouse* her method for representing the inner worlds of her characters had become beautifully supple and was seamlessly woven in with her more rhythmic, poetic voice. The method allowed her to move from the surface of their minds to the depths of unconscious feeling and hidden memory, and then back again, so effortlessly and smoothly that she had overcome any awkward-ness that remained still in *Mrs Dalloway*, and could, as its sub-sequent popularity has shown, win over a wide readership for her work in spite of its initial difficulties. Yet instead of remaining with the methods that she had crafted so carefully and successfully, she immediately went off in a whole series of new directions. In fact, and this needs emphasising for it is surely a truly extraordinary and little remarked fact, after *To the Lighthouse* she never again, in her entire remaining literary career, returned to those ways of representing consciousness that she had used in that book.

Her subsequent work was a series of anti-novels. After the 'elegy' of *To the Lighthouse*, she wrote the anti-biography *Orlando*. It is a move away from psychological realism into fantasy and parody. She reintroduces a narrator, but he is extremely unreliable. In 1929 she wrote *A Room of One's Own*, a non-fiction work of history and theory, in the form of a series of lectures by a fictional character. In *The Waves* (1931) she moved further away from mimetic realism than in any previous work. It is a poetical work in the form of a series of dramatic soliloquies interspersed with abstract, impersonal prose-poetic interludes. After *Flush* (1933), a minor work (a fictional autobiography of a dog) she worked on what was to remain an incompleted project for an 'Essay-Novel'. This work, *The Pargiters*, was to switch between fictional chapters telling the story of the Pargiter family and non-fictional historico–sociological essays on the condition of women. The inventiveness is prodigious. Two themes underlie this series of experiments. One is the rejection of the conventional novel form. The other is the history of gender roles in society and the vision of androgyny.

ESCAPADE

She had already conceived of a new mystical book, to be about a solitary woman musing as petals fell from a flower. But she was prepared to allow it to mature very slowly and while it did she decided to write something for fun. 'For the truth is I feel the need of an escapade after these serious poetic experimental books whose form is always so closely considered. I want to kick up my heels and be off. . . . I think this will be great fun to write; & it will rest my head before starting the very serious, mystical poetical work which I want to come next' (D III, 14 March 1927).

In her personal life this was a time of great contentment. Each of her two closest relationships, her friendship with Vita and her marriage with Leonard, was transgressive. They both involved unconventional gender roles. But they were both full of contentment. Each of her partners tolerated her need to be infantile. In her marriage she was a non-submissive partner. She was by now more celebrated in literary circles than her husband. She was resigned to her lack of children. Her relationship with Vita was the one serious passion of her life, though the phase of obsessive love did not last very long, and that of sexual activity was even shorter.[2] Their friendship, however, lasted through the rest of Virginia's life. Vita was ten years younger than Virginia. Both she and her husband, Harold Nicolson, had homosexual affairs, and yet their marriage remained of central importance to them. Within this circle of relationships, unconventional gender identities and degrees of androgyny flourished. Vita had had in 1918–21 a passionate affair with Violet Trefusis (on whom Sasha the Russian princess in *Orlando* was based) and would go around London with her dressed in men's clothes. That this sort of behaviour was still extremely transgressive is illustrated by the treatment of Radclyffe Hall's *The Well of Loneliness*, a novel dealing with lesbian love, which was withdrawn from circulation by its publisher, Jonathan Cape in 1928 after a torrent of outrage from the press and the Home Secretary. The book was found by the courts to be disgusting and obscene and was ordered to be destroyed. E. M. Forster, Leonard and Virginia Woolf all joined in the protests (a letter from Virginia and E. M. Forster was published in the *Nation & Athenaeum* on 8 September 1928). Virginia was relieved when the court ruled that evidence as to literary merit was inadmissible, as this meant that she would avoid being called to testify on its behalf (D III, 31 August 1928, 10 November 1928).

Vita Sackville-West was from an ancient aristocratic family. She was brought up in the huge family mansion of Knole, and the tragedy and outrage was that, being a woman, she could not inherit this house which she loved so much. On the death of her father in February 1928 it passed instead to her uncle (see D III, 11 February 1928). Vita, who had two sons, lived with her husband at Long Barn. It was here on the couch that, according to a letter from Vita, Virginia initiated their physical intimacy. In 1932 Vita moved to Sissinghurst in Kent, a more or less derelict mansion which they set about rehabilitating. It has a tower in which Vita wrote her books (the original Hogarth printing press is on view there now) and superb gardens, created by Vita. Virginia conceived of *Orlando* as a mock biography of Vita. In the book she was to be born as a male child in the fifteenth century. Only at the beginning of the eighteenth century would she become a woman. Her great poem, *The Oak Tree* (a mock version of Vita's *The Land*), would be started

in the Elizabethan age but would only be completed in the twentieth century. Without telling her what the book was, Virginia
managed to persuade Vita to pose for photographs to illustrate it.
She studied Vita's family's history and the plans of Knole. She
enormously enjoyed herself. It was written at top speed and in a
rapture. 'I walk making up phrases; sit, contriving scenes; am in
short in the thick of the greatest rapture known to me. . . . [I have]
abandoned myself to the pure delight of this farce: which I enjoy as
much as I've ever enjoyed anything' (D III, 22 October 1927). She
felt that for once she did not need to be a difficult author. She
avoided the usual problems. She never descended to the depths. It
was a deliberately superficial book. When she finished it she
worried whether it had grown too long for a joke and in the final
scenes become rather too serious. Subsequent reaction has confirmed that this unevenness of tone is a problem with the book.
The mocking, parodistic and fantastical tone with which it opens
had by the end been replaced by a more serious quest for the
character of Vita in the present day.

The full printed title of the book is *Orlando: A Biography*. Its
appearance as a biography is confirmed by the fact that it has an
index, a preface, in which the author thanks all those who have
helped her with research and encouragement (including Defoe,
Sterne and Emily Bronte), a few footnotes and eight illustrations.
Unfortunately, modern paperback editions in England, by which
many readers now become acquainted with the book, omit these
illustrations, which is a great pity as they are an important part of
the joke. Family portraits from Knole stand in as pictures of the
young Orlando and of Sherlmadine whom she marries, Angelica
Bell (Virginia's niece) in costume is Sasha the Russian princess,
and three photographs of Vita illustrate Orlando in the present
day.

The fact that it is a fantastic, comic and superficial book (in the
sense that it did not involve its author exploring her deeper
feelings) does not mean that it has nothing serious in it. Its
narrator's comments on biography provide a serious critique of the
illusions of biographical writing, which poses as factual and objective though it is actually fictional and involves the imagination.
Above all, though, its comic treatment of gender, and Orlando's
experience of switching from male to female, highlights the conventionality, the artificiality, of social assumptions about men and
women and what they are capable of. The book celebrates the

richness of Orlando's personality which, containing as it does elements and capacities normally seen as the best of both masculine and feminine, thoroughly reveals the absurdity of these social categories. It rejects the idea that a person has a fixed gender, and is limited in what they can desire and enjoy to the standard, permitted forms of pleasure. Treating such subversive themes through fantasy allows them to be aired without too much anxiety, and allows moral and cultural norms and prohibitions to be transgressed in an unthreatening way. At the same time that she pokes fun at social conventions Virginia Woolf was even relaxed enough to mock her own solemn and mystical style of writing. She makes fun of 'Time Passes'.

> Here he came then, day after day, week after week, month after month, year after year. He saw the beech trees turn golden and the young ferns unfurl; he saw the moon sickle and then circular; he saw – but probably the reader can imagine the passage which should follow and how every tree and plant in the neighbourhood is described first green, then golden; how moons rise and suns set; how spring follows winter and autumn summer; how night succeeds day and day night; how there is first a storm and then fine weather; how things remain much as they are for two or three hundred years or so, except for a little dust and a few cobwebs which one old woman can sweep up in half an hour; a conclusion which, one cannot help feeling, might have been reached more quickly by the simple statement that 'Time passed' (here the exact amount could be indicated in brackets) and nothing whatever happened. (O 69)

Readers responded to the book's irreverent fun, its cheerful celebration of unconventionality, its sheer enjoyment of invention, of making things up. They could appreciate its amusement at Orlando's having so many different selves and could go along with its observation that it is impossible to combine truth and personality in writing biography. Reviewers were relieved to find that Virginia Woolf had written such an undemanding book. It was by far her most successful book up to that time and sold particularly well in the USA, selling twice as much in the first six months as *To the Lighthouse* had sold in a whole year (Table 7.1 gives the details).

As a consequence of this, and then of the success of Vita's novels which were published by their press, the Woolfs' financial situation was, as Leonard said, 'revolutionised' in the years 1928–31.

> Up to 1928, when Virginia was forty-six, she had published five novels; she had in the narrow circle of people who value great works of literature a high reputation as one of the most original contemporary novelists. Thus her books were always reviewed with the greatest seriousness in all papers which treat contemporary literature seriously. But no one would have called her a popular or even a successful novelist, and she could not possibly have lived upon the earnings from her books. . . . She had to write a bad book [*The Years*] and two not very serious books [*Orlando* and *Flush*] before her best serious novels were widely understood and appreciated. (LW 294–5)

It is worth emphasising what Leonard is saying here, that it was not until she was forty-six years old that Virginia Woolf could live on the earnings from her books. It was not until over twenty years of professional writing that she earned from her books the £500 a year that she regarded as the minimum necessary for autonomy, for a 'room of one's own'.

For years their income had only just covered their expenditure and they had lived carefully. Now their expenditure went up slightly to about £1100 a year and remained roughly constant at that figure, but their income rose well above it (see Table 7.2 for details). Virginia's depression and crisis in the autumn of 1926, her sense of failure, had in part been to do with their lack of comfort and luxury and she had been determined to earn enough to change their situation. By the end of 1928 she had succeeded. 'For the first time since I married . . . I have been spending money. The spending muscle does not work naturally yet. I feel guilty; put off buying. . . . Yesterday I spent 15/- on a steel brooch. I spent £3 on a mother of pearl necklace – & I haven't bought a jewel for 20 years perhaps!' (D III, 18 December 1928). By the Spring of 1929 she was being offered £50 an article (instead of the usual £20) by the *New York Herald Tribune* and she knew that from now on she could earn as much as she would ever want. She decided to spend money on having an extra room for herself built at Monks House. That year the Hogarth Press made substantial profits for the first time. The staff were given bonuses and Virginia observed with pride that her writing was providing a living for the seven people they employed as servants and at the Hogarth Press. As her income rose after 1927 Leonard's decreased, as he was able to take on less journalistic work. From 1926 on she was earning more than her husband and was no longer financially dependent on his earnings.

TABLE 7.1 *Sales of Virginia Woolf's Books*

Title and date of publication	Sales data
The Voyage Out 1915	2000 in UK by 1929 not published in USA until 1920
Night and Day 1919	2338 in UK by 1929 1326 in USA by 1929
Jacob's Room 1922	1413 in UK in first year 2500 printed in USA in 1923
Mrs Dalloway 1925	First to be published simultaneously in UK and USA 2236 in UK in first year 5100 in USA in first year
The Common Reader: First Series 1925	1434 in UK in first year
To the Lighthouse 1927	3873 in UK in the first year 7600 in USA in first year
Orlando 1928	8104 in UK in six months 13 031 in USA in six months
A Room of One's Own 1929	12 443 in UK in six months 10 926 in USA in six months
The Waves 1931	10 117 in UK in six months 10 380 in USA in six months
The Common Reader: Second Series 1932	3373 in UK in six months 3271 in USA in six months
Flush 1933	18 739 in UK in six months 14 081 in USA in six months
The Years 1937	13 005 in UK in six months 30 904 in USA in six months
Three Guineas 1938	8000 in UK in first edition 7500 printed in USA
Roger Fry 1940	4670 in UK first edition 2500 in USA first edition
Between the Acts 1941	12 858 printed in 1941 in UK 12 500 printed in USA

Sources: Leonard Woolf *Downhill All the Way*, A. MacLaurin and R. Majumdar, *Virginia Woolf: The Critical Heritage*, B.J. Kirkpatrick, *A Bibliography of Virginia Woolf*.

NB. The figures, being from different sources, are given for different time periods and with different degrees of accuracy, and are therefore not strictly comparable. When sales figures are not available I have given print runs. Nonetheless, certain things stand out. First, USA sales usually outstrip UK sales. Second, *Orlando* is the turning point in her career from the point of view of sales.

From data not given in this table we know that those titles which sold in largest numbers in Woolf's lifetime, namely *Orlando*, *Flush* and *The Years*, fell off drastically in sales later. In the early 1960s they were out of print in the USA. By contrast, in the 1960s *Mrs Dalloway* and *To the Lighthouse* were regularly selling 40 000 copies a year between them. As for non-fiction, sales shot up when titles were published in very cheap editions by Penguin: *Common Reader I* in 1938 (50 000 copies printed), *Common Reader II* in 1944 (50 000 copies) and *A Room of One's Own* in 1945 (100 000 copies).

TABLE 7.2   *Leonard and Virginia Woolf, earnings 1924–39*

	VW	LW	Hogarth Press	Gross Joint Income
1924	165	569	3	1047
1925	223	565	73	1265
1926	713	499	27	1658
1927	748	352	27	1496
1928	1540	394	64	2345
1929	2936	357	380	3996
1930	1617	383	530	2875
1931	1326	258	2373	4368
1932	2531	270	2209	5331
1933	1916	263	1693	4199
1934	2130	202	930	3615
1935	801	208	741	2208
1936	721	263	637	2098
1937	2466	271	77	3184
1938	2972	365	2442	6349
1939	891	778	350	2821

Source: Leonard Woolf *Downhill All the Way*, p. 291.

Notes: The figures in columns VW and LW refer to earned income (from books, articles and other journalism). I have not listed here their other income (from stocks and shares), their income tax deductions, their net income or their annual expenditure, all of which information is given by Leonard Woolf. Their annual expenditure remained roughly constant at around £1100 per annum after 1927. Notice how Hogarth Press income jumps in 1929 (after the 1928 publication of *Orlando*) and again in 1931 (after the 1930 publication of Vita Sackville-West's *The Edwardians*).

THE DARK COUNTRY

In October 1928 Virginia travelled to Cambridge with Vita, Vanessa and Angelica Bell, to deliver the first of her two lectures on women and fiction. She returned the next week for the second. In January 1929 she and Leonard went for a week's visit to Vita and her husband in Berlin. When they returned she became ill and remained inactive for six weeks. In March, still in bed, she wrote at great speed the book that was to become *A Room of One's Own*. By May she was working on a final revision and it was published in October 1929. She was worried in case it was 'pitched in too high a voice' (D III, 19 August 1929), in case there was 'a shrill feminine tone in it which my intimate friends will dislike' (D III, 23 October 1929). At the same time, and as another indication of the change in her status as an author, the Hogarth Press began to issue a Uniform Edition of her works. Sales of *A Room of One's Own* were extremely good and by December had even overtaken *Orlando*.

Through 1929 Virginia Woolf attempted to create for herself two very different voices. It is as if she split apart into two personae who each needed their own voice and could not be contained within one fictional character. One was the seductive public lecturer of *A Room of One's Own*, whose performance involves addressing an audience and offering them an analysis of history. This part of herself was concerned with life in society, with 'grossly material things, like health and money and the houses we live in' (RO 43). The second persona or voice was that of a solitary woman, who was to be the central figure in her new novel *The Moths*. This voice was to make up stories and as it did so the sound of the waves would be heard in the background. 'The Lonely Mind' it is called at one point (D III, 4 September 1929). In October, as *A Room of One's Own* was published, she referred to this other book as *The Waves* for the first time. Whereas the former voice involved that part of Virginia Woolf which was public and concerned with grossly material life, the latter involved the secret, unshared part of herself, which was revealed in her diary: 'How I suffer, & no one knows how I suffer, walking up this street, engaged with my anguish, as I was after Thoby died – alone; fighting something alone' (D III, 11 October 1929). This solitary anguish has its positive side, for it is this that drives her to write her novels.

If I never felt these extraordinarily pervasive strains – of unrest, or rest, or happiness, or discomfort – I should float down into acquiescence. Here is something to fight: & when I wake early I say to myself, Fight, fight. If I could catch the feeling, I would: the feeling of the singing of the real world, as one is driven by loneliness & silence from the habitable world. . . . (ibid.)

We could see each of Virginia Woolf's works as composing a self-portrait of one of her selves; in these two books she was drawing at the same time two self-portraits of two parts of herself that she could not bring into contact, which would not live in easy coexistence – the sociable woman living in the habitable world and the solitary woman listening in a trance to the singing of the 'real world'. Ever since her vision of a fin in a waste of waters in September 1926, she had defined her deeper purpose as a writer as the attempt to catch that fleeting vision of 'reality':

Often down here I have entered into a sanctuary; a nunnery; had a religious retreat; of great agony once; & always some terror; so afraid one is of loneliness: of seeing to the bottom of the vessel. That is one of the experiences I have had here in some Augusts; & got then to a consciousness of what I call 'reality': a thing I see before me; something abstract; but residing in the downs or sky; beside which nothing matters; in which I shall rest & continue to exist. Reality I call it. And I fancy sometimes this is the most necessary thing to me: that which I seek . . . Now perhaps this is my gift; this perhaps is what distinguishes me from other people; I think it may be rare to have so acute a sense of something like that. . . . I would like to express it too. (D III, 10 September 1928)

Each of the voices which she created in 1929 produced a mono-logue; on the one hand a lecture, on the other a soliloquy (and eventually in *The Waves*, a series of soliloquies). There is no dia-logue. It is as if, in the pursuit of their own inner reveries or of 'the singing of the real world', her characters almost entirely stop talking to one another, or at least that their talk is beside her point.

A Room of One's Own is about the conditions in the habitable world that prevent or enable a woman to escape from that world into the solitude of creative work. This is why the book has such an air of paradox about it. The first two thirds of the book are concerned with the habitable world of the aspiring woman writer.

'Fiction is like a spider's web, attached ever so lightly perhaps, but still attached to life at all four corners . . . These webs are not spun in mid-air by incorporeal creatures, but are the work of suffering human beings, and are attached to grossly material things, like health and money and the houses we live in' (RO 43). For a woman to write, the material conditions of her life must not obstruct her. She must have money, education, time, a room of her own. She must not be exhausted by domestic labour and child rearing. But the removal of these external obstacles is not enough. Once inside her own room, with the door locked, the writer can still be obstructed. There are cultural and psychological obstacles to her work which she takes with her into her room. There are rules of decorum telling her what she can and cannot write about without giving offence. There are habits of concern which stand in the way of her hurting men by damaging their self esteem. When she gave a talk on the subject to the National Society for Women's Service in January 1931, she portrayed these barriers to a woman's writing in the figure of the Angel in the house, who would hover at her shoulder and warn her to behave herself. The Angel must be killed.[3] The third obstacle preventing the woman writing is the lack of a vitalising tradition. Historians must remove this obstacle and enable women to 'think back through their mothers' (RO 76). Virginia Woolf herself in her essays contributed enormous, invaluable amounts of work of this kind so that if women can now appreciate that they have a literature of their own this is in no small measure thanks to her efforts.

Mary Beton, the fictional character whose voice we hear in *A Room of One's Own*, is a vehicle for that part of Virginia Woolf that was fascinated by women's lives, and particularly by what it has been like to be a woman who wants to write, in different historical periods. This part of Virginia Woolf was fascinated by the details of the material conditions of women's lives, their houses, their work, the social and cultural pressures weighing down on them. It is a part of her that we hear also in many of her essays, and in the 'Introductory Letter' which she wrote in 1931 to *Life As We Have Known It*. This is a collection of memoirs by working women, organised by the Women's Cooperative Guild. In *A Room of One's Own* it is the part of her that researched the lives of women writers such as Lady Winchilsea and Margaret of Newcastle, and which imagined the lethal conditions in which Judith Shakespeare would have been forced to live and die. When this part of her mind split off and temporarily pushed her other selves aside it sent her running to the British Museum to read history, sociology and anthropology. It drove her to read biographies, to find out about 'the lives of the obscure' (the title of one of her essays in *The Common Reader* I). It compelled her to write essays on the oddest books, not just the canonised literature but all sorts of memoirs, letters, diaries and travel books. Much of the freshness, the idiosyncrasy, of the *Common Reader* collections (she was at this time preparing the second series and it was published in 1932) derives from this irrepressible curiosity. In *The Common Reader: Second Series* she seems positively to prefer to write about obscure individuals, wayward lives and informal or eccentric writings. Her interest was, in fact, not limited to the lives of women. As examples, there is a wonderful essay on the life of the Rev. John Skinner, who wrote ninety-eight manuscript volumes recording the stream of village life before he went out into the woods and shot himself. Other essays which rescue the lives of the obscure or the less well known include a study of the strange relationship between Geraldine Jewsbury and Jane Carlyle and anecdotes from the works of the sixteenth-century Gabriel Harvey.

When this part of Virginia Woolf thought about the future of women's fiction she became excited by the possibility that after centuries of neglect the conditions of women's lives could now be written about. As she argues in 'Women and Fiction', because men's values and priorities are different from women's, what they will emphasise in their writing will be different.

> Thus, when a woman comes to write a novel, she will find that she is perpetually wishing to alter the established values – to make serious what appears insignificant to a man, and trivial what is to him important . . . Often nothing tangible remains of a woman's day. The food that has been cooked is eaten; the children that have been nursed have gone out into the world. Where does the accent fall? . . . For the first time, this dark country is beginning to be explored in fiction. (WW 49)

Moreover, women are now no longer restricted to domestic life; they are entering the professions and political life, and these experiences must also be recorded and the social conditions obstructing them criticised. In *A Room of One's Own* Virginia Woolf adds to this. She imagines Mary Carmichael, a woman novelist, wanting to explore in fiction the lives of contemporary women. She will most likely want to throw the main emphasis upon her women characters at work, perhaps in a laboratory; and then in relation with each other. Women have before only been portrayed in their relation to men, but they do also befriend and love one another, and these relationships are part of the dark country which needs to be explored. In 'Professions for Women' her definition of the problem is a little different. A woman writer must be free to tell the truth, and she has been prevented from telling the truth by rules which have prohibited her from throwing light upon certain areas of her experience. These rules are internalised and the woman writer's reach into her own unconscious mind is obstructed by them. Her imagination is blocked. The great problem for the woman writer now is to learn how to overcome these obstacles so that she can tell the truth about her passions and about her body: 'telling the truth about my own experiences as a body, I do not think I solved. I doubt that any woman has solved it yet' (WW 62).

Now, however, we find that there are forces pulling her argument in a completely different direction. There is another part of Virginia Woolf, and it is the part which speaks, for example, in *The Waves*. She is not in the end satisfied with the kind of fiction which she has imagined for Mary Carmichael. After all, she had argued in 'Mr Bennett and Mrs Brown' against the Edwardian novel because of its interest in the houses that we live in, in grossly material things like health and money. She had complained about novels which take on the functions of government departments by taking upon themselves the tasks of social investigation and criticism. She felt that this kind of 'materialism' omitted something important. More recently, in 'The Narrow Bridge of Art', which I described above as her modernist manifesto, she declared that in future the novel 'will make little use of the marvellous fact-recording power . . . It will tell us very little about the houses, incomes, occupations of its characters; it will have little kinship with the sociological novel or the novel of environment' (CE II 225). What she seems to be describing here is her own future novel, *The Waves*, in which, more even than in any of her other novels, she refused to show the slightest interest in the material conditions of life. It leaves the dark country of both men's and women's lives completely uncharted. About Bernard, the central character, we never learn what he does for a living. That he marries and has children are mentioned only in passing. The novel is silent about his passions and his body. What seems trivial and what seems important do not correspond at all to the views about women and fiction expounded by that other part of Virginia Woolf who speaks through the lecturer Mary Beton.

In fact, however, this conflicting view is also to be found in *A Room of One's Own* itself and in 'Women and Fiction'. In the latter, having welcomed the fact that women's novels can now deal with the dark country of women's everyday lives, and with the social evils which women confront in public life, she goes on to say that there is another change in the novel which is 'more interesting to those who prefer the butterfly to the gadfly – that is to say, the artist to the reformer'. This is that women's lives now enable them to achieve an impersonal perspective and will encourage the poetic spirit.

> It will lead them to be less absorbed in facts and no longer content to record with astonishing acuteness the minute details which fall under their own observation. They will look beyond the personal and political relationships to the wider questions which the poet tries to solve – of our destiny and the meaning of life. (WW 51)

This very revealing remark shows us that Virginia Woolf, or at least this part of Virginia Woolf, gave relatively low priority to the kinds of prose which represent and imaginatively investigate personal relationships, private emotions and social life. Another kind of literature, which she calls poetry, though it includes some kinds of novels, has a higher value for her. The reason for this is that the mission of poetry is a very ambitious one indeed – to solve the problems of 'our destiny and the meaning of life'. When Virginia Woolf wrote in this way she was at her closest to that kind of modernism that is represented by the Bloomsbury painters and art critics, Roger Fry and Clive Bell. She was expressing that side of herself that valued the mystical, the spiritual, in experience. There was always a conflict in her between the belief that life is profuse, chaotic and disordered, full of unpredictability and accident, and another kind of belief which she felt in moments of vision, a belief in pattern and order, a belief that we are not transitory but that we connect and interpenetrate each other, a belief that time does not exist. Thinking about her brother Thoby, and he was often on her mind while she was writing *The Waves*, she wrote, 'I think of death sometimes as the end of an excursion which I went on when he died. As if I should come in & say well, here you are' (D III, 26 December 1929).

In *A Room of One's Own* she developed this argument in much greater detail, and it is here that her idea of androgyny has its place. Having presented us with a picture of what it is to be a woman writer, with a woman's values and traditions and using a woman's sentence, she springs on us the idea that to write freely, without impediment, is to write 'as a woman who has forgotten that she is a woman', as someone in whom 'sex is unconscious of itself'. Only thus can one write not as someone immersed in the world's concerns but 'as if one had gone to the top of the world and seen it laid out, very majestically beneath' (RO 92). There are within the mind, she argues, two sexes, and to write without effort or distortion it is necessary that they be in harmony with each other. Only when the fusion or intercourse between the woman and the man in her mind takes place can the mind use all its faculties. This state of androgyny prevents the mind from being separated into different chambers. A writer must be woman–manly or man–womanly. Otherwise, in writing s/he will be repressing some part of herself in giving voice to some other part. As so often, Virginia Woolf sketches here an erotics of the soul, sexual figures for the soul's craving for unity: 'Some marriage of opposites has to be consummated. The whole of the mind must lie wide open if we are to get the sense that the writer is communicating his experience with perfect fullness' (RO 103).

What is this fullness? It is a myth. But it is a myth which Virginia Woolf clung onto from her early days as a writer and throughout her career. In 1924 she wrote that the Greeks had enjoyed perfect expression, that their language was a perfect vehicle for their emotions, so that their inner lives poured effortlessly out through their mouths. She imagined a state of language and of the soul which would allow one to give voice to all those meanings and feelings that we carry inside ourselves and which we cannot bring out except in the partial and distorted forms of our speech and our writing. She imagines a perfect language in which we could release ourselves whole and entire, incandescent as she says, melted down into a pure liquid fluent form. It is a strange and disconcerting leap that she takes, from the materialism of her analysis of writing as a woman to the mythology of the disembodied, fluent and androgynous soul.

THE SINGING OF THE REAL WORLD

The Waves was the most hard-won of all Virginia Woolf's novels since *The Voyage Out*. The original seed was planted in her mind, as we have seen, during her crisis autumn of 1926. Over the next three years she returned again and again to her idea of a solitary woman's flow of thought. It was not until after she had written *Orlando* and *A Room of One's Own* that she began to write a draft of this new novel in July 1929. She gave up and started afresh in September of that year, completing a first draft in April 1930. She worked on a second draft from May 1930 until February 1931. The novel was published in October 1931.[4]

She found writing this novel, compared with *To the Lighthouse*, slow and hesitant work. At first she had a problem with the basic conception. 'Here's my interesting thing; & there's no quite solid table on which to put it' (D III, 5 November 1929). This 'Lonely Mind' or solitary woman, was she to be a soliloquist or a narrator? Would she muse on life or tell stories? In fact stories, about six characters, first as children then grown up, came to be the main material. Only when she was well into the second draft did the story-teller disappear and the six characters themselves take over with their own soliloquies. But she could not find a way of doing it that seemed right. Astonishingly, it was only at the very latest possible moment, after years of searching and frustration, at the very last revision before the typescript was dispatched to the printers, that she hit upon the structure of the novel that we are familiar with. There are six voices or characters. Through these voices we hear the stories of their lives from childhood to middle age. In the long final section, however, one of the voices, that of Bernard, seems to take over all the others, or at least their separate existence is thrown in doubt. Moreover, there are other sections, printed in italics, which are not spoken by any character. In these sections, which she called interludes and which are interspersed between the soliloquies throughout the book, we follow the passage of a single day from sunrise to sunset. These interludes in this form, with their own passage of time and their own distinct typography, were only introduced at the very last minute in preparing the fourth typescript of the book, in July 1931.[5] Throughout its composition, Virginia Woolf struggled to find a structure or a device which could contain her vision.

In the end she was satisfied that she had done what she had set out to do, and after so much anguish and uncertainty it at last felt right.

> I must record, heaven be praised, the end of The Waves. I wrote the words O Death fifteen minutes ago, having reeled across the last ten pages with some moments of such intensity & intoxication that I seemed only to stumble after my own voice, or almost, after some sort of speaker (as when I was mad). I was almost afraid, remembering the voices that used to fly ahead. Anyhow it is done; & I have been sitting these 15 minutes in a state of glory, & calm, & some tears, thinking of Thoby & if I could write Julian Thoby Stephen 1881–1906 on the first page . . . I have netted that fin in the waste of waters which appeared to me over the marshes out of my window at Rodmell when I was coming to an end of To the Lighthouse. (D IV, 7 February 1931)

Of all her novels *The Waves* is the least mimetic, the least 'realist'. The voices do not correspond to any real possible form of speech, either inner or public. Their eloquent, poetic effusions are openly artificial. Like the abstract geometries of Kandinsky or the floating, dreamlike images of Chagall, they do not disguise the fact that they are made up, not copied from experience but fabricated by an artist. Moreover, there is the problem of the interludes which bracket the soliloquies. Who speaks them? Sometimes they contain lines from the soliloquies as if a ventriloquist were rehearsing his parts. Of all Virginia Woolf's novels it is the one which has most often been read as mythic, and been interpreted in terms of mythic schemes and meanings.

Probably many readers find, as did Vita and other of her close friends, that it is quite hard to keep reading through the first one hundred pages of the book. Those who persist, however, find that in the long final section, Bernard's one-sided 'conversation' in a restaurant, suddenly all the hard work and bafflement that has led up to this has been very worth while. For, many readers find, these strange fifty pages of prose, however one interprets them, are among the greatest that she ever wrote. It is as if she has cunningly managed to create an impossible situation (a man sums up in monologue his own and five other lives as he sits at a restaurant table with a silent acquaintance), through which she can dramatise a voice which corresponds to her deepest desires and fantasies. It is a voice which speaks outwardly and fluently, in the most wonderful poetic rhythms, for that silent, lonely inner self that she had always wanted to find a way of releasing through her writing. Through Bernard she can speak to us. The strange inter-mixing of conversational with almost ritualistic rhythms is an important part of the power of Bernard's monologue. Through this device she can give voice to inarticulate but deeply felt experi-ences. She has created a way of coaxing into words visions, intuitions and memories which she had valued above all others but which had remained locked in silence. Some of these were child-hood memories (an apple tree associated with death, a puddle which she could not bring herself to step over). Others were more recent, especially her meditations on the death of her brother, the fin in a waste of waters at Rodmell, and her repeated experience of waking in the morning and saying 'Fight! fight!' as if that effort of going on were the key to her being. Each of these is incorporated, in Bernard's monologue, into a verbal context which allows them to release their meanings. Her aim, in other words, was not to record facts nor simply to make fine phrases, but to create a voice which could speak the unspeakable, the 'singing of the real world'. To accomplish this she had to make good her aim – to 'make prose move – yes I swear – as prose has never moved before' (D IV, 7 January 1931).

The Bernard 'character' is a writer. We can see him as one of Virginia Woolf's most self-conscious self-portraits. His voice pro-vides her with a vehicle for her reflections on the purposes and limitations of writing. He shares her distrust of stories and of fine phrase-making.

> . . . there are so many, and so many – stories of childhood, stories of school, love, marriage, death and so on; and none of them are true. Yet like children we tell each other stories, and to decorate them we make up these ridiculous, flamboyant, beauti-ful phrases. How tired I am of stories, how tired I am of phrases that come down beautifully with all their feet on the ground! (W 204)

Not the least interesting are Bernard's remarks about biography, a form about which his author had a life-long curiosity, amplified no doubt by her dissatisfactions with the biographic style as practised by her father and later, in a more modern mode, by her friend Lytton Strachey. Her scepticism was to some extent voiced in 'The New Biography' which she wrote in 1927, at the time when she was making fun of biography in *Orlando*. Bernard expressed her belief that not only was the accepted way of writing people's lives mistaken, but that it was complicit with patriarchal forms of social discipline.

> After all, one cannot find fault with the biographic style if one begins letters 'Dear Sir,' ends them 'yours faithfully'; one cannot despise these phrases laid like Roman roads across the tumult of our lives, since they compel us to walk in step like civilised people with the slow and measured tread of policemen though one may be humming any nonsense under one's breath at the same time – 'Hark, hark, the dogs do bark,' 'Come away, come away, death'. (W 223)

She was convinced that the decisive influences acting to shape a life are mostly invisible to, and hence ignored by, biographers. It is to emphasise this, and to highlight other, more subtle and hidden forces, that she excludes from the stories of her characters' lives in *The Waves* so much that would normally be given prominent consideration (parents, social groups, work, domestic life, marriage and so on). In the novel, the single most influential event in the characters' lives is the death of Percival. The emptiness that is left when he dies stands behind all of their experiences. Other experiences are also given prominence, especially, in Bernard's life, a moment of vision in response to which his perception of the world seems to undergo a crucial though subtle change. It corresponds to Virginia's vision of the fin in Rodmell in 1926, and another experience about which we know even less that seems to have happened in 1932 (which I discuss below).[6] 'Here am I shedding one of my life-skins, and all they will say is, "Bernard is spending ten days in Rome"' (W 161). This is a line of reflection to which she returned in 1938, when faced with the task of writing a biography of Roger Fry.

The price that she paid for this achievement, however, was that she led the novel into a cul-de-sac. She had been accused of this when she wrote *Mrs Dalloway*, but then it had been untrue, for her discoveries in that novel could be developed both in her own work and by many subsequent writers. But *The Waves* has led nowhere. It was unrepeatable by Virginia Woolf and inimitable by anyone else. It was so abstracted from all the usual material of the novel that, as one perceptive reviewer put it, 'it comes close to going out of bounds' (MM 273). Less than any other of her books is it concerned with 'the houses that we live in', with the material reality of our lives or with the psychological reality of our relationships. It is almost a disembodied book, 'eyeless' as she said. The same reviewer said that 'Mrs Woolf, so far as the novel is concerned, has almost reached the jumping off place', for pushed any further in this direction her work would pass beyond the novel and into something else – poetry, poetic drama or perhaps song. To continue as a novelist her work would have to take a radically new direction.

The other danger that she ran in choosing such an abstracted style, was that she would be widely misunderstood. It is certainly her most demanding book and she was anxious that it would be dismissed as exquisite but unreal. She was made nervous by the review in the *TLS* for it 'praised my characters when I meant to have none' (D IV, 8 October 1931). The next day she wrote: 'Really, this unintelligible book is being better "received" than any of them. . . . And it sells – how unexpected, how odd that people can read that difficult grinding stuff!' She began to receive quite ecstatic reactions. Winifred Holtby wrote to her saying that 'It is a poem, more completely than any of your other books, of course. It is most rarely subtle. It has seen more deeply into the human heart, perhaps, than even To the Lighthouse. . . .' (D IV, 22 September). Harold Nicolson phoned to say that it was a masterpiece. Although she was sure that it could not be a popular book it sold well, as well as her 'popular' books, *Orlando* and *A Room of One's Own*.

However, the positive reaction was based on a consistent response which gave her pause. What she wanted was 'to be told that this is solid & means something' (D IV, 22 September). She felt that in writing it she had aimed not merely at beauty but had 'tried to speak the truth' (D IV, 15 September). Overwhelmingly, however, readers reacted to it as beautiful poetry. 'Poetic' was by far the most common adjective that it elicited. The book consolidated her reputation for being an ethereal writer, hypersensitive but without substance. The reviewer in *The Times* wrote: 'Like some old Venetian craftsman in glass, Mrs Woolf spins the coloured threads, and with exquisite, intuitive sensibility fashions ethereal frailties of enduring quality'. Vanessa was 'overcome by the beauty' (D IV, 15 September–15 October 1931). A more unkind version of the same response was that 'there is something pale, mild, wistful, sentimental about its poetic feeling' (MM 275). The book's difficulty and its style were getting in the way of readers' appreciating that, for all its beauty, it is a hard book about hard experiences; about madness and despair, about growing old, about bereavement and suicide. It attempts to face life with no illusions. It poses questions and gives no answers. As life is renewed in Susan's pregnancy, Bernard says 'It goes on, but why?', the authentically unanswerable modernist question. The exquisite fabric of the prose distracts attention from the harshness of the experiences and the restlessness of spirit, the endless movement from exultation to despair. Where could Virginia Woolf go from here?

8

1932–37: The Outsider

*'An outsider – and it is part of a writer's profession to be an outsider –
can see aspects of things that are not visible from the inside.'* (P 7)

BREAKING THE MOULD

The publication of *The Waves* in 1931 brought to an end Virginia
Woolf's most productive decade. She reached a turning point in
her career, as drastic as anything since her abandonment of the
conventional novel after *Night and Day*. The story of the last ten
years of her life is an ambiguous one. Most people have seen these
years as a sad falling away from success. In the rest of her life, she
did not publish a single novel which she herself felt to be successful. She found it impossible to settle on a satisfactory style of
writing, and wasted her last years with unfinished or minor works.
The one acknowledged success, *Between the Acts*, was never revised for publication and was only published after her death.
However, there is another way, which I prefer, of telling the story
of these years. My emphasis will be not on her failures but the fact
that after 1931 she progressively abandoned the more restricting,
formalist aspects of Bloomsbury ways of thinking about her work.
She turned her attention more towards the recording of what she
thought of as 'non-being', and away from the lofty, mystical
aspirations of *The Waves*. She became less concerned with formal
elegance and poetic beauty and more with the comedy and absurdity of everyday life. Her technical inventiveness never ceased.
In the 1930s she suffered crushing disillusionment, but she drew
on this to win for literature some of her most daring prose, much of
it published after her death.

In the twelve months after the publication of *The Waves* she was
mostly occupied in writing essays. She completed *The Common
Reader: Second Series* (it was published in October 1932). Since she
had become a celebrated author she had acquired a variety of
lucrative outlets and forms of publication for her essays. She was

not above trying to make money. She could, through the Hogarth Press, invent ways of maximising income from her minor works. Many of her essays were originally published not only in magazines but also as pamphlets or short, cloth-bound books. B. J. Kirkpatrick's indispensible bibliography contains many fascinating details of such publications.[1] For example, 'On Being Ill', a short essay of some 4000 words, first published in 1926 in *The New Criterion*, was republished by Hogarth in 1930 in boards and with a dust jacket. It was printed in purple ink and the type was set by Woolf herself. 250 copies were sold at £1 15s 0d each and the edition was, according to Leonard, heavily oversubscribed. At this price it cost more than twice as much as her cloth-bound novels at the time. In 1934 her essay 'Walter Sickert: A Conversation', first published in the *Yale Review* that year, was issued in Britain as a booklet, in paper wrappers illustrated by Vanessa Bell, at 1s 6d each, in an edition of 3800 copies. As another example, Kirkpatrick also lists an American edition of 'Street Haunting' in 1930 issued by a company in San Francisco. In addition to these special publications, Woolf was by the early 1930s able to attract as many lucrative commissions for magazine articles as she could handle. Note, for example, her series of six articles on 'London Scenes' for *Good Housekeeping* magazine, written in 1931. 'Articles & more articles are asked for. For ever I could write articles' (D IV, 11 April 1931).

Her 'Letter to a Young Poet' illustrates yet another form of publication, for this was one of a series of 'Letters' written by different authors for Hogarth. This was a publishing gimmick thought up by Leonard Woolf and John Lehmann, who was then manager at the Press. They appeared as 30 page pamphlets in an edition of 6000, selling at one shilling each, and were later republished in book form.[2] In this work for the first time we can see Virginia Woolf not as a young writer in the literary vanguard, opening up the path of modernism in the novel for those who will come after, but as a senior author addressing a young, up and coming generation of writers, with their own quite different priorities and anxieties. She was fifty years old in 1932. The cultural situation was changing fast and she was in danger of seeming dated and out of touch.

In 1931 she had begun to write *Flush*, a minor work, which was eventually published in 1933. This little book is, like *Orlando*, a parody biography, though it has none of the earlier book's excitement or magic. It is the life story of a spaniel belonging to Elizabeth

Barrett Browning, intended as a light-hearted parody of the biographic methods of Lytton Strachey (L V, 23 February 1933). It had endnotes and a list of sources and nine plates (of which four were drawings by Vanessa Bell and one a photograph of the Woolfs' dog Pinka, standing in for Flush). Virginia came to think of it as 'a silly book' and 'a waste of time' (D IV, 29 April 1933). It was selected by the Book Society in England and in America. It was her biggest selling book to date and made £2000 for its author at high speed. The majority of reviewers were not impressed and dismissed it as a slight little joke of a book. As throughout the decade, Virginia Woolf enjoyed increased fame and wealth and a wider readership, at a time when she was least certain of the value of her own work.

In January 1932 Lytton Strachey died of cancer at the age of fifty-two. He was the first of the Bloomsbury friends to die and it was a great shock to Virginia. Vanessa, Duncan Grant and Virginia sobbed together in Vanessa's studio. In March Dora Carrington, who had lived with Strachey, killed herself. Virginia found herself thinking how little fame meant. Her father, very famous at the time of his death, counted for nothing now only thirty years later, his 'solid statue' existing no longer (D IV, 4 February 1932). There was no funeral ceremony for Lytton Strachey. Virginia felt that it was wrong that he had gone with nothing definite to mark the fact, no ceremony or stone. Keynes agreed that this was carrying unconventionality too far. In September 1934 Roger Fry died suddenly, of a heart attack. Though he was older this was even more of a shock. 'I think the poverty of life now is what comes to me. a thin blackish veil over everything' (D IV, 12 September 1934). The Woolfs went to the funeral service which consisted entirely of music. In the immediate aftermath she experienced the same swing from despair to exultation that she had described in *The Waves*. She felt that we all fight, with our brains and with our loves, and yet must be vanquished. 'Then the vanquisher, this outer force became so clear . . . & we so small fine delicate. A fear then came to me, of death. Of course I shall lie there too before that gate, & slide in; & it frightened me. But why? I mean, I felt the vainness of this perpetual fight, with our brains & loving each other. . . .' A week later the other feeling begins to appear: 'the exalted sense of being above time & death which comes from being again in a writing mood. And this is not an illusion, so far as I can tell' (D IV, 19/20 September 1934). Perhaps more than for most writers, writing was the means by which she went on living.

Virginia Woolf herself saw that her attitudes and work had undergone a crucial transformation after the publication of *The Waves*. She dated this change to the autumn of 1932 when she had, as she told the story later, an experience of 'revelation' or 'conversion'. We know even less about this experience than we do about that of 1926, which again confirms her view that the influences that shape a life are often invisible to biographers. The context for the experience was provided by Lytton Strachey's death and her own age. Reaching fifty and having pursued to a limit her artistic intentions of the previous decade, having achieved fame and wealth and having, it seems, emotionally accepted her childlessness, she was now freed from those life narratives which until then had given her struggle for identity its shape. She needed to concern herself no longer with either the socially accepted narratives of women's lives nor her own eccentric narrative of becoming a woman writer.[3] She had an audience. In fact, she had different audiences, for with *Orlando*, *A Room of One's Own* and *The Common Reader* volumes, her work was accessible to far more readers than would have been drawn to her novels by themselves. This situation made it possible for her to give voice to concerns which until then she had felt the need to restrain. She now felt free to express her anger about the damage done to people's lives by men and their desire to dominate, both to women through the institutions and culture of patriarchy, and to men as well through militarism and war. The new identity that she adopted, in October 1932, was that of the 'outsider': 'It is part of a writer's profession to be an outsider' because an outsider 'can see aspects of things that are not visible from the inside' (P 7).

The eventual outcome of this new identity was her book *Three Guineas*, and as she waited anxiously for its publication, in June 1938, she looked back to the time when it was conceived, dating it to 1933 or 34.

> I am an outsider. I can take my way: experiment with my own imagination in my own way. The pack may howl, but it shall never catch me. And even if the pack – reviewers, friends, enemies – pays me no attention or sneers, still I'm free. This is the actual result of that spiritual conversion (I cant bother to get the right words) in the autumn of 1933 – or 4 – when I rushed through London, buying, I remember, a great magnifying glass, from sheer ecstasy, near Blackfriars: when I gave the man who

played the harp half a crown for talking to me about his life in the Tube station. (D V, 20 May 1938)

At other times she dates her 'conversion' to an earlier year. On the last day of 1932 she wrote:

Yes, of course this autumn has been a tremendous revelation. You will understand that all impediments suddenly dropped off. It was a great season of liberation. Everything appeared very distinct, amazingly exciting. I had no restrictions whatever, & was thus free to define my attitude with a vigour & certainty I have never known before. . . . I secured a season of intoxicating exhilaration . . . If one does not lie back & sum up & say to the moment, this very moment, stay you are so fair, what will be one's gain, dying? No: stay, this moment. No one ever says that enough. (D V, 31 December 1932)

'Freedom' is the key word in expressing her new attitude to life. She thought that she had freed herself from her fear of men, their social condemnation, their ridicule and contempt. She also felt free of unwanted social obligations. She had freed herself from any need to create a public reputation for herself and she no longer cared about reviewers' judgements on her books. On 29 October 1933, when reviewers of *Flush* announced that she was finished as a live force in literature, she shrugged it off: 'I have at last laid hands upon my philosophy of anonymity . . . How odd last winter's revelation was! freedom; . . . I will not be 'famous' 'great'. I will go on adventuring, changing, opening my mind & my eyes, refusing to be stamped & stereotyped. The thing is to free ones self'. Again, on 14 March 1937, when *The Years* was being reviewed: 'And now I can put my philosophy of the free soul into operation . . . All the falsities can drop off'. Her philosophy of freedom was perhaps most sorely tested when she was attacked by Wyndham Lewis in *Men Without Art*, an unpleasant, abusive book. Her response was to say: 'I think my revelation 2 years ago stands me in sublime stead, to adventure and discover, & allow no rigid poses: to be supple & naked to the truth. . . . the feeling of being dismissed into obscurity is also pleasant and salutary' (D IV, 14 October 1934).

The exhilaration of the autumn of 1932 came also from the successful beginning of a new book, which she first mentioned as an idea in January 1931, before *The Waves* was published. 'I have this moment, while having my bath, conceived an entire new book – a sequel to a Room of Ones Own – about the sexual life of women: to be called Professions for Women perhaps – Lord how exciting!' (D IV, 20 January 1931). The inspiration was her speech to the National Society for Women's Service the next day, when she would share the platform with her new friend Dame Ethel Smyth, a militant, rumbustious feminist, a composer who put up a fierce fight for entry into the man's world of music performance. She was, in Virginia Woolf's description, 'an ironclad' of a woman, and she proved to be a very demanding friend. The meeting attracted a huge audience and the speakers were, according to Vera Brittain's report in the *Nation*, 'hilariously serious' (P xxxv). When she at last set about writing her new novel, in October 1932, she went back to the typescript for this speech as her starting point, and by now her plan had broadened out. Her new book was to be about the social, political and cultural lives of women from the Victorian period to the present. The book that was born at this time went through many changes; starting in 1932 as a 'Novel-Essay' *The Pargiters* or *Here and Now*, it eventually, after many other provisional titles, divided into two books which were published as *The Years* (1937) and *Three Guineas* (1938).[4]

She wrote, at great speed and with enormous confidence and excitement, 60 000 words between October and December 1932. This great 60 000-word outpouring was a first draft of only the first chapter of the book. Her plan was an extraordinary one. She would write a book following the history of a family from 1880 to the present day. It was to consist of fictional episodes dramatising the conditions of women's lives and interspersed between them would be essays in which the author would discourse on the factual history which provided the social context for the fiction. The resulting manuscript, abandoned by her later but now published as *The Pargiters*, contains what are presented as five 'extracts' from a novel alternating with six essays. The 'extracts' concern the Pargiter family, the father Colonel Pargiter, a retired army officer, and his seven children and they trace the influence on them of a variety of Victorian attitudes. The young daughter Rose sees a man exposing himself in the street and is too terrified and confused to mention the episode to anyone. The other daughters are trapped in a life of narrow expectations while the boys are educated and trained for independence and work. One of the sons is a student at Oxford learning Greek and repressing his sexual thoughts about his cousin Kitty. Edward has no real knowledge or understanding of women, and he transforms Kitty in his imagination into a purified and idealised figure. Kitty meanwhile is bored and dissatisfied with the life which is offered to her as a daughter of the upper middle class. She seeks out an education on the fringes of the university and meets, in the family of Joseph Wright, some of the few people who have escaped the deforming influences of Victorian patriarchy and who can stand as an embodiment of the ideals of honest scholarship and healthy relations between the sexes. The essays expand on the historical facts and meaning of this pathological culture. Even from Virginia Woolf, whose every novel was an innovation in form, this was an extraordinary invention. Unfortunately she decided that it was a mistake and abandoned it.

It is worth pointing out explicitly the astonishing turnabout that she had been trying to perform in *The Pargiters*. Ever since 'Mr Bennett and Mrs Brown' in 1924 she had been arguing that the novel should not concern itself with the external facts of life, with the houses that we live in, nor should it preach doctrines or try to impose a particular view upon the world. In 'The Narrow Bridge of Art' she had argued that the novel should take over the duties of poetry and not concern itself with houses, incomes and occupations. She thought that in the future the novel would distance itself from the sociological novel. In her own novels she had represented social life only indirectly, as it is perceived by her characters. She had developed new, enriched ways of representing the world from the characters' point of view and of representing their own inner worlds. Yet here in *The Pargiters* she was suddenly attempting apparently to reverse the whole direction of her work. In a totally unanticipated move, the novel opens with a description of 56 Abercorn Terrace, the house that the Pargiter family lives in. She poured into her new novel the social facts and observations that she had accumulated over twenty years. She aimed to portray 'everything, sex, education, life &c' (D IV, 2 November 1932). She was writing not about the characters' inner worlds but about the social world as it influences and forms them. The direction of her attention and emphasis could not have altered more drastically. In terms of method, she was now exploiting the skills she had learned writing *Orlando* ('In truth the Pargiters is first cousin to Orlando', she wrote on 19 December 1932). She was writing narrative. She uses a narrator and a point of view external to the characters. For the first time since *Night and Day* she was using the impersonal narrator of the traditional novel. 'I find myself infinitely delighting in facts for a change, & in possession of quantities beyond counting: though I feel now & then the tug to vision, but resist it' (D IV, 2 November 1932). As it turned out, she found, after this exhilarating start, that it was appallingly difficult to find a convincing way of doing what she wanted to do, to combine facts with vision and to portray social life without preaching.

The trouble was that she could not yet let go of Bloomsbury ways of thinking. She equated 'art' with beauty. The disclosing of social and historical truth was 'preaching'. She was trapped in this dichotomy. If she was to express herself freely she would need to expel from her room not only the angel of her own femininity with her insistence on purity, but also her Bloomsbury 'brothers', Roger Fry and Clive Bell. She would have to free herself from their intolerance of 'materialism', and their insistence on the purity of art, which they did not want contaminated by the extraneous material of comment on manners and morals. If she was to succeed in her new project she was going to have to be prepared to dirty her mind. With her new sense of freedom she wished to break away from the elegiac, lyrical poetry of her previous novels. Beautiful though they were, they had a narrow readership and did not confront directly the forces in life about which she had such strong bottled up feelings. But in trying to invent a new kind of novel she came again and again up against her old horror of 'preaching'.

INTERRUPTIONS

At the beginning of 1933 Virginia Woolf changed her design for the new novel, leaving out the 'interchapters' and trying to absorb the historical material into the fictional scenes. Her basic objective remained the same: 'I am breaking the mould made by The Waves' (D IV, 28 July 1934). Instead of creating for the characters' thoughts and feelings an internal context of memory and imagination to saturate them with meaning, she now aimed to create for them an external context, a view of the world outside the window. She moved ahead with the writing, still confident that it was on the right lines, even though it was by far the most ambitious project she had ever attempted.

> But The Pargiters. I think this will be a terrific affair. I must be bold & adventurous. I want to give the whole of the present society – nothing less: facts, as well as the vision. And to combine them both. I mean, The Waves going on simultaneously with Night & Day . . . It should aim at immense breadth & immense intensity. It should include satire, comedy, poetry, narrative, & what form is to hold them all together? Should I bring in a play, letters, poems? I think I begin to grasp the whole. And its to end with the press of daily normal life continuing. And there are to be millions of ideas but no preaching – history, politics, feminism, art, literature – in short a summing up of all I know, feel, laugh at, despise, like, admire hate & so on. (D IV, 25 April 1933)

Two years after her first start on this immense project she completed a first draft. She had sometimes been in despair, wondering how she could hold the whole thing together, but more often she had felt confident and the writing had poured out, 'in full flood'. The provisional title had become 'Here and Now'. As she approached the end she was triumphant. She had, she wrote, never been so excited over a book. By the end she had written 200 000 words and was happy with the basic design. She set about revising the book. She changed the title regularly. She was, by January 1935, still predicting that it would be finished and published that year and that she would be able to start on a biography of Roger Fry. Something went wrong, for it was not in the end published until March 1937 and then only after a period of terrible crisis. There had never been in her entire career so great a gap between her novels as this.

Part of the problem was that politics intruded on her life and made calls on her time with increasing urgency from 1935 on. She was swept up into political activity as never before in her life. I describe some of the details of this below. The political arguments, about pacifism and fascism, revived her desire to write a sequel to *A Room of One's Own* and more and more frequently she felt frustrated at having to hold back from thinking about this new book. In 1932 she had thought of calling it 'Men are Like That?'.

Now that the idea was active again the book was conceived as including not only the psychology of the masculine mind but also ideas about war and fascism. In 1935 it was regularly on her mind, now called 'On Being Despised' or 'The Next War'. Since 1932 she had been collecting material for the book (she thought then already that she had 'enough powder to blow up St Pauls', D IV, 16 February 1932). By the end she had accumulated three bound volumes of cuttings, manifestos, extracts, letters, pictures and other material relating to the questions of men, war and fascism. These volumes, now in the Monks House Papers at the University of Sussex Library, provide a marvellous collage of material from the political life of the thirties, documenting the clash of attitudes and the changing currents of argument.[5] Much of the material found its way eventually into the notes in *Three Guineas*.

As far as *The Years* (as it became known in 1935) was concerned, the problem was that Virginia Woolf was extremely anxious to avoid what she called 'preaching'. 'This fiction is dangerously near propaganda', she wrote (D IV, 14 April 1935). She wanted to split off all her anger and her thoughts about society and politics into the other book, so sure was she that the novel must not be a vehicle for ideas, that it must remain 'impersonal'. This insistence was to prove very damaging, for her original clarity of intention was lost and the book became unfocused and rambling. There has been surprisingly little comment on just how odd Virginia Woolf's resistance to 'propaganda' was. While one can understand why she would reject the idea of having a strident or moralising narrator laying down a line, it is not clear at all why she could not invent, as other authors would have done, strident or assertive characters who could represent different points of view. These would allow the reader to imagine how people come to adopt these points of view or just what it is that they argue for. Even if she felt that firmly held opinions on such issues as feminism somehow necessarily imply angry, dogmatic propagandistic ways of speaking (and this is surely a very strange assumption), yet it would still be quite possible, even normal, to have one-sided, angry or dogmatic characters without having a one-sided novel. Perhaps what is involved here is Virginia Woolf's unwillingness or inability to dramatise such characters, to represent their points of view, through dialogue. Perhaps it was her incapacity as a writer rather than her fastidiousness, or a failure of nerve, that stood in her way. Whatever the reason, the result was that in *The Years* we find not only a scrupulously impersonal narrator but also characters, such as the suffragist Rose Pargiter and the eccentric, poetic Sara who, however militant or forceful in their opinions, are never allowed by their author the opportunity to speak their minds. It seems that this problem was made worse by the extensive revision which she did while writing the second draft. Grace Radin,[6] who has studied the original manuscript and compared it with the galley proofs as well as the printed text, gives extensive evidence that in the drafts the conversations between the characters were very much fuller and more revealing than they are in the published novel. Elvira (Sara as she becomes in the novel), Rose and Maggie take much more clearly defined and argued points of view. Rose struggles politically to win the vote for women, whereas Elvira/Sara is determined to remain a spectator, feeling that it would be corrupting to enter into the social process at all. Maggie is in favour of contraception and is shocked that Elvira is so ignorant of the ways of the world that she does not even know that the dissemination of contraceptive techniques was against the law. Elvira, who is a partial self-portrait of Virginia Woolf, is a writer and a visionary; she is physically deformed and childless; she has definite attitudes towards sex, politics and religion. Almost all of these details of conversation and character are lost in *The Years*. Sara in particular has become strangely sketchy and insubstantial.

In January 1936, as she finished a second draft, she began to swing between satisfaction that the book had achieved what she wanted and terrible panic, thinking it nothing but 'feeble twaddle' (D V, 16 January 1936). In March she did something that she had never done before; she sent the typescript off to the printers in Edinburgh without Leonard having read the book. She usually received page proofs from the printers, but on this occasion she ordered galleys, feeling that she would have to make further extensive revisions.

I have never suffered, since The Voyage Out, such acute despair on re-reading, as this time. On Saturday for instance: there I was, faced with complete failure: & yet the book is being printed. Then I set to: in despair: thought of throwing it away; but went on typing. After an hour, the line began to taughten. Yesterday I read it again; & I think it may be my best book. (D V, 16 March 1936)

At the beginning of April she sent the last pages to the printers. There is a gap of two whole months in her diary. She had collapsed. These and the following months of strain and depression brought her close to suicide. It was her worst time since 1913. It was not until October that she was again well enough to work. Then she read through the proofs. She despaired. She was completely convinced that the book was so obviously a mistake and a failure that she gave it to Leonard to burn. She worked out that she had wasted three years of her life plus some £300 on the proofs. Leonard, knowing that she was unstable, decided that for the first time he must lie to her about his reaction to one of her books. He was relieved when he read it for though it was, he thought, the worst book she ever wrote, it was publishable, though too long. But he told her that it was 'a most remarkable book', better than *The Waves*. She could see that he read it with tears in his eyes (D V, 5 November 1936 and LW 299f).

She could not entirely trust his judgement of the book. Her drastic instability continued. But his praise was enough to enable her to proceed to a final revision. As with *The Waves*, she added in at this very latest possible time, the lyrical descriptive passages with which each chapter opens. These provide a very distant, inhuman point of view, as if some extra-human intelligence were concentrating on the passage of the seasons but then could swoop down at will, to take a very close-up view of the particular human dramas that occur at widely distant times. These passages help to adjust the reader to the great leaps in time between each section. Moreover, she also introduced or brought back into the text many repeated images and phrases, thereby providing the novel with its echoing or 'reverberative' structure.[7] As a result of these changes the book did become much tighter, with the hint of a symbolic rather than a purely narrative pattern.

However, she also made two very major excisions. Leonard described her revisions: 'She revised the book in the most ruthless and drastic way. . . . The work which she did on the galleys is astonishing. She cut out bodily two enormous chunks, and there is hardly a single page on which there are not considerable rewritings or verbal alterations' (LW 302).[8] The two chunks, about 120 pages of text, are among the darkest, most pessimistic episodes in the novel and their exclusion alters its balance. Virginia Woolf in her work always attempted to express her experience of endlessly swinging from a belief that there is solidity and pattern in life to a

belief that life is transitory and without order, and her correspond-
ing moods of exaltation and despair. As a result of these two major
cuts in *The Years*, the overall weight of feeling in the novel shifted
towards the more optimistic view. She wondered about whether
she should not restore these sections for the Uniform edition of the
book, but unfortunately decided not to.

How does the novel measure up to her own intentions and her
hopes for the future novel as defined in 'Women and Fiction' and
'Professions for Women'? Does *The Years* explore the dark country
of women's daily life? Does it tell the truth about women's passions
and their bodies? As for the former, *The Pargiters*, in its portrayal of
the Victorian family as an institution which trapped or confined
women and thereby disabled or deformed them or prevented them
from developing to their full capacity, was a successful start. But
after the 1880 section *The Years* seems to lose touch with this
objective. It does not focus on a portrayal of women as active
agents in society, and the possibilities and constraints which affect
their activity, but on family conversations. For example, we are
never given an exploration of the charity work of Eleanor, her
house-building projects, nor of the political work of her sister
Rose, her suffragist campaigning or her experience in prison. The
narrative tells us that women move into new positions in society
(Peggy becomes a doctor) and that the old upper middle class
family, with eight children and living-in servants, vanishes after
the war. But these social changes are obliquely hinted at, not
focused on in the way that the original Novel–Essay had promised.
As for the latter, the truth about women's passions and their
bodies, Virginia Woolf did at first make an attempt to throw some
light onto these matters in her initial portrait of Rose Pargiter, but
Rose's lesbian sexuality and the discussions about passions and the
body to which it gives rise were all deleted from the published novel.

As it progressed the novel became much more oblique and
abstract. The novel which, in some ways, it most resembles is not
Night and Day but *Jacob's Room*, with its musing on how impossible
it is to know anybody, on the difficulties that stand in the way of
breaking through the barriers that hold us apart. Its emotional
centre shifts from being a woman's anger (for this is relocated in
Three Guineas) to the primal sadness of individuality, of apartness,
and of our feeble and clumsy attempts to overcome it. This theme
is signalled in the quotation from Dante which seems to stand as
the novel's motto (in the 1911 section):

For by so many more there are who say 'ours'
So much the more of good doth each possess.

This theme is dramatised most often in the novel in conversations. In writing the novel Virginia Woolf returned to dialogue which she had not written extensively since *Jacob's Room*. She began noting down conversations in her diary as practice. But dialogue is not used, as it conventionally was, to represent successful communication. Talk is portrayed rather as the failure of communication. Over and over again members of the family meet and talk only to find their efforts to arrive at a shared meaning frustrated. They are interrupted by noise, by other people, by the telephone ringing. People cannot hear or will not listen. Or they fail to find the right words and their thoughts are lost. Lack of concentration or exhaustion prevents the verbalisation of feeling. At other times talk is itself used as an instrument of repression of unwanted thoughts, a means for turning the mind away from something difficult that threatens to be communicated. Whether it is because of interruption, fear, repression, shyness or exhaustion, it is shown that speaking the truth is almost impossible. It does happen occasionally but when it does it is hard-won, a triumph against the norm. In her modernist novels, from *Mrs Dalloway* to *The Waves*, Virginia Woolf shared the aspirations of her character Terence Hewet in *The Voyage Out*, who said, 'I want to write a novel about Silence . . . the things people don't say' (VO 220). She wanted to fill the silence with meaning. *The Years* by contrast is about the things that people do say; it is a novel about talk. But it highlights the interference, the noise, that prevents talk from being filled with meaning. 'All talk would be nonsense, I suppose, if it were written down', says Rose Pargiter (TY 139).

When the book was published the reviews and the reactions of her friends were in the main very favorable. She was amazed, perhaps because she knew how far she had moved from her original intentions, and she found it hard to trust her readers' reactions. She still thought it an 'odious rice pudding of a book' and was not surprised when Edwin Muir's review in *The Listener* dismissed it as a dead and disappointing novel (D V, 2 April 1937). So she found it curious when the review in *The Times* called it a masterpiece, and Maynard Keynes and Stephen Spender both told her that they thought it her best book. Muir was himself a visionary poet and must have found the book's resolute superficiality a disappointment after her earlier, visionary novels. Spender on the other hand was of the more politically engaged generation whose impatience with Bloomsbury aesthetics was to be so important in the thirties. For him the book may have represented a welcome return to realism.

Although Virginia Woolf referred to it as her Arnold Bennett novel, *The Years* is in many ways more like *Jacob's Room* than *The Old Wive's Tale*. It reads like a deconstruction of the family chronicle novel and its reader's expectations are constantly frustrated as information, meaning and narrative continuity are withheld. For those who prefer the aesthetics of interruption to the aesthetics of visionary rapture, *The Years* is a great relief after *The Waves*. In spite of its oddity, it immediately became her best selling book, particularly in the USA where it sold over 30 000 copies in six months. Surprisingly she had become not just a famous but a popular author. With this novel Virginia Woolf had her greatest though most ironic success when, after her death, it was issued in 1945 in an American Armed Services edition. Given the central, though muted, anti-war theme of the book, it is wonderful to contemplate the thought of all those GIs with copies of *The Years* in their pockets. Priced at one cent, it sold 156 700 copies.[9] Subsequently the reputation of the book fell as that of her more difficult novels increased. By the mid-sixties it was out of print in the USA. In 1968, astonishingly, it was reissued in Britain as a Penguin Modern Classic. But its critical reputation remained low and it remains probably the least known and the least read of her novels. There are many books on Virginia Woolf's novels which ignore it altogether. Only since the emergence of feminist readings of Woolf in the seventies have there been attempts to reappraise it.[10]

ART AND POLITICS

According to her husband 'Virginia was the least political animal that has lived since Aristotle invented the definition' (LW 204). We know that often in her life she took a small part in political work, addressing envelopes for the women's suffrage movement in 1910, joining and going to meetings of, at different times, the Fabian Society, the Women's Cooperative Guild and the Labour Party. But her attitude to politics was ambivalent, and this ambivalence is clearly expressed in *The Years*. She had no trust in any political discourse or organisation. On the other hand she was not a quietist like her Quaker Aunt Caroline (or as Elvira, in the first draft of *The Years*, seems to be), content to let the world go its way while she attended to higher, more spiritual things. In the figure of the Outsider she found an identity which expressed her spirit of resistance and refusal, her desire to make a public stand for certain values and political attitudes while being unwilling to commit herself to the programmes and disciplines of organised political life. It is a position which has more recently been called 'anti-politics', a militant distrust of power, party and propaganda. The refusal to take part in society's rituals, without wishing to impose anything in their place, is a typical Outsider's move, as when Virginia Woolf turned down academic and civic honours. It is a principled and thought-out position, though it was not recognised as such by her husband nor by her Bloomsbury friends. It is true that in Virginia Woolf it is not always easy to distinguish it from something else, her snobbery, sometimes her racism and xeno-phobia, and her distaste for the physical presence of people except for those of her own race and class.

She thought that art and politics were two quite separate things and that art was damaged if they were not kept distinct. In the end she found it impossible to include her political thoughts and her anger in *The Years* and they were split off into a separate book. Sometimes, however, the situation is so bad that the artist is obliged to take note of what is going on and to participate in it, even though this is a distraction from his or her more universal, artistic purposes. This, at any rate, was her argument about the situation in Europe from the mid-thirties, as she expressed it in her rather slight article 'Why Art Today Follows Politics', which was published in the Communist Party newspaper *The Daily Worker* in 1936 (it is reprinted as 'The Artist and Politics' in CE II). In general, she argued, the artist should have 'no regard for the political agitations of the moment'. But in times of chaos the artists' isola-tion and detachment is disturbed, and they have to join in, to take sides, to fight for the survival of art. In these conditions the artist cannot concentrate on art. She represents this situation as a matter of loss for the artist. There is no sense that art might gain some-thing from being forced to attend to the voices and pleas of other people, from being brought down to earth. As with *The Years*, this is the view of material life of someone who would really much rather be attending to something else.

The political ideal implicit in this position is a society in which politics is no longer necessary. The aesthetic ideal implicit in her position is one which sees art as elevated above all other discourses, all ideologies. In this she was showing herself true to her Bloomsbury origins and quite out of step with the younger generation of writers, film makers, painters and photographers who in the thirties argued for a view of art as partisan, as one form of ideology among others, as having political duties. They argued not only for a different understanding of art but for a different aesthetic. Battle raged between surrealists and realists, between documentary and fictional realisms, between proletarian forms of art and elitist forms of art such as, in painting, formalism and abstraction. Modernism came to be denounced as a short-lived and now defunct bourgeois form which would give way to more popular and accessible kinds of art and writing. One of the organisations in which these debates were conducted was the Artists International Association (AIA), and it was this group which had solicited Virginia Woolf's article on art and politics.[11] The AIA, formed in 1933, provided for a time an umbrella which could shelter groups whose loyalties were otherwise quite different. It was a pacifist and anti-fascist organisation and the Bloomsbury painters Duncan Grant and Vanessa Bell were among its members. As the political temperature rose through the 1930s and the activity of the intellectuals became more hectic these painters also joined in the meetings and protests organised by Bloomsbury's more political members, Adrian Stephen, Leonard Woolf, Quentin Bell and Margery Fry. They made posters, organised exhibitions and sales, went to meetings and signed declarations. Vanessa, just like her sister, was not happy to have been manoeuvred by history into this uncomfortable role of artist–agitator. Speaking of the AIA she wrote to her other son Julian, 'It's a hopeless mixture of politics and art I think – they can't be mixed'.[12] The younger generation, Julian and Quentin Bell as well as the young poets Spender, Auden and Day Lewis, being both men as well as of a different age, rejected the categories on which this distinction was based. Quentin Bell, Virginia's nephew, who was a member of the Hogarth Group (which took its name from the artist and had nothing to do with the Hogarth Press), a group of artists proclaiming the ideal of socially committed realist art, expresses well the impatience of the young men faced with that dated old woman, his aunt, and he makes the connection between her literary style and her distaste for their style of politics: 'Her gift was for the pursuit of shadows, for the ghostly whispers of the mind and for Pythian incomprehensibility, when what was needed was the swift and lucid phrase that could reach the ears of unemployed working men or Trades Union officials' (QB II 186).

In spite of her hesitations Virginia Woolf allowed herself to be drawn into political activity in the 1930s on a much bigger scale than ever before in her life. The turning point for her was the Labour Party Conference in October 1935, at which she listened to the disarmament debate. It was a decisive moment in British politics. Since 1918 there had been an enormous groundswell of pacifist opinion, and disarmament was the commonsense of the Left. In this sense, Virginia and other Bloomsbury pacifists like Lytton Strachey had been in the mainstream of Left-wing opinion. Leonard Woolf, who was not a pacifist, and had supported the League of Nations and sanctions as the best means of preventing aggression, began by 1935, along with many others in the Labour Party, to change his position, and his political differences with Virginia from this time became more visible. At the Party Conference the leader, the pacifist George Lansbury, was defeated by Ernest Bevin. 'Tears came to my eyes as L[ansbury] spoke. And yet he was posing I felt – acting, unconsciously, the battered Christian man. Then Bevin too acted I suppose. He sank his head in his vast shoulders till he looked like a tortoise' (D IV, 2 October 1935). She agonised over whether it was really her obligation to struggle to change the state of society. She supported the speakers who were arguing for the pacifist position of non-resistance.

Two days later Mussolini launched an attack on Abyssinia and the League of Nations voted for sanctions against Italy. Virginia wrote a letter to Ottoline Morrell: 'I wish public affairs wouldn't jerk their ugly heads up. When even I cant sleep at night for thinking of politics, things must be in a fine mess. All our friends and neighbours talk politics, politics . . . Now Leonard has turned on the wireless to listen to the news, and so I am flicked out of the world I like into the other. I wish one were allowed to live only in one world, but thats asking too much' (L V, 4 October 1935). Nothing could illustrate so well her reactions to political events, the combination of strong conviction with irritation, distrust and a longing to withdraw. For three days, she says in her diary, she was wildly excited about 'The Next War', as the book that was to become *Three Guineas* was then called: 'the result of the L[abour]

P[arty] at Brighton was the breaking of that dam between me & the new book, so that I couldn't resist dashing off a chapter' (D IV, 15 October 1935). Two weeks later: 'Then theres my Next War – which at any moment becomes absolutely wild, like being harnessed to a shark; & I dash off scene after scene' (D IV, 27 October 1935). However, the book had to wait until she had finished *The Years*. She was caught up in political argument sufficiently to go to a National Peace Council conference on the relation of the general problem of peace to colonial problems: 'Went to Peace Conference, by way of a joke, yesterday, & saw several baboon faced intellectuals; also some yearning, sad, green dressed negroes & negresses, looking like chimpanzees brought out of their cocoanut groves to try to make sense of our pale white platitudes' (D IV, 30 October 1935). Thus adequately illustrates some of her less attractive attitudes.[13] Remaining a pacifist, Virginia was committed to a political position with which her husband and her two nephews disagreed and for which they felt, as the situation deteriorated and fascism advanced in country after country, considerable contempt. Leonard's retrospective view of the rise of fascism was that it was 'the destruction of civilisation by a gang of murderous hooligans' (LW 371). 'Civilisation' was the word which summed up everything that Bloomsbury had been about, the belief in progress through the gradual dissemination of civilisation, and the influence of civilised individuals. Virginia's response was to see fascism as the unrestrained masculine lust for domination. She became ever more isolated in her views within her own circle of friends.

For the time being, however, the pacifists, the communists and the socialists could all just about work together in the anti-fascist committees. At the beginning of 1935 Virginia became a member of a communist-dominated committee which was organising an anti-fascist exhibition, in which capacity she met and worked with such artists and critics as Anthony Blunt, Herbert Read and Henry Moore; 'respectable Bohemia' she baptised this circle (D IV, 20 February 1935). Later in the year she was invited by Forster to go with him to Paris for meetings of Vigilance, a French organisation of anti-fascist intellectuals:

Oh my dear Virginia, fancy if you and Leonard came after all! What a delight, and what a fortification against communists who will probably try to do the silly! . . . I don't suppose the conference is of any use – things have gone too far. But I have no doubt as to the importance of people like ourselves *inside* the conference. We do represent the last utterances of the civilised. (QB II 188)

The two Woolfs did serve on this committee for a while, but Virginia resigned in July of 1936, leaving Leonard to do the work. Charles Mauron, Bloomsbury's representative in France and a member of Vigilance, visited England to attend the equivalent English committee, which was called Intellectual Liberty. Through much of that year Virginia was preoccupied with the final preparation of *The Years* and for months ill and incapacitated. The Spanish Civil War broke out in July 1936 and the volumes of material that she was collecting for her next book began to reflect this fact. They include a letter to the editor of the *Daily Telegraph* from July 1936, which was also published in the *New Statesman*, expressing sympathy with the Spanish government and people and signed by thirty-three people including Leonard and Virginia Woolf. There are also many newspaper clippings and, from November 1936, a document calling a meeting of the International Association of Writers for the Defence of Culture, chaired by the poet C. Day Lewis. Also in November she received from the Spanish government the packet of photographs of dead children, killed by the bombing in Spain, which play an important part in the argument of *Three Guineas*. Her letter to Julian Bell, who was in China, of 14 November 1936, conveys well how the Woolf and Bell circles had been swept into this storm of political activity and contestation. At the height of her illness in 1936 and after a particularly unpleasant meeting of the Vigilance committee, she hoped that she could withdraw from politics completely, but things were not to turn out that way. 'Did I tell you of my great political shindy, in the worst too, of my coma, when I was drowsy and painful as a crushed snake? How I was hauled out to Committees and meetings and abused and rooked and at last resigned, and now will never sign a petition or even read a report let alone attend a conference again?', she wrote to Ethel Smyth (L VI, 22 July 1936).

The situation came even closer to home when Julian Bell returned from China determined to go and fight in Spain, in spite of desparate pleas from his mother. Divisions between pacifists and those who believed in fighting against fascism now ran right through the middle of the family, reflecting the general split on the

British Left. With British volunteers fighting in Spain the issue was no longer merely theoretical. As the historians of the Artists International Association put it: '. . . the Communist Party had been withdrawing from its previous association with the peace movement and the unconditional pacifists were to become an increasingly isolated minority within the left as ultimate military confrontation with Fascism became all the more apparent'.[14] This was the context in which Virginia Woolf at last began to write *Three Guineas*, from an embattled minority position both generally and within her own circles and family, in January 1937. She had become an Outsider. She wrote it between January and October 1937, and the strange thing is that she wrote it in very high spirits, and suffered none of the anxiety in anticipation at being ridiculed or rejected that had plagued the writing of her fiction. She was very determined to state her case.

1937 was the most political year of Virginia Woolf's life, dominated by the writing of *Three Guineas* and, from July, by the catastrophe of Julian Bell's death in Spain. He had been persuaded not to join the International Brigades as a fighter but had gone instead as an ambulance driver. He was killed by a shell on 18 July. Vanessa, his mother, was devastated. For months Virginia visited and looked after her. The situation in Spain had gone from bad to worse. In April Guernica was bombed by the Germans. The correspondent of *The Times* wrote: 'In the form of its execution and the scale of the destruction it wrought, no less than in the selection of its objective, the raid in Guernica is unparalleled in military history. Guernica was not a military objective . . . The object of the bombardment was seemingly the demoralisation of the civil population and the destruction of the cradle of the Basque race'.[15] A new chapter of military history had opened, of the deliberate terror bombing of civilian populations. People began to predict the most appalling prospect of all-out destruction of cities, and hence of civilisation, by aerial bombardment. The question to which all intellectuals were addressing themselves, and which was the subject of *Three Guineas*, of how to prevent war, became of greater urgency than ever.

Within a few days of the bombing Picasso, a communist who had no Bloomsbury scruples about the mixing of art and politics, began to make a series of pencil sketches. He went on to produce at amazing speed the large painting *Guernica* and the series of etchings and aquatints *The Dream and Lie of Franco*. *Guernica* was finished in time to be exhibited at the Paris World Fair in the summer of 1937. Earlier Duncan Grant with Vanessa and Quentin Bell visited Picasso at his studio in Paris where they saw, but were not especially impressed by, the unfinished *Guernica*.[16] Quentin's mission was to persuade Picasso to come as a speaker to a meeting at the Albert Hall in London in support of the Basque children. He did not attend but he donated one of his *Dream and Lie of Franco* etchings which was auctioned at the meeting together with a drawing by Miro. The immediate occasion for the meeting was the fall of Bilbao, on 18 June. Some 4000 children had already been evacuated from Bilbao and brought to England, and Virginia Woolf recorded in her diary the sight of one group walking through Tavistock Square in London on their way from one train station to another:

> As I reached 52 [Tavistock Sq.], a long trail of fugitives – like a caravan in a desert – came through the square: Spaniards flying from Bilbao, which has fallen, I suppose. Somehow brought tears to me eyes, tho' no one seemed surprised. Children trudging along; women in London cheap jackets with gay handkerchiefs on their heads, young men, & all carrying either cheap cases, & bright blue enamel kettles, very large, & saucepans, filled I suppose with gifts from some Charity – a shuffling trudging procession, flying – impelled by machine guns in Spanish fields to trudge through Tavistock Sqre, along Gordon Square, then where? (D V, 23 June 1937)

The meeting at the Albert Hall was held the next day. The programme, with a *Guernica* sketch on the cover and a note by J. B. Priestly, lists as sponsors of the meeting Virginia Woolf, Vanessa Bell, Duncan Grant, Jacob Epstein, Barbara Hepworth, Julian Huxley, Henry Moore, H. G. Wells, Rebecca West, and Ralph Vaughan Williams, among others. Paul Robeson flew from Moscow for the meeting and sang to tremendous applause. The Woolfs, who sat on the stage with the other stars behind the speakers, donated £1 each. Virginia chatted with Forster and Auden. It was one of the most remarkable assemblies of progressive intellectuals and performers, of many political tendencies, to have been triggered by the Spanish Civil War. Virginia Woolf's reaction was typically less than whole-hearted.

I have had no more experiences in the great world, unless sitting behind the Duchess of Atholl on the platform at the Albert Hall 2 nights ago can count. Oh what a bore those meetings are! We sat for 3 hours behind the Duchess and talked about Spain – I mean we listened; and they talked, but into megaphones, so that not a word came singly but in a kind of double division to us behind. However, by hook or crook, really by means of a fat emotional woman in black velvet called Isabel Brown they collected £1500 for the Basque children. (L VI, 26 June 1937)

The paths of Picasso's *Guernica* and Bloomsbury were to cross again and again, and Bloomsbury usually reacted with faint praise and condescending attitudes. Forster visited the Paris Exhibition that summer and reported that

Picasso has done a terrifying fresco in the Spanish Pavillion, a huge black and white thing called 'Guernica'. Bombs split bull's skull, woman's trunk, man's shins. The fresco is indignant, and so it is less disquieting than the potato-feeders of Van Gogh. Picasso is grotesquely angry, and those who are angry still hope. He is not yet wise, and perhaps he is not yet a creator. Nevertheless, he too succeeds in saying something about injustice and pain.[17]

Perhaps it would not be worth remarking on this were it not for the fact that it throws such eloquent light on the problem that Virginia Woolf herself had faced when setting out to write *The Pargiters*, which was meant to be an angry and protesting book. She would have anticipated from her purist Bloomsbury friends just this tone of superiority, of being ticked off for naively mixing up art with political emotion. Perhaps this helps to explain just why she had given up her original plan and was now engaged in writing out her anger not in an artistic work but in pamphleteering style. She could anticipate head-shaking and disagreement, but at least she had not muddied her art with too much private anger. It also helps to emphasise the fact that in the 1930s choice of style in art, whether writing or painting, was subjected to political interpretation. Virginia Woolf's move away from the abstraction of her latest modernist work did not take place in a cultural vacuum or only in response to private considerations.

Unfortunately there appears to be no way of knowing exactly why, surprisingly, both Virginia Woolf and E. M. Forster allowed their names to be associated with Picasso the following year. Perhaps she felt that he was a fellow spirit, since he was attacked by the 'realist' party, as Bloomsbury had been so often, for appealing only to aesthetes. *Guernica,* which was championed by the surrealists against attacks by the Socialist Realists, was brought to London's Burlington Gallery by Herbert Read and Roland Penrose in 1938. It then travelled on to Leeds and Oxford and returned to London to be exhibited at the Whitechapel Gallery, where it was seen by 12 000 people. The tour was sponsored by the Labour Party and the Stepney Trades Council, to raise money for the Million Penny Fund to pay for a food ship for Spain. The list of patrons of the exhibition at the Burlington includes Virginia Woolf, Fenner Brockway, Hugh Sykes Davies, E. M. Forster, and Naomi Mitcheson.

Through June and into July 1937 the writing of *Three Guineas* was 'in full flood' and Virginia's indirect contact with events in Spain went on, almost daily. She met with Christopher Isherwood to discuss sending a message to the Second International Writers' Congress, which was to be held in Madrid in July. She talked with Vanessa, who was anxious about Julian who was now in Spain. On the evening of 20 July she heard the news of Julian's death. *Three Guineas* came to a standstill. She wrote a moving memoir of Julian, with whom she had had an affectionate relationship and, in recent years, had exchanged lengthy letters.[18] In September she read a document which Julian had written trying to explain and defend his political choices and his values, so different from those of his mother and his aunt. This was his 'War and Peace: A Letter to E. M. Forster',[19] a long apologia in which he argues that fascism has its origins in class and economic changes, and that civilisation must be defended against fascism by every means including war. 'At this moment, to be anti-war means to submit to fascism, to be anti-fascist means to be prepared for war.' To be prepared for war means to recognise and encourage the military virtues, the ability to confront death without flinching, the efficient, unemotional pursuit of objectives. We must recognise and accept that human nature includes barbarian emotions, the excitement of physical combat and bodily commitment. It is dangerous to base one's values only on the contemplative and reflective virtues. In addressing his remarks to Forster and in arguing in these terms,

Julian Bell was clearly aiming to criticise both the Cambridge and the Bloomsbury ideals which so many members of his own generation had found unrealistic and disabling in the political strife of the 1930s. In this document, which she read as she returned to the writing of her book, Virginia Woolf was confronted with beliefs and arguments which countered her own at every turn. She must have felt yet more in danger of finding no audience for her own writing, a fear which she expressed more and more often in the last years of her life. She pressed on, however, and even though *Three Guineas* is at many points a direct reply to her nephew's arguments, it remained the most uncompromisingly angry and partisan book she ever wrote. It was as if she had in her a pressure to give voice to her views on men, women and war that simply could not be denied. She had something in her that absolutely had to be released: 'I wanted – how violently – how persistently, pressingly, compulsorily I cant say – to write this book' (D V, 12 April 1938). It was finished in October and published in June 1938.

The question which *Three Guineas* tries to answer is 'How can the daughters of educated men help to prevent war?' War, she argues, is caused by something in the psychology of men, and the important thing is to ensure that as women gradually force an entry into the male world of the professions and higher education, they do not suffer the psychological damage of themselves becoming, like men, competitive, hungry for domination, jealous of their property and power. Women can prevent this from happening by holding on to their position as outsiders and refusing to be corrupted by the wealth, prestige and power that nurture men's egotism and their desire to dominate. Her argument depends on her being able to persuade us to view men from an unfamiliar angle. She wants us to practice a huge act of reinterpretation, and to see the world in terms of meanings quite different from those fostered by the dominant culture. When we see judges in their robes or generals in their uniforms we should learn to see not the majesty of state authority but the narcissism of vain people who, like primitive tribesmen, love to decorate their bodies with bits of coloured stuff. Imagine the naked man underneath and the 'savage' motivation that puffs him up with self-importance and pleasure as he covers his nakedness with his medals and his feathers. To support her argument she included five photographs (unfortunately now left out of modern editions of the book). They show us, for example, a general with a long feather in his hat and his chest covered in medals, a judge in wig, ermine and lace cravat, and a procession of university dignatories, also in extraordinary costume. It is difficult not to see these men as ridiculous. Her disrespect in making fun of them infuriated many of Woolf's male readers.

This perspective, she hopes, will help us also to think differently about men's motivation. When we see them at their professions, we should see not dedicated public servants, but men driven by greed for wealth, ruthless competition for power, and blind self-satisfaction. She imagines a woman watching, from outside of course, as a procession of privileged professional men, with a few junior women now joining in at the rear, passes by. What is the psychological motor that drives the procession forward? What are the motivations that women are being invited to share and to respect? 'Let us never cease from thinking – what is this "civilisation" in which we find ourselves? What are these ceremonies and why should we take part in them?' (TG 73). She tries to show that there is a connection between the psychology of the professional life and war, because the professions 'make the people who practise them possessive, jealous of any infringement of their rights, and highly combative if anyone dares dispute them . . . And do not such qualities lead to war?' (TG 77). Above all the practice of the professions makes people so sure that they know best, that they are right, that they develop the kind of arrogant self-confidence, the unquestioning trust in their own judgement, that she had always found both laughable and ludicrous, whether she saw it in the doctors who sent people off to the asylums without having heard a word of what they said, or the politicians who preach their solutions from their platforms when they are talking about things which they cannot possibly understand. There is something very liberating about being reminded that inside every authoritative, judgemental and powerful man there is a naked little boy driven to make his one-sided pronouncements and confident decisions not by the expertise of which he is so proud but by infantile psychological urges and primitive drives. Women, she appears to argue, are different only because their social history has been different: 'In another century or so if we practise the professions in the same way, shall we not be just as possessive, just as jealous, just as pugnacious, just as positive as to the verdict of God, Nature, Law and Property as these gentlemen are now?' (TG 77).

The great and abiding value of the book is the clarity with which it defines the basic premises of the social psychology of gender, of masculinity and femininity. Masculinity is perceived not as an innate form of personality but as a socially and culturally reproduced form of pathological immaturity. Men are victims of a system that creates and values unhealthy psyches. However, her argument suffers from damaging over-simplification. Her conception of the psychology of masculinity is crude and one-sided and blinds her to the more complex motivations behind male social behaviour. Moreover, and this was especially damaging because of the political context of the time, her analysis of the *politics* of masculinity was simplistic. Men, she argues, enjoy power over other people. Therefore they are dictators. Patriarchy and dictatorship are one and the same. Dictatorship she equates again and again with fascism (or more specifically with Hitlerism, as she calls it in her 1940 article 'Thoughts on Peace in an Air Raid'). She had, in 1937, no idea at all of just how unspeakably murderous fascism was to be. Even at the time her equation of the patriarchal family with the fascist state must have seemed a serious lapse of judgement. It encouraged her to think about the causes of war entirely in terms of the psychology of masculinity. This seemed to many of her readers sadly over-simplistic, and in the immediate political context, in which the main question was how to respond to and defend against fascism, worse than useless. Her nephew's diagnosis was that she was trapped in thinking about the Second World War in terms of motivations that had been active in the First and wrote 'as though she had to rebuke the passions of 1914'.[20]

Her prescription was that women should remain outside the system of social rewards and privileges which encourage the dictatorial psychology, while cultivating their own alternative civilisation. The evil that results when infantile fixations are allowed to flourish in fascist politics and in warfare can only be resisted by a kind of anti-politics and pacifism. By the time the book was published, Hitler had invaded Austria and the threat of war was very real. Her argument for resistance by a Society of Outsiders who would practise private experiments in civilised living, takes it for granted that that social space, of financial independence and cultural freedom that women win when they earn their own living, would survive fascism. But the social space occupied by active, independent citizens, 'civil society' as it is called, is the first thing that totalitarian regimes abolish.

The book did have a positive response from many women

readers who were excited by the idea of a Society of Outsiders and who wrote to Virginia Woolf with their ideas and experiences. A nun wrote to her asking her to hold a rally of Outsiders in Hyde Park. She had found herself a wider audience. But her friends and her old audience among the intellectuals were almost unanimously hostile. Keynes was, says Quentin Bell 'angry and contemptuous' (QB II 205). Vita wrote that she found the book exasperating because of its misleading arguments. Forster thought it the worst of her books. The reviews were mixed, perhaps not as bad as she had anticipated. In *Scrutiny*, never a journal friendly to her, Q. D. Leavis wrote a fierce attack calling the book dangerous, preposterous and nasty. *Time and Tide*, after a respectful review, published a cartoon showing a circle of men critics dashing down the book and jumping upon it in their frustration, being caught between their reviewers' code of decorum and their private loathing of the book.[21] By the end of the year it had sold 8000 copies but not one of her friends had talked with her about it. Through it all Virginia remained completely calm and unbothered, thankful that she had relieved the pressure that had compelled her to write. 'But I think I can sit calm as a toad in an oak at the centre of the storm', she predicted, and she was right (D V, 30 May 1938).

9

1938–40: Life-Writing

'If you are old, the past lies upon the present, like a thick glass, making it waver, distorting it.' (CE II 293)

SCEPTICAL BIOGRAPHER

Before *Three Guineas* was published Virginia Woolf had already started, in April 1938, on two new books. One of them, the biography of her friend Roger Fry, was to be the last of her books published in her lifetime. She had, since 1935, been reading her way through a mountain of documents relating to his life in preparation for this book. It was finished in February 1940 and published in July of that year. The other, *Pointz Hall* (or *Between the Acts* as it came to be called) was finished but not yet revised for publication when she killed herself in March 1941. In April 1939, she began, in addition, to write notes for a memoir. This was later published as 'A Sketch of the Past' in the posthumous collection of autobiographical pieces called *Moments of Being*. Thus, quite apart from other lectures, articles, reviews and stories which she also wrote in these three years, she was usually actively working on two, and sometimes three, major projects simultaneously. Her will to write never faltered until perhaps the very last month of her life. Each of these works is different in conception both from anything she had ever written before and from each other. She still took each new project, whenever she could, as an opportunity to refashion the conventions of prose literature.

Roger Fry was the exception. Being a biography, it was the book which allowed her least scope for inventive unconventionality. It involved her in fidelity to the facts of his life (except where decorum decreed otherwise), and to a massive amount of documentation and research, reading old letters and soliciting information from friends and family. She had never felt work to be such drudgery. She had to make delicate decisions about just which episodes in Fry's life would have to be left unrecorded. His love affair with Vanessa was not to be mentioned. So writing the book posed for her many problems which she had never had to confront before. Never had her diary been so full of complaint about the hard grind and the difficulty of concentrating on her work.

But her greatest problem was that she did not believe in biography at all. All her working life she had rejected biography as a form. She had mocked it in *Orlando* and *Flush*, she had argued against it in 'The New Biography', she had chosen to write her novels in the ways that she did because she rejected the idea that the truth about a person can be told by writing a life story. For her, the conventions of life-writing, both in her father's work but also in that of the new biographers such as Lytton Strachey, falsified and evaded the truth about their subjects' lives. This was partly a matter of censorship, the way that the conventions simply refused to admit certain crucial but private facts about a person's life into their written life story. But this was not the most difficult problem. We can see from the way that she wrote her novels, as well as from comments about her own life that we have found in her diary, that the facts about a person's life which she regarded as crucial, which would allow one to understand what their experiences meant to them and how they perceived the world, are not normally accessible to the biographer and are not given a place in the conventional life story. She had emphasised these decisive but inaccessible facts about experience in her fiction when she had focused on characters' inner worlds and moments of being. The former she portrays as caverns and tunnels of private meaning which reverberate with memory, fantasy and anticipation so intimate and subtle that they usually escape verbalisation even by the person whose experiences they are. The latter she portrays as moments of revelation or illumination in which are preserved some glimpse of 'reality' and which are narrated in the form of condensed images which hold together many complex strands of meaning. As Bernard points out in *The Waves*, these moments can be crucial turning points in a person's life and yet the biographer usually knows nothing of them.

She returned to these problems as she began to work on her biography of Roger Fry, in 'The Art of Biography', an article which was written in November 1938 and published in *Atlantic Monthly* magazine in April 1939. She argued there that whereas the biographer is tied to the documented facts the novelist is free to imaginatively create moments of intensity for the characters, and in this way to get closer to the rhythm that actually governs people's lives. For the central problem is that of *time*. The conventions of biographical narrative artificially divide up a life into chapters, and these time divisions correspond to artificial ideas about how to construct books, not to the flow of time in the stream of lived experience. 'The real current of the hero's existence took, very likely, a different course' (CE IV 226).

She wrote *Roger Fry* and *Between the Acts* in tandem so that she could keep 'switching from assiduous truth to wild ideas' (D V 4 August 1938). Later, she took to writing her own autobiographical 'Sketch of the Past', and she used it to express her worries and scepticism about life-writing. It was as if she wrote *Roger Fry* with her right hand, according to conventional good form, while simultaneously, with her left hand, noting all the reasons for not believing a word of it. It was a strange exercise in self division. She was relieved, when *Roger Fry* was finished, that both Vanessa and Fry's sister Margery were moved by it and convinced that it should not be altered. When it was published she had a strong sensation of the oddity of biography, that a writer replaces a person with a made-up image which they have conspired together to create.

> What a curious relation is mine with Roger at this moment – I who have given him a kind of shape after his death – Was he like that? I feel very much in his presence at the moment: as if I were intimately connected with him; as if we together had given birth to this vision of him: a child born of us. Yet he had no power to alter it. And yet for some years it will represent him. (D V, 25 July 1940)

What shape had she chosen to give him? The life story of public figures traditionally took the form of a story about character, how it was formed and tested, how it developed in spite of obstacles and hurdles, how in the end it flourished and in doing so embodied certain virtues and values for the public good and thus accomplished the life's meaning. The story has a linear, causally linked structure in which the meaning of every episode is derived from its relation to the end or overall accomplishment of the life. Virginia Woolf's biography of Roger Fry has precisely this structure. What makes it specific is that the life, instead of being a personification of Victorian morality, is the personification of the values of 'Old Bloomsbury'. The hero of the story is the free, civilised individual, exemplifying those values of aesthetic contemplation and friendship, and the rational pursuit of truth and beauty, for which the group stood in its earliest days.[1]

As she tells the story, even as a child Fry was already a sensitive, potentially free spirit, bewildered by the despotism of Victorian family and school life. The catalogue of horrors to which he was subjected is certainly impressive, but so is the way in which they are woven into a narrative which aims to vindicate his rebellion and his choice of identity. Her story simply reproduces Fry's own account of his childhood in which his self-scrutiny, in contrast with that in her own 'Sketch', is aimed entirely at confirming and justifying adult identity rather than at throwing disturbing and dissolving light upon it. Fry tells how even as a small child it was beauty which most stimulated his passion. He loved a particular poppy plant and would sit in his private patch of garden patiently watching it:

> I had a general passion for red . . . I remember on one occasion the plant was full of fat green flower buds with little pieces of crumpled scarlet silk showing through the cracks between the sepals. A few were already in flower. I conceived that nothing in the world could be more exciting than to see the flower suddenly burst its green case and unfold its immense cup of red. (RF 13)

His mother mocked his passion, and he learned the lesson that a passion for beauty exposes one to the ridicule of the philistines. The anecdote is one to which Virginia Woolf several times returns in the course of telling his life story, perhaps because it already contains within itself in embryo the full meaning of his adult life. It is the epitome of Roger Fry, for there he was seeking a private space in which he could freely devote himself to his calling, the disinterested contemplation of aesthetic beauty, purified, he thought, of all possible hidden meanings of a more disturbingly sexual kind in the disclosing of those red lips, and having to learn to expect, but not to be diverted by, the intrusions of unjust authority. His whole life is told as the enactment of this plot.

As a student he discovered his life's work and in the following years he tested his capacity and his courage while waiting for the flowering of his self, for his moment of self-confirmation and triumph. This moment arrived, of course, in 1910 with the first Post-Impressionist Exhibition when Fry both established a public identity as a champion of modern culture and at the same time discovered his way as a painter. He had found both public recognition and private self-assurance. 'He had found himself at last.' It was as if all his life had been tending towards this point. In narrating it Virginia Woolf hints that there may be one of those moments of vision which, if only we understood them, might throw in doubt the whole linear time-bound scheme of the story which she is engaged in telling, when time seems to circle around to take in its own tail. But being a biographer, she is not in a position to pursue such speculation.

> Such moments of vision, when a new force breaks in, and the gropings of the past suddenly seem to have meaning, are probably familiar to most artists. But most artists leave them unexplained . . . The origin of these moments of vision lies too deep for analysis. A red poppy, a mother's reproof, a Quaker upbringing, sorrows, loves, humiliations – they too have their part in moments of vision. (RF 140)

The whole past stands behind such a moment and shadows its surface. This is something that she would explore in her own autobiographical memoir, and which she had portrayed in her novels, but which in the biography has to stand as a reminder that the writer is constrained by ignorance. Forced to exclude imaginary solutions, the writer has to restrict the narrative to a more traditional form.

It is to this more conventional story-telling that she returns. The hero, the now triumphant civilised individual, enjoys public honours and rewards. He becomes, in effect, an Insider. He gains professorships and wealth. He can now act with his full force as a public champion for a certain vision of life and society. His life represents a moral ideal, that of the autonomous individual battling for social and cultural reform. This combination of retreat into private individuality with engagement in public life, is very precisely caught in Virginia Woolf's metaphors: Roger Fry's studio in the early 1920s was

> both an ivory tower where he contemplated reality, and an arsenal where he forged the only weapons that are effective in the fight against the enemy. More than ever it was necessary to oppose the emotionalism and chaos of the herd by reason and

order. If the political man . . . is a monster, then the artist must be more than ever independent, free, individual. (RF 207)

At its end the story becomes positively hagiographic. It is perhaps the most thoroughly conventional moment in her entire oeuvre, when she pronounces Fry 'a saint who laughed; a saint who enjoyed life to the uttermost' (RF 259).

Her scepticism about the story which she had been constrained to tell must have been increased not only by the enforced silence on the subject of some of the publicly less acceptable episodes in Fry's life, and her general disbelief in the biographic form of life-writing, to which I shall return, but also by the disintegration of the 'Old Bloomsbury' world-view under the pressure of historical events. Fascism and war made the optimistic story of the salvation of mankind by the civilised individual less credible than her friends had once found it. In 1938, as she was writing *Roger Fry* and worrying about the meaning of her own life, this was confirmed by two important statements by Bloomsbury figures, and they are also present, as it were, in silent dialogue with Virginia Woolf between the lines of 'A Sketch of the Past'. One evening in September 1938 Maynard Keynes read a paper to the Memoir Club called 'My Early Beliefs'. The Memoir Club had been going since 1920 and it was to continue meeting until 1956. It was a gathering of Bloomsbury friends who met to hear each other tell tales about their earlier experiences. Three of Virginia Woolf's essays in *Moments of Being* were Memoir Club contributions. Few of the papers read at the Club over the years could have been as important and as serious as this one by Keynes. He challenged his Bloomsbury friends to review their earlier beliefs and to admit that they had been mistaken. In particular he poured scorn on the Cambridge men and their worship of Moore. They had, he now claimed, taken being good more seriously than doing good. They were more interested in the contemplation of beauty than in activity to improve the world. Their views had rested on beliefs about human nature which were disastrously mistaken. Their extreme individualism and belief in the progressive role of people like themselves in history were naive. They were ignorant of all the dark, volcanic forces in individuals and societies, which constantly threaten to disrupt civilised life and social order. 'I can see us as water-spiders, gracefully skimming, as light and reasonable as air, the surface of the stream without any contact at all with the eddies and currents underneath.'[2]

Of course Virginia Woolf, who had always been an Outsider even within Bloomsbury, and who had sufficient acquaintance with what Keynes called 'the vulgar passions', both in her madness and in a life of 'being despised' as a woman, had always had reason to treat the Old Bloomsbury–Cambridge narrative with incredulity. Her own 'credo', *Three Guineas*, which had just been published, was itself meant as an exposure of some of the illusions of that 'civilisation', and of the vulgar passions on which it rests. As they all listened to Keynes's paper that evening there was a very real possibility that Britain would be at war with Germany within a few days, as Hitler was poised to strike at Czechoslovakia. Virginia noted in her diary: 'Maynard read a very packed profound & impressive paper so far as I could follow, about Cambridge youth; their philosophy; its consequences; Moore; what it lacked; what it gave. The beauty & unworldliness of it' (D V, 12 September 1938). Perhaps Keynes's image for those naive young men, the water-spiders skimming the surface of the stream, was in her mind a few months later when, writing her 'Sketch of the Past', she thought about the impossibility of life-writing:

> Consider what immense forces society brings to play upon each of us, how that society changes from decade to decade; and also from class to class; well, if we cannot analyse these invisible presences, we know very little of the subject of the memoir; and again how futile life-writing becomes. I see myself as a fish in a stream; deflected; held in place; but cannot describe the stream. (MB 80)

By coincidence, there was published that very week yet another Bloomsbury self-examination, and this one would also confirm Virginia Woolf in her scepticism about the official Bloomsbury narrative that she was writing in *Roger Fry*. It was E. M. Forster's 'Credo', which was published in the *London Mercury* in September 1938.[3] Virginia's first response was to be depressed by the praise which Forster's credo received while her friends were still silent about her own. Forster's seems characteristically quiet and unassuming compared with hers or Keynes's. He remained defiantly an individualist, a liberal, and a believer in 'civilisation'. He argued that this is a necessary antidote to the violence which erupts into history. His is a quiet refusal of the aggressive certainties of both communism and fascism. But this civilisation, in which it is necessary to believe and from which everything of value in human life derives, is, he says, an illusion. 'The people I respect most behave as if they were immortal and as if society were eternal. Both assumptions are false: both of them must be accepted as true if we are to go on eating and working and loving, and are to keep open a few breathing holes for the human spirit.'[4] This sad image of the writer as the defender of a civilisation in which he no longer believes, as the spokesman for a necessary but illusory humanism, is perhaps not a surprising terminus for Bloomsbury's idealism. In each of the three credos, Keynes's, Forster's and Woolf's (*Three Guineas*), the authors found themselves confronted by a problem to which they had no solution, of civilisation's refusal to live peacefully with its discontents.

BEING AND NON-BEING

If writing *Roger Fry* was drudgery and a hard grind, writing 'A Sketch of the Past' was a painful and sobering exercise in excavation and self-scrutiny. 'Let me then, like a child advancing with bare feet into a cold river, descend again into that stream' (MB 98). The differences between *Roger Fry* and 'A Sketch of the Past' are extreme. The former tells a conventional story. Only the author's tone of muted mocking irony signals her scepticism about the whole enterprise. The latter is self-consciously questioning and unconventional in method. Because it was not revised for publication, it is unguarded, uncensored, and relatively uncontrolled. It is not just an autobiographical memoir but also a diary in which the author registers her anxieties and gives the life-writing activity itself a context. Because it is in a raw state, it is less self-protective than the published works, less apt to use beautiful writing as a screen.

The difference between the two is precisely that designated in critical theory by the terms 'the classic realist' and the 'interrogatory' texts.[5] The narrator of 'Sketch' does not simply tell the story of Virginia Woolf's upbringing. She constantly questions whether or not she has got it right. She uses the search for her own life story as an opportunity for questioning whether life-writing is possible at all. Our lives are shaped by many important influences, and some of them are not included in the conventional plots that life stories are supposed to follow. Virginia Woolf gives as an example her own obsession with her mother, whose presence she felt and whose voice she heard until she was in her mid-forties.

My mother was one of those invisible presences who after all play so important a part in every life. This influence, by which I mean the consciousness of other groups impinging upon ourselves; public opinion; what other people say and think; all those magnets which attract us this way to be like that, or repel us the other and make us different from that; has never been analysed in any of those Lives which I so much enjoy reading, or very superficially. (MB 80)

In another typical passage, having just told stories about some incidents in her childhood (one was an incident of sexual abuse and another was about her feelings of shame and fear at looking at herself in a mirror), she emphasises how hard it is to define the person to whom things happen, for the person is such an inexplicable complex of inherited instincts and powerful but unanalysable experiences.

Though I have done my best to explain why I was ashamed at looking at my own face I have only been able to discover some possible reasons; there may be others; I do not suppose that I have got at the truth; yet this is a simple incident; and it happened to me personally; and I have no motive for lying about it. In spite of all this, people write what they call 'lives' of other people; that is, they collect a number of events, and leave the person to whom it happened unknown. (MB 69)

Moreover, not only are one's explanations of remembered incidents unsure, but one's memories are selective, and the things one does not remember are as important, perhaps more important, as those one does.

It is easier to discover the story of a person's life if one has a clear sense of who he or she had in the end become. If we know where the story ends we can recount earlier parts of the life as stages which lead up to this achieved identity. In the case of Roger Fry it was easy to select and interpret past events in his life and fit them into his life story once she had accepted that his was the story of a free, civilised individual whose commitment to painting was eventually vindicated by both his private success as a painter and his public role as a reformer of social values. Virginia Woolf, surveying her own life, does not have such a clear final identity. The present 'I', the person who is exploring the past and trying to make sense of it, is fractured and dispersed. She knows that she is a writer, but she is not sure just what that amounts to, either psychologically or in terms of public values. So part of her attempt to trace her path though life becomes a questioning of her present self as she enters into old age. There are always alternative interpretations jostling for attention and approval in her mind and muddying the narrative waters. In this kind of life-writing the dramatic situation of the present 'I' is as important as are the adventures of the past 'I'. The writer tells us that as she writes an air battle is going on over her head. Every night there are bombing raids. It is quite possible that she will die. Apart from the bombs, an invasion is expected shortly, and she and her husband have arranged ways of killing themselves when that time comes. The last mention in her diary of 'memoir writing' is on 21 January 1941, just two months before her death, when she killed herself because she was afraid that she was once again going mad. She had been reading through her parents' letters to each other. She had been thinking again about the deaths of her mother, her half-sister and her brother, though resisting stepping again into those cold waters. This means that there is no stable, reliable narrator telling the story of her childhood. Rather, the activities of remembering and narrating are attempts to clarify the narrator's present identity. It is not so much a search for lost time as an attempt, through memory, to ease her present predicament.

In this 'sketch', the writing is not so much designed to record or recall an already established history, as to attempt to create a coherent identity, by holding together in a pattern the various parts of herself, or different identities, that she feels are all authentically part of who she is. She wants to create a story that will bring these parts together into an intelligible whole. In particular the narrator is anxious to exhibit for us her will to write as a kind of unexplained oddity at the heart of her life. There are different possible ways of understanding the will to write. She prefers one particular life story, one way of making sense of it, but she cannot tell us with certainty that it is true.

The preferred story weaves together into one single narrative thread four different self-images to each of which she is attached and each of which she has explored in fictional self-portraits. There is the damaged young girl whose normal development had been made impossible by sexual abuse and by the trauma of loosing her mother (Rachel Vinrace in *The Voyage Out*); there is the girl who is peculiarly susceptible to shocks of terror, to suicidal impulses but also to visionary revelations (Rhoda in *The Waves*); there is the modern woman artist, autonomous and unconventional (Lily Briscoe in *To the Lighthouse*) and the social Outsider, uncorrupted by society's rewards (the narrator of *Three Guineas*). These characters are discovered in her own life-story, in her 'mutilation', as she calls it, as a young girl and her subsequent fantasy of disembodiment, in her multiple bereavements and subsequent madness, but also in her ability, as she cracks, to allow 'reality' to flood in, so that she experiences moments of being in which some pattern is revealed behind the cotton wool of everyday life. Finally, there is the central mystery, the will to write. This was so strong that she rebelled against the conventional social narrative for which her half-brother attempted to train her. Instead she took to her room to read and write. The story as it is told in 'A Sketch of the Past' ends with a scene of radical disconnection, of Victorian tea parties downstairs, intellectual activity upstairs in the study and sexual interference in the bedroom. The whole of her subsequent life had been a flight from this scene of Victorian oppression into her own chosen form of modern womanhood.

The central definition of herself that this preferred life story gives her and which she wants to shore up against the eroding force of her doubts, links together three things – her susceptibility to 'shocks', her visionary tendency to 'moments of being' and her will to write.

I only know that many of these exceptional moments brought with them a peculiar horror and a physical collapse; they seemed dominant; myself passive. This suggests that as one gets older one has a greater power through reason to provide an explanation; and that this explanation blunts the sledge-hammer force of the blow. I think this is true, because though I still have the peculiarity that I receive these sudden shocks, they are now always welcome; after the first surprise, I always feel instantly that they are particularly valuable. And so I go on to suppose that the shock-receiving capacity is what makes me a writer . . .

[a shock is not simply] a blow from an enemy hidden behind the cotton wool of daily life; it is or will become a revelation of some order; it is a token of some real thing behind appearances; and I make it real by putting it into words. (MB 72)

From this story she wants to derive a conclusion, a statement of the higher meaning of her life, a context that will allow her to understand her life's dedication to writing as having contributed to a greater, impersonal truth.

From this I reach what I might call a philosophy; at any rate it is a constant idea of mine; that behind the cotton wool is hidden a pattern; that we – I mean all human beings – are connected with this; that the whole world is a work of art; that we are parts of the work of art. *Hamlet* or a Beethoven quartet is the truth about this vast mass that we call the world. But there is no Shakespeare, there is no Beethoven; certainly and emphatically there is no God; we are the words; we are the music; we are the thing itself. (MB 72)

This intuition or conception, that there is a pattern behind the cotton wool, is, she says, the rod that holds all her life together, makes it coherent, provides its centre. It is what explains her will to write and what would, if she could really trust it, make her autobiography into a coherent story.

I prove this, now, by spending the morning writing, when I might be walking, running a shop, or learning to do something that will be useful if war comes. I feel that by writing I am doing what is far more necessary than anything else.

All artists I suppose feel something like this. It is one of the obscure elements in life that has never been much discussed. It is left out in almost all biographies and autobiographies, even of artists. (MB 73)

Virginia Woolf would like to believe this story, but she offers us plenty of hints that there is an alternative interpretation of her life which she could make up. She knows that we make up ourselves, as her father made up himself through the story of frustrated genius, in order to justify our passions and our will to power. We make ourselves up to defend ourselves against the gratuitousness of our passions. Our identities are necessary illusions. We never stop attempting to patch them up, and to provide them with some plausibility, but they are always threatening to fall into dereliction or to explode with the force of unresolved contradictions. Whereas Roger Fry's written life story had clear outlines, an unambiguous outcome and an untroubled narrator, Virginia Woolf's own life story, as she tells it in these raw notes, is disturbed by many questions, hesitations and doubts. She is not entirely confident of the meaning of those famous 'moments of being'. She does not entirely trust her susceptibility to delight and ecstasy. Is it true, she wonders, that when she cracks up reality floods in?

> to cut short an obscure train of thought, about the other voice or voices and their connection with art, with religion: figuratively, I could snapshot what I mean by fancying myself afloat, [in an element] which is all the time responding to things we have no words for – exposed to some invisible ray: but instead of labouring here to express this, to analyse the third voice, to discover whether 'pure delights' are connected with art, or religion: whether I am telling the truth when I see myself perpetually taking the breath of these voices in my sails, and tacking this way and that, in daily life as I yield to them – instead of that, I note only this influence, suspect it to be of great importance, cannot find how to check its power on other people; and so erect a finger here, by way of signalling that here is a vein to work out later. (MB 115)

She has not definitely settled in her own mind how to understand her peculiar 'sensitivity'. She plays with the idea that she is like a device for detecting emanations from an invisible zone of Being, like a mystical dish aerial picking up signals too weak for other people to be aware of. She wants to think of her writing as giving words to this 'singing of the real world', but she is unsure. There is another possibility. Perhaps what really drives her writing is obsession and delusion. She started to read Freud in the last years of her life and this may have helped to confirm for her the possibility that unconscious wishes and illusions are central in the creative life. She was aware of the worm of obsession lurking in the rose of artistic genius. She sometimes talked about her fascination with her parents as pathological and obsessive. This obsession energised her writing of *To the Lighthouse*:

I wrote the book very quickly; and when it was written, I ceased
to be obsessed by my mother. I no longer hear her voice; I do not
see her.

   I suppose that I did for myself what psycho-analysts do for
their patients. I expressed some very long felt and deeply felt
emotion. And in expressing it I explained it and then laid it to
rest. (MB 81)

The ambiguity (what results from obsession, is it insight or is it
delusion?) is one that haunts much of the art of the modern age.
There is no sure way of distinguishing between creative insight
and disease.

   Consider another ambiguity – this one is personified beautifully
in Virginia Woolf's final self-portrait, the writer Miss La Trobe in
Between the Acts, whom she created at the same time that she was
writing 'A Sketch'. Should she consider herself a success or a
failure in her literary career? She had achieved international fame,
wealth and the admiration of many friends and critics. Yet she had
her own doubts. By 1941 it was ten years since she had published a
novel that she herself really believed in. In 'A Sketch' she seems
fairly confident that she had succeeded as a writer as long as she is
discussing her 'moments of being' or 'revelations', which she took
to be

   A token of some real thing behind appearances; and I make it
   real by putting it into words. It is only by putting it into words
   that I make it whole; this wholeness means that it has lost its
   power to hurt me; it gives me, perhaps because by doing so I
   take away the pain, a great delight to put the severed parts
   together. (MB 72)

However, in one very interesting passage she admits that she
must consider herself a failure. There is something that she always
aimed to achieve in her writing but never succeeded in, and that is
the writing of non-being in her fiction. She has never solved the
problem of how to describe non-being. Her fiction is unbalanced,
weighted towards the poetic, the visionary. She does not know
how to give non-being its due force. Her focus, in her writing, on
Being, could itself be given a negative interpretation, as having its
origin in her life-long denial of her own body. In any case, she had
accepted that the challenge for the novelist is to describe the

coexistence of and the movement between these different kinds of experience, Being and Non-Being. In this she takes herself to have failed. 'The real novelist can somehow convey both sorts of being. I think Jane Austen can; and Trollope; perhaps Thackeray and Dickens and Tolstoy. I have never been able to do both. I tried – in *Night and Day*; and in *The Years*' (MB 70).

This diagnosis should remind us of other objectives that she had set herself as a writer: to tell the truth about a woman's passions and about a woman's body, and to explore the dark country of women's daily lives. We can easily imagine that she might count herself a failure in these respects also, especially given the history of *The Pargiters*. Moreover, she would have felt that her failure must have had its origin in her childhood, and that in sketching her past, especially everything in it that had led her to adopt her existential stance of disembodiment, she was identifying the sources of her incapacity. She traced her fear and shame at her own body to an episode of sexual abuse that she suffered at the hands of one of her half-brothers. So once again, the life story becomes diverted into a diagnosis of failure.

We do not know, of course, what form her autobiography would have taken had she composed it for publication. We do not know whether she would have exposed these doubts and hesitations. Perhaps it was only in the privacy of these notes that she could have brought herself to expose so much. It is hard not to take this unconventional, formally inventive and painfully honest life-writing as among the great successes of her career, even though it was almost lost among her papers and only published thirty-five years after her death. Perhaps this sketch, along with her diaries, was all part of a *ruse* that she played on herself, that allowed her to disclose her secret history and uncertain identity without wholly admitting to herself that she was doing so.

'A Sketch of the Past' is such a wonderful work precisely because it was written as notes. Fortunately, she never did compose it, as she planned to, into an orderly work of art 'where one thing follows another and all are swept into a whole' (MB 75). It provides a satisfying counterweight to all that is excessively composed in her fiction. Perhaps she came close to recognising this herself.

I dipped into my memoirs: too circuitous & unrelated: too many splutters: as it stands. A real life has no crisis: hence nothing to tighten. It must lack centre. It must amble on. All the same, I can

weave a very thick pattern, one of these days out of that pattern
of detail. (D V, 1 November 1940)

Perhaps this throws some light on the fact that with Virginia
Woolf the reader feels a much greater impulse than with many
other authors to move on from reading her novels to reading not
only her unpublished memoirs but also her private documents, her
diary, her letters and the drafts of her novels. Just as she never
settles nor do we. We go backwards and forwards from the fiction
to the non-fiction. It is as if we need to balance the 'Being' in the
novels with the 'Non-Being' in the diary and letters. That combination, which she never achieved within her fiction to her satisfaction, is available to us because her literary career did not finish
with her death, but continues to this day with the publication of
previously unpublished documents. The most important of these,
her diary, was not published only for its biographical or historical
interest or for purely scholarly purposes, but because it is a fine
work of literature in its own right. It was published first in condensed form, as *A Writer's Diary*, by her husband in 1953, and from
1977 onwards the full diary has been published in five volumes.

It was not her conscious intention that her oeuvre should take
this form and her literary career have this unusual posthumous
trajectory. She regarded her diary as the raw material for the
memoirs that she hoped one day to write. She was so 'trained to
silence' that we cannot imagine her consciously writing the diary
for publication. Her resistance to personal life-writing was very
strong. She wrote to Ethel Smyth in 1931:

> For months on first knowing you, I said to myself here's one of
> these talkers. They don't know what feeling is, happily for them.
> Because everyone I most honour is silent – Nessa, Lytton,
> Leonard, Maynard: all silent; and so I have trained myself to
> silence; induced to it also by the terror I have of my own
> unlimited capacity for feeling. . . . (L IV, 29 Dec 1931)[6]

She was deeply reticent. In everything which she wrote for
publication the masking outweighed the disclosure. There were
many parts of her life that could only be written if she thought that
the writing would not be seen. This is a theme of her letters to her
very unreticent friend Ethel Smyth. 'I hate any writer to talk about
himself; anonymity I adore. And this may be an obsession. I blush,

I fidget, I turn hot and cold. I want to pull the curtain over this indecency' (L V, 6 June 1933). In response to Ethel Smyth's autobiography in 1940 she wrote, 'It's a curious light on your psychology; that you can confess so openly, what I should have hidden so carefully. And of course as I see, you're absolutely right' (L VI, 9 July 1940).

Lorrie Goldensohn has argued that, 'When reading her books . . . we seem always committed to peering into and behind them for contexts, sub-texts and sub-vocalisations. It occurs to me, though, that we might do this a little less relentlessly if the feelings were not strong within us that she withheld so much, swept so much out of her novels and essays with the one hand, and back into her diaries and letters with the other. What can we do, when there is always such a clear track of words, but follow?'[7] Her diary exposes sides of herself that she tidies away out of sight in the fiction – her malice, her sense of fun, her snobbery, her contentment with domestic life, her tolerance of triviality, her delight in her sister's children, her friendships with Vita and Ethel Smyth. The diary usually stays on the surface and that is its virtue. 'Once more, as so often, I hunt for my dear old red-covered book, with what an instinct I'm not quite sure. For what the point of making these notes is I dont know; save that it becomes a necessity to uncramp, & some of it may interest me later. But what? For I never reach the depths; I'm too surface blown. And always scribble before going in – look quickly at my watch' (D V, 17 December 1939).

The last volume of her diary conveys very movingly the feel of life in war-time England. Perhaps more than any carefully composed novel she could have written, the diary tells us what it was like to live through the air raids and the fear of invasion in 1940–41. She makes no attempt to order the experiences into any overarching shape. The daily reality we realise was a strange coexistence of everyday concerns with life-threatening danger. Perhaps it is because I, as a small child, shared this strange experience of a world that was at one and the same time quite ordinary and absolutely terrifying, that I am so moved by this record in her diary of the last months of her life. Virginia had to think about cooking. Leonard got on with the gardening. They played games of bowls and Leonard carefully recorded the results. They went for walks. They wrote letters. As they did there were constant reminders that they could die at any minute. Planes roared overhead. Bombs fell so close that the pen jumped from Virginia's hand. As they walked they were suddenly forced to throw themselves to the ground. They lived without a future, 'with our noses pressed to a closed door' (D V, 26 January 1941). Sometimes the feeling that she conveys is not so much terror as a profound sadness or bleakness.

> Walking today . . . saw my first hospital train – laden, not funereal, but weighty, as if not to shake bones. Something what is the word I want: grieving & tender & heavy laden & private – bringing our wounded back carefully through the green fields at which I suppose some looked. Not that I could see them. And the faculty for seeing in imagination always leaves me so suffused with something partly visual partly emotional, I can't though its very pervasive, catch it when I come home – the slowness, cadaverousness, grief of the long heavy train, taking its burden through the fields. Very quietly it slid into the cutting at Lewes. (D V, 29 May 1940)

The diary is where '[I] get down some of the myriad impressions which I net every day' (D III, 9 April 1925). When writing her diary she has no audience except herself. She has no need to create a mask. She creates a voice quite different from any of the others which she invented. The writing is speedy, full of abbreviations, ampersands and semi-colons. She allows herself to enjoy what in a more solemn mood she would count as non-being. She jots down curious conversations, anecdotes, impressions of acquaintances, exasperation with the servants. Everything is sketched in a rush that is not often much slowed down by thought or analysis. This is a different kind of life-writing from autobiography. Of all her writing it is that which is most like the impressionistic writing she had described in her essay on Dorothy Richardson and in 'Modern Fiction', descriptions which have often wrongly been taken as defining her novelistic method. The diary takes an ordinary mind on an ordinary day and records the myriad impressions, the shower of atoms, that fall upon it. It discloses life in what is small and trivial. It celebrates 'non-being' rather than dismissing it as a sham. The reader, holding the composed, elegant novels in one hand and the profuse diaries and letters in the other, comes as close as one can to bringing the severed parts together.

10

1941: The Illusion Fails

'It was the primeval voice sounding loud in the ear of the present moment.' (BA 99)

'COMMONERS AND OUTSIDERS'

It has been suggested that there was a revolution in Virginia Woolf's thinking in 1940, detectable in two interventions in public debate that she made that year.[1] In the spring she gave a lecture to a Worker's Education Association meeting in Brighton, which was then published as 'The Leaning Tower' (CE II 162). It is remarkable that she agreed to give this lecture at all, since her few other public lectures had all been to audiences of university or professional women. It seems to have been important to her to reach out to a wider audience. It is quite astonishing that in this lecture she addressed her audience in the first person plural as if she and they, regardless of their differences of class, accent and culture, had enough in common to see the world in similar terms. The target of her criticism was the group of young writers who had come into prominence in the 1930s. They all viewed the world from a distinct position of privilege, for they stared down on the rest of society from a height which derived from their being men, wealthy, and expensively educated. In the 1930s these privileged young poets had become self-conscious of their privilege and hence of their limited vision. In compensation they began to write political poetry in a didactic, preaching strain. In the future, she hoped, writing would not be left to this privileged class, but would be taken on by 'commoners and outsiders like ourselves'. This remarkable, and quite unconvincing, declaration of solidarity, of community, with the underprivileged and uneducated (she consistently said 'we', referring to both herself and her audience of working people) indicates certainly a very real desire on her part to overcome the narrowness of her social life, which had exposed her to harsh and, she felt, unfair criticism. However, whatever her desires in the matter, there were serious obstacles, and these she could not overcome. It is hard to think of any writer more thoroughly cut off, by experience, wealth, attitude and imagination, from working people. Never in her life, and nowhere in her fiction, did she ever succeed in overcoming her limitations in this respect. Her 'Memories of a Working Women's Guild' (CE IV 134f) described quite honestly the limitations of imagination and experience that made it impossible for her to conceive what it was like to be a working woman. On the very few occasions when she attempted to represent the voices or perceptions of working women in her fiction, she failed miserably. The creeking, moaning Mrs McNab in *To the Lighthouse* is among the worst examples. Perhaps what the lecture helps us to see is just how unsatisfactory the idea of 'Outsiders' is as a tool for thinking about society, since it collects together under a single label too many quite different kinds of people.

Although the publication of *Three Guineas* had connected her with an enthusiastic new audience from whom she received many letters of support, the book had at the same time opened her to attack. A working woman from Huddersfield, Agnes Smith, wrote to her. She was initially quite hostile and suspicious and accused Virginia Woolf, quite fairly, of having very little idea of how people really lived. In response to Virginia's friendly reply, Agnes Smith undertook to provide Virginia Woolf with a kind of correspondence course on the subject. She sent her a series of letters containing much detailed information. She tried to explain the difficulties that cramped people's lives. One of her themes was the hunger that some working people felt for books, art and travel, and the importance to them of such sources as exist, for example the municipal libraries and the WEA.[2] Perhaps it was Agnes Smith's letters that persuaded Virginia Woolf to speak to the WEA in Brighton.

Another attack came in a review of *Three Guineas* in *Scrutiny*, in which Q. D. Leavis accused Virginia Woolf of being a social parasite, of belonging to a narrow, propertied élite, who should not claim to be able to speak on behalf of her sex. Virginia Woolf could perhaps comfortably disregard this abuse. However, there was another line of attack which must have worried her and which had become quite common in the 1930s. According to this, English fiction had undergone, since the days of Hardy and Conrad, a very damaging split. It was now divided into two quite distinct classes. On the one hand there was esoteric fiction, difficult to read and avant-garde in form, read by a very small highbrow élite, and on the other there was popular, mass-market fiction, selling in huge editions to wide audiences but of very little literary merit. This view had been stated and documented in Q. D. Leavis's book *Fiction and the Reading Public* (1932) in which *To the Lighthouse* featured as a prominent example of a highbrow work that is not accessible to the common reader. Q. D. Leavis argued that not only is this novel's style baffling to an audience not accustomed to reading poetry, but its '*tone* is prohibitive to anyone who does not share the author's cultural background'.[3]

A similar view of problems of modern literature and of Virginia Woolf's place in it was argued in 1938 by Cyril Connolly in *Enemies of Promise*, in which he distinguished between those who, like Virginia Woolf, wrote in mandarin style and those who wrote in the vernacular. Virginia's reaction was to think that perhaps her reputation had reached its height with *To the Lighthouse* and that subsequently she had been discarded as second-rate. She had been attacked by Wyndham Lewis, Gertrude Stein and now Cyril Connolly. E. M. Forster's reputation, she thought, was much higher than her own (D V, 22 November 1938). In February 1940 Connolly again irritated her by describing her as one of 'the ivory tower dwellers' (L VI, p. 384).

In August of that year she received yet another blast of criticism, this time from one of Vita Sackville-West's sons, Benedict Nicolson, who wrote to her in response to her biography of Roger Fry. He accused Fry and his friends of living in a fool's paradise, shut away from all disagreeable actualities, and cultivating a private world which 'could only be communicated to a few people as sensitive and intelligent as himself'. The artist, instead of 'retreating into his tower', should try to persuade as many other people as possible to fight against stupidity and untruth (L VI, 13 August 1940). Virginia was stung into writing long, carefully considered replies, and in doing so she spelled out some of the ways in which she had herself attempted to reach out to a broader audience. She had taught at Morley College. Meetings of the Women's Cooperative Guild had been held at her house. She defends her non-fiction books and says, 'I did my best to make them reach a far wider circle than a little private circle of exquisite and cultivated people' (L VI, 24 August 1940). Although she did not mention this to Nicolson, *The Common Reader: First Series* had in fact in 1938 been published by Penguin, at the price of 6d. in an edition of 50 000 copies.

Penguin books were an extremely important publishing innovation in the 1930s, being very cheap paperback editions that made
serious books accessible to a wide audience. By way of illustration,
the price of the Hogarth Press edition of *Common Reader I* was 12s
6d., that is, twenty-five times the price of the Penguin edition. A
few months after the exchange of letters with Nicolson, the popularity of *The Common Reader* was confirmed for her when she came
across a copy of it in the Free Library in Lewes, with plenty of
evidence of its having been frequently out on loan. There she also
came across a book by John Buchan in which he judged that
Virginia Woolf was the best critic since Matthew Arnold.

In spite of these successes, she was goaded by Nicolson into
surveying her whole career and testing it against the accusation
that she had failed in her duty to communicate beyond her class. It
is clear that the accusation both irritated and worried her. She had
a real anxiety about it. Although she came out fighting and put up
a reasonable defence, the argument must have left her confused
and uncertain.

> But I do feel myself that I ought to have been able to make not
> merely thousands of people interested in literature; but millions.
> Why have I failed to do that? The other day I went and lectured
> to the WEA at Brighton, and felt that it was hopeless for me to
> tell people who had been taken away from school at the age of 14
> that they must read Shakespeare . . . My puzzle is, ought artists
> now to become politicians? My instinct says no; but I'm not sure
> that I can justify my instinct. (L VI, 24 August 1940)

The letters to Nicolson seem to me to be an honest defence of her
career, but probably the correspondence did nothing to discourage
her increasing tendency to think of her career in terms of failure. It
was by now nearly ten years since she had published a book that
she felt satisfied with. She was working on *Between the Acts* and no
doubt wondering whether this was to be yet another disappointment. Moreover, she must have known, as a result of these various
exchanges of letters and her lecture, that her self-image as 'common reader' and 'outsider' did not represent any effective community with others. She was in fact increasingly isolated, particularly
after she and Leonard could no longer return to London because
their flats had been bombed. She felt herself to be misunderstood.
The argument flared up again at the beginning of 1941 when

Desmond MacCarthy reviewed 'The Leaning Tower' in the *Sunday Times*. He picked up her confusion of identity, arguing that 'she ought not to have used the pronoun "we" in addressing an audience of working men'. Virginia was furious that he could not see what a difference her lack of university education had made for her, nor understand why she should feel that she had the right to claim unity with the working class. She argued with Leonard about it. She must have felt rejected by everybody.

READING FREUD

In the summer of 1940 she was asked to contribute to a Women's Symposium in the USA and she took this opportunity to take another public stand, and to reach out beyond her purely literary audience. She wrote 'Thoughts on Peace in an Air Raid' (CE IV 173), in which she argued that while the pilots were fighting against tyranny with their bodies, her contribution would be to fight with her mind. She would fight to free men from the tyranny of their 'subconscious Hitlerism'. For men are driven, she argued, by ancient instincts of aggression, instincts which are fostered rather than diverted and tamed by education and training. Her argument was influenced by the fact that in 1939 she began, for the first time in her life, to read the works of Sigmund Freud. In spite of the fact that the English translations of his works had been published by The Hogarth Press in association with the Institute of Psycho-analysis, and that Bloomsbury had many connections with psychoanalysis (her brother Adrian trained as an analyst; James Strachey, Lytton's brother, was the translator of Freud's *Collected Papers* and an analyst) she had not before read any of his work. In 1938 Freud, at the age of 82, had escaped from Vienna and had settled in London. Leonard and Virginia, as his publishers, visited him in January 1939. He gave Virginia a narcissus and they discussed politics. He was, she wrote, 'an old fire now flickering' (D V, 29 January 1939). She mingled in psychoanalytic circles in 1939. She met Anna Freud. She went to a formal dinner of the British Psycho-Analytical Society at the Savoy Hotel, where she met and invited to dinner Melanie Klein, whose books the Hogarth Press was also publishing.

Reading Freud had an important impact on her thinking. She was both disturbed and excited by it: 'Freud is upsetting: reducing

one to whirlpool; & I daresay truly. If we're all instinct, the
unconscious, whats all this about civilisation, the whole man,
freedom &c? His savagery against God good' (D V, 9 December
1939). She was gratified to learn that Freud had a word, 'ambivalence', for a phenomenon which she had both experienced and
written about at length, of feeling intensely both love and hate at
the same time for the same person. Perhaps through Freud she
learned for the first time to give the body its due. Moreover,
through reading Freud she was able at last to throw off the Old
Bloomsbury ideology of 'civilisation'. She came to appreciate that
civilisation is not so much the cultivation of a distinct aesthetic
sensibility, but the ability to delay gratification of the instincts
through their sublimation into other forms of activity. Art has its
roots in the instincts and not in a distinct, purely incorporeal taste
for beauty.

The youths of Cambridge–Bloomsbury had been, according to
Keynes, like water-spiders skimming the surface of a pond, oblivi-
ous of the forces at work beneath the surface. Reading Freud
helped Virginia Woolf to direct her and our attention to the depths.
After hearing Keynes read his memoir she had penned a counter-
image, in 'A Sketch of the Past'. She proposed that the individual
is like a fish in a stream, held in place, or thrown this way and that,
by invisible forces like currents in the stream. Her perception of
those forces had certainly deepened when, in *Between the Acts*, the
image of a fishpond was given central place. She was distancing
herself even more from the Old Bloomsbury world-view.

> Water, for hundreds of years, had silted down into the hollow,
> and lay there four or five feet deep over a black cushion of mud.
> Under the thick plate of green water, glazed in their self-centred
> world, fish swam. . . . Silently they manoeuvred in their water
> world, poised in the blue patch made by the sky, or shot silently
> to the edge where the grass, trembling, made a fringe of nod-
> ding shadow. On the water-pavement spiders printed their
> delicate feet. (BA 35)

At the end of 1939 she read and made notes on Freud's *Group
Psychology and the Analysis of the Ego* (RN 115f). In this she found
confirmation for her views about men, women and war. She noted
down a thought that would reappear in her 'Thoughts on Peace'

article the next summer, that men all have subconscious 'Hitlerism' in their heads. She equates masculinity with 'Hitlerism', and thereby provides the answer to her question as to what women can do to help prevent war, namely that they should fight against 'Hitlerism in England'.

It is very likely that she read also a collection of Freud's writings called *Civilisation, War and Death*, which was edited for the Hogarth Press by John Rickman (whom she met and liked) and was published in 1939. There is no direct evidence that she read this anthology, but given that she was setting out to read Freud for the first time, and given that she met socially with the editor of the volume, which was produced specifically for the layperson, and that it was published by her own press at exactly this date, and that it was addressed to the very issue which was also at the time at the top of her mind, 'Why war?', it seems very likely that she would have started her reading of Freud with this volume. It contains a 1915 paper 'Thoughts for the Times on War and Death', an edited version of *Civilisation and its Discontents*, and the 1932 letter to Einstein, 'Why War?' The latter especially is one very likely source for whatever is new in her thinking in 'Thoughts on Peace' and her new emphasis, which is a campaign to emancipate men from their aggression and their desire to enslave women. Freud argued that we are driven by two instincts, called in his letter to Einstein Love and Hate (a very similar thought occurs to Isa in *Between the Acts*). Love, or Eros, Freud explains, is comprised by the erotic instincts, taking 'erotic' not in a narrow sexual meaning but in the broader connotation that it has in Plato's *Symposium*. Virginia Woolf, reading this, must have felt vindicated, for she had all her life thought of the erotic in just these terms. There is no prospect of being able to eliminate humanity's aggressive tendencies (Freud does not attribute them only to men!). All we can do is to attempt to divert them into channels less damaging than warfare, by increasing the extent to which Eros is enabled to produce ties of sentiment binding men together.

From our mythology of the instincts we may easily deduce a formula for an indirect method of eliminating war. If the propensity for war be due to the destructive instinct, we have always its counter-agent, Eros, to our hand. All that produces ties of sentiment between man and man must serve as war's antidote. . . . All that brings out the significant resemblances between men calls into play this feeling of community, identification, whereon is founded, in large measure, the whole edifice of human society.[4]

She would have found in Freud, then, both a congenial way of thinking about war and masculinity, and also a way of connecting this with her desire for community, for overcoming her sense of isolation and loss of audience.

MISS WHATSHERNAME

In April 1938, before she had read Freud, Virginia started her new novel, called at first *Poyntzet Hall*, as a relief from the drudgery of writing *Roger Fry*. Its emphasis was to be the community built or invoked by literature. She wanted to avoid anything too ambitious, after the appalling experience of *The Years*.

Through 1940, as she read and drafted her different works, the ideas that she had in her mind migrated from one work to another, and sometimes she even moved passages from one to another too. She was thinking about war and the instincts, for her essay 'Thoughts on Peace in an Air Raid'; she was from November 1940, thinking about and drafting her new book on the history of English literature, which starts with 'Anon'. She came to think more and more, as she wrote *Between the Acts*, about the role of the writer in building the wall of civilisation, in forging those 'erotic' connections between men which counteract the aggressive instincts, and so about art generally as rooted in village life and in the primeval sediment of our biologically inherited instincts. The Freudian idea of the sublimation of primeval instincts underlies all three works. They were all variations on the theme of the writer's role in society, particularly in time of war. She was struggling to find some way of thinking about her work that gave it a social significance, so as not to understand it entirely in terms of her own personal obsessions. In 'A Sketch of the Past' (yet another work on which she was engaged at this same time) she analysed her will to write solely in its relation to her personal history of traumatised childhood, and her susceptibility to visionary experience. In the other three works of 1940 she looked rather to her social role. She portrayed the writer as having a vital function in the life of the community, seeing literature as a form of combat against the forces of destruction. 'I will not cease from mental fight', she quotes from Blake in 'Thoughts on Peace', even though with the destructive instincts so rampant and with the isolation imposed by the war she felt increasingly that she could no longer communicate with her audience.

As we have seen, Virginia Woolf was at this time sunk deep into her own past. She was reading her parents' letters, she had been reading letters of Roger Fry, she had been fishing in her own infancy while writing 'A Sketch of the Past', and she was now quite used to the idea of the presence of the past – the permanence of some past experiences that she discovered she could retrieve after fifty years. Indeed, as she says, moments of her childhood 'can still be more real than the present moment' (MB 67). But she is used to thinking of these preserved 'moments' in a non-corporeal way. They come from outside the body and are preserved because they are traces of a non-bodily reality. They come like water into a cracked vessel. Through reading Freud she came, perhaps for the first time, to think of the presence of the past, both one's personal past and the past of our historical and prehistorical origins, as stored in and transferred from one generation to another, through the body. We live, in our nerves and brains, in our blood and bones, with instincts which are a form of bodily memory and which make us, more thoroughly than she had ever portrayed before, at one with nature, with the animals and the earth (birds, fish and cows all have star roles in *Between the Acts*). All her life she had been portraying human beings as animals, but until now this was always in a spirit of fun or a defensive mechanism which she used as a way of reducing people to less frightening proportions. Indeed, sometimes, as with *Flush*, it was a way of humanising animals. Now, in these late works, she began to see people and animals as joined in a common instinctual heritage.

Her portrait of the writer and her community in *Between the Acts* is deeply affected by these ideas. The theme is now not the permanence of moments of being, but the imperishability of the primitive, of our biological inheritance. In the Rickman Freud anthology, in a section called 'The Disillusionment of War', she would have read that in the development of mind, earlier stages do not disappear as later stages form, but persist alongside the later stages.

The earlier mental state may not have manifested itself for years, but none the less it is so far present that it may at any time again become the mode of expression of the forces in the mind, and that exclusively, as though all later developments had been annulled, undone. . . . It may well happen that a later and higher stage of evolution, once abandoned, cannot be reached again. But the primitive stages can always be reestablished; the primitive mind is, in the fullest meaning of the word, imperishable. (What are called mental diseases inevitably impress the layman with the idea of destruction of the life of mind and soul. In reality, the destruction relates only to later accretions and developments. The essence of mental disease lies in a return to earlier conditions of affective life and functioning.)[5]

This must have made extremely alarming reading for Virginia Woolf, given her mental history, and given her present immersion in her own damaged past, and could have contributed to her sense of defeat when she felt that her madness was returning in early 1941. The remarkable thing is that in her novel, which had by now expanded into a portrayal of the imperishable instincts of mankind played out in village life, as well as a portrait of the artist as an old woman, that she was able to preserve a tone, of light, mildly comic celebration.

Between the Acts portrays a simple drama. There is a battle between forces of dispersal and forces of togetherness, forces which tear things apart and those which, by bringing things together, produce and reproduce life and community. On the one hand, 'Dispersed are we', on the other 'I' rejected, 'We' substituted. '*Unity – Dispersity*' (BA 140) All of life is reduced to this simple plot, however much we may wish it otherwise. 'Love and hate – how they tore her asunder! Surely it was time someone invented a new plot, or that the author came out from the bushes . . .' (BA 150). Miss La Trobe's pageant celebrates literature, which through history has repeated over and over again this very same plot. On the one hand, the love story of Valentine and Flavinda, on the other the invocation of the wars, the cities flattened by war, and the families destroyed by murder – Babylon, Nineveh, Clytemnestra, Agamemnon, Troy. Before there were people, the drama was played out among the animals. Now, and since human time began, the old struggle between Eros and Thanatos goes on. At the end of the day Giles and his wife find themselves alone together. 'Alone, enmity was bared; also love. Before they slept, they must fight; after they had fought, they would embrace. From that embrace another life might be born. But first they must fight, as the dog fox fights the vixen, in the heart of darkness, in the fields of night' (BA 152). In Giles's wife Isa, who lusts after farmer Haines, we come as near as anywhere in Virginia Woolf's entire oeuvre to a depiction of a woman who experiences sexual desire.

Between the Acts, like *The Tempest*, is a late work. When she wrote it Virginia Woolf was conscious not of her impending suicide but of old age. 'So the land recedes from my ship which draws out into the sea of old age', she wrote (D V, 6 May 1940). It is as if in a late work the writer does not have to wrestle so strenuously with the conventions of art, but can accept them, and play with them, or invent dazzling ways of transcending them, as in Prospero's final speech in *The Tempest*, or in the unexpected last lines of *Between the Acts*. The author can enjoy the illusion, the magic of performance. In spite of the seriousness of the subject matter of the novel, *Between the Acts* holds on to a certain simplicity, charm and even a spirit of fun. Miss La Trobe attempts to weave her spells on her audience, and she succeeds, but only with a little help from another quarter, from the omnipotent magic of the author who so arranges it that whenever the enchantment of Miss La Trobe's music threatens to vanish, help arrives from nature, which, in this enchanted plot, is a benign and cooperative force. When the playwright's words are swept away by the wind, the illusion fails. But she is saved by the God-like author's contrivance of animal music. If Shakespeare, in *The Winter's Tale*, can make Hermione come alive again after sixteen years, then why should not Virginia Woolf make the cows sing?

Then suddenly, as the illusion petered out, the cows took up the burden. One had lost her calf. In the very nick of time she lifted her great moon-eyed head and bellowed. All the great moon-eyed heads laid themselves back. From cow after cow came the same yearning bellow. The whole world was filled with dumb yearning. It was the primeval voice sounding loud in the ear of the present moment. Then the whole herd caught the infection. Lashing their tails, blobbed like pokers, they tossed their heads high, plunged and bellowed, as if Eros had planted his dart in their flanks and goaded them to fury. The cows annihilated the gap; bridged the distance; filled the emptiness and continued the emotion.

Miss La Trobe waved her hand ecstatically at the cows. 'Thank Heaven!' she exclaimed. (BA 99)

Like Prospero conjuring his storms, the author contrives that nature should play its part, should join in the drama. When Miss La Trobe again stands facing the audience in an impotent panic, the author this time provides a shower of rain. 'Down it poured like all the people in the world weeping. Tears. Tears. Tears' (BA 125). When the music resumes the birds and the dogs join in the dance: 'the reticence of nature was undone, and the barriers which should divide Man the Master from the Brute were dissolved' (BA 128). Nowhere else does Virginia Woolf so play with the idea of the artifice and the illusionism of art, and indeed with the Freudian idea that art, like religion, is an illusion based on wish-fulfilment, on our willingness to believe in benign omnipotence.

This novel was, and not just in a technical sense, quite different from anything she had previously written. She had abandoned both the visionary aesthetics of *To the Lighthouse* and the comedy of interruption of *The Years*. She maintained her extraordinary record of formal innovation right up to the end. 'I am a little triumphant about the book', she wrote when she finished it. 'I think its an interesting attempt in a new method. I think its more quintessential than the others. More milk skimmed off. A richer pat, certainly a fresher than that misery The Years. I've enjoyed writing almost every page' (D V, 23 November 1940).

Yet no more than a few months later her confidence had vanished completely. When she read through the manuscript in March 1941, she found the novel unpublishable. She wrote to John Lehmann: 'Its much too slight and sketchy. Leonard doesnt agree. So we've decided to ask you if you'd mind reading it and give your casting vote'. She added 'I feel fairly certain it would be a mistake from all points of view to publish it' (L VI, 20 March 1941). She wrote again a week later that 'I cant publish that novel as it stands – its too silly and trivial'. It was published in July 1941, after her death, with a note from Leonard Woolf explaining that the typescript had not been finally revised for publication. On the basis of her work on other novels, we can say that it is quite likely that she would have considerably tightened up the metaphoric network of the book and given it a greater poetic resonance.[6]

How then was Virginia Woolf thinking about the writer and her role in society in these last years? We can draw on evidence from both the picture of Miss La Trobe, or Miss Whatshername as she is known to some of her audience, and that of, as it were her namesake, Anon. The writer is the handmaid of Eros, forging links between people, building the wall of civilisation, and thus thwarting the powers of destruction. She is like a cow with a dart in its flanks, singing the music of universal yearning, driven by an instinct as powerful as that of self-preservation.

> The song has the same power over the reader in the 20th century as over the hearer in the 11th. To enjoy singing, to enjoy hearing the song, must be the most deep rooted, the toughest of human instincts comparable for persistency with the instinct of self preservation. It is indeed the instinct of self preservation. Only when we put two and two together – two pencil strokes, two written words, two bricks . . . do we overcome dissolution and set up some stake against oblivion. The passion with which we seek out these creations and attempt endlessly, perpetually, to make them is of a piece with the instinct that sets us preserving our bodies, with clothes, food, roofs, from destruction.[7]

In writing for her audience the writer creates community by reproducing their common beliefs, their history, and therefore their sense of themselves as a common tribe, as does Miss La Trobe by providing the village with its history in the pageant of English literature. She also provides for her audience a language which, as Lucy Swithin says, stirs in them their own unacted parts, those parts of themselves which lie dormant for never having been assigned any role in life, but which remain potent as blocked up dams, as unfulfilled wishes, aggravating fantasies, a reminder that who we are and who we could have been are two different things. Similarly with the audience at Elizabethan drama, amazed to hear on the stage their own silent, inner lives spelled out loud in words: 'They saw themselves splendidly dressed. They heard themselves saying out loud what they had never said yet. They heard their aspirations, their profanities, their ribaldries spoken for them in poetry.'[8] This verbal art is a paradoxical mirror, for it reflects back to the audience a verbal image of themselves which they recognise, though it is 'saying out loud what they had never said'. As long as this truthful illusion is sustained, then art has served its purpose, for gaps are filled, where there was silence there are words, the 'orts, scraps and fragments' are held together in a precarious unity.

But when the illusion fails the audience breaks up. The writer cannot work without an audience. The importance of the reader, Virginia Woolf wrote, 'can be gauged by the fact that when his attention is distracted, in times of public crisis, the writer exclaims: I can write no more'.[9]

Virginia Woolf did feel that she could write no more and she drowned herself on 28 March 1941. When *Between the Acts* was published a few months later it was war-time and scarcely a time for considered literary judgement. The reputation of Bloomsbury was at its lowest. It is easy to imagine that it could have seemed a rather slight work, a feeble reflection to give back to a nation at war. Certainly, an accumulation of anti-Bloomsbury scorn was released in a dismissive review in *Scrutiny*, in which F. R. Leavis wrote that 'But for the name on the cover, and the mannerisms associated with that name, no one could have supposed it to be by an author of distinction or achievement' and went on to scoff at its 'extraordinary vacancy and pointlessness'.[10] The *TLS* found it 'a rarefied touching and imperfect book', and David Cecil wrote that '. . . it must be confessed that Mrs Woolf does not make her meaning altogether clear. . . . it must be counted as in part a failure' (MM 436). Only Edwin Muir, reviewing it in *The Listener*, praised it highly, and announced that it was her finest novel. The bafflement of early readers reflects the fact that in some ways it was Virginia Woolf's most audacious experiment, and that it was not easy to see how it fitted in with her earlier work. It has subsequently become, of course, one of her most admired novels.

In 1941, after her death, E. M. Forster gave a lecture in Cambridge about her work. His words remind us of what must be, from the point of view of her literary career, the single most important fact of her life: she liked writing. 'These words, which usually mean so little, must be applied to her with all possible intensity. . . . She liked writing with an intensity which few writers have attained or even desired. . . . She had a singleness of purpose which will not recur in this country for many years, and writers who have liked writing as she liked it have not indeed been common in any age.'[11]

11

Conclusion

In 1938 Virginia Woolf formally gave up her part in the Hogarth Press. They were earning so much money that she did not need to spend time on the Press any longer. They sold a partnership to John Lehmann, who also took over as manager (LW 438). It had been an unqualified success, remaining, as they wanted, modest in its output (publishing about twenty books each year). During the war the press was bombed out of its premises in Tavistock Square and had to be moved out of London. Paper was rationed and publishing became very difficult. Leonard continued in his connection with the press until his death in 1969. He supervised the publication of many volumes of Virginia's stories and essays. He produced a volume of extracts from her diary, *A Writer's Diary*, in 1953. Subsequently, the Hogarth Press has continued to publish Virginia Woolf's work, notably her complete *Diary* and her *Letters*. The complete *Essays of Virginia Woolf* is now in the course of publication.

In the immediate aftermath of her death there were respectful obituaries. The common opinion was that Virginia Woolf was a fine stylist in an impressionist mode, who suffered from great limitations. Stephen Spender summed it up in his obituary in *The Listener*: 'Her strength – and perhaps also her weakness – lay in her rare mind and personality. . . . the quality of what she created had the undiluted purity of one of those essentially uncorrupted natures which have been set aside from the world for a special task by the strangest conjunction of fortune and misfortune' (MM 426). That her work was too rarefied and not quite of this world, that some essential humanity was lacking in it, was a common complaint. Storm Jameson had said already in 1929: 'She sees as an artist sees, listens as a musician does, to common suffering, crying, laughing, doing good and doing mischief. Doubtless she suffers, weeps, laughs, herself – but not as a man [sic] does. As a fallen angel might. Or a changeling. She has no roots in our common earth' (MM 244–5). It was only much later that readers began to discover in her something altogether tougher, more critical, more perceptive, than this implies. There is in her work a whole dimension of social and psychological understanding that has now been highlighted especially, but not only, by feminist readers.[1] While no one would want to call her 'earthy', it is not too much to say that now she can be seen as having been, after all, of this world.

After the war, her readership began to grow. Her non-fiction books were published by Penguin. *The Common Reader: Second Series* was printed in an edition of 50 000 copies at 9d each in 1944, and 100 000 copies of *A Room of One's Own* at 9d each were printed in 1945. Her readership is now immense. Interest in Bloomsbury revived. Feminists, thinking back through their mothers, discovered in Virginia Woolf a highly valued member of their family. Curiosity about her life increased with the publication in 1972 of Quentin Bell's biography of his aunt. An immense academic industry has grown up around her work. A British television series on the Ten Great Modern Writers included Virginia Woolf as the only woman. Monks House in Rodmell now belongs to the National Trust. In short, Virginia Woolf has been absorbed into our 'heritage'. The difficulty for her now is not to find an audience for her work but to escape from the suffocating attentions of the heritage and academic industries, which threaten to smother her in false and sentimental piety. Everything, at least in Britain, contrives to encourage her to be read with, of all things, nostalgia. Bloomsbury fabric designs are on sale at Liberty's. *To the Lighthouse* appears on television as period costume drama. The Beresford photographs are on sale at the National Portrait Gallery. Tourists buy guided tours of her home. None of this is objectionable in itself, but the combined result is that there is removed from her work all of its challenging, critical, disturbing, disorienting qualities. She is read as an accepted, if eccentric member of the cultural ruling class. She has been made safe. The challenge now, for those who teach or read her work, is to rediscover in it the voice of the angry, combative, difficult, demanding and dangerous Outsider.

Why write books?, she asked herself. 'How much part does "coming out" play in the pleasure of writing them? Each one accumulates a little of the fictitious V.W. whom I carry like a mask about the world' (D V, 28 July 1940). Of all the fictitious V.W.s which she created in her novels, the one which I prefer, in present circumstances, is that of the dotty but embattled, determined, driven Miss La Trobe, settling down over a pint in the pub, her mind already buzzing with new work. We might think, though, that there was too much of wish-fulfilment about this mask, for Miss La Trobe had about her, as Virginia Woolf did not at all, more than a touch of vulgarity. So perhaps we should choose to conjure up a version of her produced by somebody else. The Irish writer Elizabeth Bowen stayed with Virginia Woolf in the last year of her life, and what she recalled of her was a feature which many others have also commented on, her attractive, slightly demented laughter:

> . . . her laughter was entrancing, it was outrageous laughter, almost like a child's laughter. Whoops of laughter, if anything amused her. As it happened, the last day I saw her I was staying at Rodmell and I remember her kneeling back on the floor – we were tacking away, mending a torn Spanish curtain in the house – and she sat back on her heels and put her head back in a patch of sun, early spring sun. Then she laughed in this consuming, choking, delightful, hooting way. And *that* is what has remained with me.[2]

Notes

Introduction

1. E. M. Forster, 'Virginia Woolf', *Two Cheers for Democracy* (Penguin, 1965) p. 250.
2. Phyllis Rose, *Writing of Women: Essays in a Renaissance* (Wesleyan University Press, 1985) p. 69, emphasis added.
3. Ibid., p. 71. See also Carolyn Heilbrun, *Writing a Woman's Life* (Norton, 1988). This model of identity is attributed to Erik Erikson. Both Rose and Heilbrun discuss its importance for the writing of biography.
4. MHP B11.

Chapter 1

1. Vanessa Bell, 'Notes on Virginia's Childhood', cited by Louise De-Salvo, *Virginia Woolf: The Impact of Childhood Sexual Abuse on her Life and Work* (Women's Press, 1989) p. 138.
2. Cited by Lyndall Gordon, *Virginia Woolf: A Writer's Life* (Oxford University Press, 1986) p. 15.
3. *A Cockney's Farming Experience*, ed. Suzanne Henig (San Diego State University Press, 1972). This juvenile work is quoted extensively by Louise DeSalvo, op. cit., but her analyses seem to me to be fanciful.
4. See Noel Annan, *Leslie Stephen: The Godless Victorian* (University of Chicago Press, 1984) p. 105f; also *Moments of Being*.
5. Annan, op. cit., p. 107.
6. Julia Margaret Cameron, *Victorian Photographs of Famous Men and Fair Women*, with Introductions by Roger Fry and Virginia Woolf (Hogarth Press, 1926): see also ed. Graham Ovenden, *A Victorian Album: Julia Margaret Cameron and Her Circle* (Secker and Warburg, 1975).
7. Noel Annan, op. cit., p. 119–20.
8. Monks House Papers MH/A.5c (University of Sussex Library), cited and discussed in Martine Stemerick, 'Virginia Woolf and Julia Stephen: The Distaff Side of History' in eds Elaine K. Ginsberg and Laura Moss Gottlieb, *Virginia Woolf: Centennial Essays* (Troy, New York: Whitston, 1983).
9. On Dr Savage and his role in Woolf's life see Stephen Trombley, *'All that Summer She was Mad': Virginia Woolf and Her Doctors* (Junction Books, 1981).
10. Annan, op. cit., p. 305.
11. Ibid., p. 113.
12. Add. MSS 61973 British Library.
13. Ibid.
14. Alice Fox, *Proceedings of the Modern Languages Association of America*,

1982, vol. 97, p. 103–4; this is in reply to Katherine Hill, 'Virginia Woolf and Leslie Stephen: History and Literary Revolution', *PMLA*, 1981, vol. 96, pp. 351–62.

15. Annan, op. cit., pp. 130–1. See also Louise DeSalvo, 'As "Miss Jan Says": Virginia Woolf's Early Journals', in ed. Jane Marcus, *Virginia Woolf and Bloomsbury* (Macmillan, 1987), p. 96f. and *Virginia Woolf: The Impact of Childhood Sexual Abuse on her Life and Work* (Women's Press, 1989). DeSalvo quotes extensively from the early diaries. In my opinion her speculations about Woolf often go far beyond anything that could be supported by the known evidence.
16. See the works cited in note 6 above. Woolf's essay was the introduction which is referred to there. See also *Freshwater: A Comedy* (Hogarth Press, 1976).

Chapter 2

1. See Madeline Moore, *The Short Season Between Two Silences: The Mystical and the Political in the Novels of Virginia Woolf* (George Allen & Unwin, 1984).
2. See Jane Marcus, 'The Niece of a Nun: Virginia Woolf, Caroline Stephen, and the Cloistered Imagination' in her *Virginia Woolf and the Languages of Patriarchy* (Indiana University Press, 1988). In my view Marcus seriously exaggerates the influence of Caroline Stephen on Woolf by neglecting the fundamental differences between them on questions of religion. Nonetheless, this chapter contains much useful information.
3. 'A Dialogue upon Mount Pentelicus', *Times Literary Supplement*, 11–17 September, 1987, p. 979.
4. These details I owe to the generosity of Andrew McNeillie who has informed me of 44 recently discovered Woolf essays in the *TLS* archives. They will be printed as an appendix to a future volume of *The Essays of Virginia Woolf*.
5. See Louise DeSalvo, 'Shakespeare's Other Sister' in ed. Jane Marcus, *New Feminist Essays on Virginia Woolf* (Macmillan, 1981).
6. See note 3.
7. 'Friendship's Gallery', *Twentieth Century Literature*, vol. 25, nos 3–4, Fall/Winter 1979, with an introduction by Ellen Hawkes. See also Ellen Hawkes, 'Woolf's "Magical Garden of Women"' in ed. Jane Marcus, *New Feminist Essays on Virginia Woolf*.
8. See, for example, S. P. Rosenbaum, *Victorian Bloomsbury: The Early Literary History of the Bloomsbury Group*, volume 1, St Martin's Press, 1986, pp. 161, 224.
9. Leonard Woolf, *Sowing*, in ed. S. P. Rosenbaum, *The Bloomsbury Group: A Collection of Memoirs, Commentary and Criticism* (University of Toronto Press, 1975) p. 104.
10. G. E. Moore, *Principia Ethica* (Cambridge University Press, 1962) p. 15.
11. J. M. Keynes, 'My Early Beliefs', in *Two Memoirs* (Rupert Hart-Davis, 1949) p. 85, reprinted in ed. S. P. Rosenbaum *The Bloomsbury Group*, p. 54.

Chapter 3

1. For the history of *The Voyage Out* and its various drafts see Virginia Woolf, *Melymbrosia: An Early Version of The Voyage Out*, ed. Louise DeSalvo (New York Public Library, 1982) and Louise DeSalvo, *Virginia Woolf's First Voyage: A Novel in the Making* (Macmillan, 1980).
2. The concept of the 'moratorium' derives from the work of Erik Erikson and is discussed in relation to Virginia Woolf by Carolyn Heilbrun, *Writing a Woman's Life* (Norton, 1988). Alex Zwerdling, *Virginia Woolf and the Real World* (University of California Press, 1986) applies the concept to the case of Jacob Flanders in *Jacob's Room*.
3. Leonard Woolf, *The Wise Virgins* cited Roger Poole, *The Unknown Virginia Woolf* (Cambridge University Press, 1978) p. 95.
4. Frances Spalding, *Vanessa Bell* (Macmillan, 1984) p. 61.
5. Cited by S. P. Rosenbaum, *Victorian Bloomsbury*, p. 66.
6. For more details see George Spater and Ian Parsons, *A Marriage of True Minds: An Intimate Portrait of Leonard and Virginia Woolf* (Jonathan Cape and the Hogarth Press, 1977) chapter 6.
7. J. M. Keynes, 'My Early Beliefs', op. cit., also in ed. S. P. Rosenbaum, *The Bloomsbury Group*, p. 64.
8. Gerald Brenan, *Personal Record 1920–72* (Jonathan Cape, 1974) p. 156. For another excellent account of Virginia Woolf and her Bloomsbury friends by Gerald Brenan see the extract from his *South from Granada* reprinted in ed. S. P. Rosenbaum, *The Bloomsbury Group*, p. 283f.
9. Roger Poole, *The Unknown Virginia Woolf*, p. 62.
10. S. P. Rosenbaum, *The Bloomsbury Group*, p. 77.
11. Ibid., p. 67.
12. From a draft of *The Voyage Out* cited by Louise DeSalvo, *Virginia Woolf's First Voyage*, p. 43.
13. For the best class analysis of the Bloomsbury Group see Raymond Williams, 'The Bloomsbury Fraction' in *Problems in Materialism and Culture* (Verso, 1980).
14. Roland Barthes, *A Lover's Discourse: Fragments* (Hill and Wang, 1978) p. 73.
15. Cited by Louise DeSalvo, *Virginia Woolf's First Voyage*, p. 47. Compare the 'censored' version, VO 139.

Chapter 4

1. Jane Marcus is right to emphasise the analogy with *The Magic Flute* in her 'Enchanted Organ, Magic Bells: *Night and Day* as a Comic Opera' in *Virginia Woolf and the Languages of Patriarchy* (Indiana University Press, 1988) p. 18f.
2. Sally Dennison, *Alternative Literary Publishing: Five Modern Histories* (University of Iowa Press, 1984) p. 73.
3. Eileen Traub, 'The Early Years of the Hogarth Press', *American Book Collector*, vol. 7, October 1986, pp. 32–6.
4. Peter Ackroyd, *T. S. Eliot* (Cardinal, 1988) p. 127.

5. See Phyllis Rose, *Woman of Letters: A Life of Virginia Woolf* (Routledge & Kegan Paul, 1978) p. 279, note 17.
6. Suzette Henke, 'Virginia Woolf Reads James Joyce: The *Ulysses* Notebook', in eds Morris Beja, Phillip Herring *et al.*, *James Joyce: The Centennial Symposium* (University of Illinois Press, 1986) pp. 39–42.
7. Richard Ellmann, *James Joyce* (Oxford University Press, 1982) p. 403.

Chapter 5

1. On the drafts of *Jacob's Room* see E. L. Bishop, 'The Shaping of *Jacob's Room*: Woolf's Manuscript revisions', *Twentieth Century Literature*, vol. 32, no. 1, Spring 1986, pp. 115–35. For useful contributions to other topics relevant to my discussion of *Jacob's Room* see Barry Morgenstern, 'The Self-Conscious Narrator in *Jacob's Room*' in *Modern Fiction Studies*, vol. 18, no. 3, 1972, p. 351f., and Judy Little, '*Jacob's Room* as Comedy: Woolf's Parodic *Bildungsroman*' in ed. Jane Marcus, *New Feminist Essays on Virginia Woolf* (University of Nebraska Press, 1981). Alex Zwerdling's discussion in his *Virginia Woolf and the Real World* (University of California Press, 1986) is particularly good and in tune with the basic strategy of the present book, as he discusses Woolf's innovations in form in relation to her purposes as a writer, as means to her broader ends.
2. Phyllis Rose, *Writing of Women*, op. cit., p. 69.
3. See above, note 1.
4. John Mepham, 'Mourning and Modernism', in eds Patricia Clements and Isobel Grundy, *Virginia Woolf: New Critical Essays* (Vision Press, 1983) pp. 137–56.
5. Richard Jenkyns, *The Victorians and Ancient Greece* (Oxford University Press, 1980) p. 338.
6. Peter Parker, *The Old Lie: The Great War and the Public School Ethos* (Constable, 1987) p. 218.
7. Ibid.
8. Ibid., p. 219. See also John Mepham, 'Mourning and Modernism', op. cit. (note 4) on the 'Greek' theme in *Jacob's Room* and the significance of Woolf's 1924 essay 'On Not Knowing Greek'.
9. On Rupert Brooke see Samuel Hynes, *Edwardian Occasions: Essays on English Writing in the Early Twentieth Century* (Oxford University Press, 1972) pp. 144–52.
10. E II, p. 203; see also p. xiii.
11. B. J. Kirkpatrick, *A Bibliography of Virginia Woolf*, 3rd edn (Clarendon Press, 1980) p. 16.
12. This and many other letters from Forster to Virginia Woolf are in Monks House Papers, Sussex University Library and in eds Mary Lago and P. N. Furbank, *Selected Letters of E. M. Forster*, vol. 2, 1921–70 (Collins, 1985).
13. The protracted battle between Woolf and Bennett is surveyed in Samuel Hynes, 'The Whole Contention Between Mr Bennett and Mrs Woolf' in his *Edwardian Occasions*, pp. 24–37. See also Beth Rigel

Daugherty, 'The Whole Contention Between Mr Bennett and Mrs Woolf Revisited' in eds Elaine Ginsberg and Laura Moss Gottlieb, *Virginia Woolf: Centennial Essays* (Whitston, 1983).

Chapter 6

1. On the various drafts of *Mrs Dalloway* and the notebook from which this quotation comes, see C. G. Hoffmann, 'From Short Story to Novel: the Manuscript Revisions of Virginia Woolf's *Mrs Dalloway*', *Modern Fiction Studies*, vol. 14, Summer 1968, pp. 171–86 and Jacqueline Latham, 'The Manuscript Revisions of Virginia Woolf's *Mrs Dalloway*: A Postscript', *Modern Fiction Studies*, vol. 18, Summer 1972, pp. 475–6. See also Virginia Woolf, *Mrs Dalloway's Party: A Short Story Sequence*, with an Introduction by Stella McNichol (Harcourt Brace Jovanovich, 1973).
2. They are in *Mrs Dalloway's Party* (see note 1) and now also in CSF.
3. E. M. Forster, 'The Novels of Virginia Woolf', originally published in *The New Criterion* in 1926 is now, as 'The Early Novels of Virginia Woolf', in *Abinger Harvest* (Penguin, 1967): the quoted phrase is on p. 124.
4. See Maria DiBattista, 'Joyce, Woolf and the Modern Mind', in eds Patricia Clements and Isobel Grundy, *Virginia Woolf: New Critical Essays* (Vision Press, 1983) pp. 96–114.
5. Virginia Woolf originally wrote this is in 1931 in a series of articles on London for *Good Housekeeping* magazine. They are now available as *The London Scene* (Hogarth Press, 1982) p. 20. See also Raymond Williams, *The Country and the City* (Chatto & Windus, 1973) p. 233–47.
6. The history of the conception and revisions of *To the Lighthouse* together with details of notebooks is given in Susan Dick's edition of the holograph drafts of the novel (Hogarth Press, 1983), referred to here as TL/MS.
7. J. A. Lavin, 'The First Editions of Virginia Woolf's *To the Lighthouse*', in ed. Joseph Katz, *Proof: The Yearbook of American Bibliographical and Textual Studies*, vol. 2 (University of South Carolina Press, 1972) pp. 185–211. Most significant, to my mind, is the difference in section 9 of Part III, which is enclosed in round brackets in the US edition but in square brackets in the UK edition. The former is surely a mistake which Woolf failed to spot. On the significance of square brackets in the novel see John Mepham, 'Figures of Desire: Narration and Fiction in *To the Lighthouse*' in ed. G. D. Josipovici, *The Modern English Novel* (Open Books, 1976).
8. The photograph is reproduced in Lyndall Gordon, *Virginia Woolf: A Writer's Life*, and discussed by her on pp. 197–8. On Julia Margaret Cameron, see Amanda Hopkinson, *Julia Margaret Cameron* (Virago, 1986).
9. See eds Louise DeSalvo and Mitchell Leaska, *The Letters of Vita Sackville-West to Virginia Woolf* (Hutchinson, 1984); Leaska's 'Introduction' provides a useful short history of the relationship.

10. See Kate Flint, 'Virginia Woolf and the General Strike', *Essays in Criticism*, vol. 36, October 1986, pp. 319–34.
11. See James M. Haule, '"Le Temps passe" and the Original Typescript: An Early Version of the "Time Passes" Section of *To the Lighthouse*', *Twentieth Century Literature*, vol. 29, no. 3, 1983, pp. 267–311.
12. See Morris Beja, 'Virginia Woolf: Matches Struck in the Dark', in his *Epiphany in the Modern Novel* (University of Washington Press, 1971).
13. Ibid., p. 126.
14. Cited in Haule, see note 11 above, p. 268.
15. This photograph is reproduced, for example, in QB II, as 'Virginia, c.1925'.
16. John Lehmann, *Virginia Woolf* (Thames & Hudson, 1975) p. 63. The three Man Ray photographs of Woolf are reproduced together in George Spater and Ian Parsons, *A Marriage of True Minds*, p. 85f.
17. Man Ray, *Self Portrait* (Bloomsbury 1988).
18. Richard Kennedy, *A Boy at the Hogarth Press* (Penguin, 1978).
19. For further details of the Hogarth Press at this time see LW 303f.

Chapter 7

1. See E. M. Forster, 'The Early Novels of Virginia Woolf', *Abinger Harvest* (Penguin, 1967).
2. See eds Louise DeSalvo and Mitchell Leaska, *The Letters of Vita Sackville-West to Virginia Woolf* (Hutchinson, 1984) and Nigel Nicolson, *Portrait of a Marriage* (Weidenfeld & Nicolson, 1973).
3. The figure of the angel in the house derives from a poem by Coventry Patmore. Woolf's speech is printed as 'Professions for Women' in WW. A much longer, typescript version of the same speech is printed in P.
4. The extant drafts of *The Waves*, together with Woolf's notes and an 'Introduction' which discusses the history of the writing of this novel in detail, are all in Virginia Woolf, *The Waves: The Two Holograph Drafts*, transcribed and edited by J. W. Graham (Hogarth Press, 1976).
5. Ibid., p. 36.
6. The importance of such moments in shaping a life and the implications of this for biography are central to Lyndall Gordon's treatment of Woolf's life in her *Virginia Woolf: A Writer's Life*. See also Gordon's 'Our Silent Life: Virginia Woolf and T. S. Eliot' in eds Patricia Clements and Isobel Grundy *Virginia Woolf: New Critical Essays* (Vision Press, 1983).

Chapter 8

1. B. J. Kirkpatrick, *A Bibliography of Virginia Woolf*, 3rd edn (Oxford University Press, 1980).
2. *The Hogarth Letters*, with an Introduction by Hermione Lee (Chatto & Windus, 1985).

3. See Carolyn Heilbrun, *Writing a Woman's Life* (Norton, 1988) chapter 7.
4. For some details of this history see D IV, 20 January 1932, note 8.
5. They are described by Brenda Silver in RN p. 22f.
6. Grace Radin, *Virginia Woolf's* The Years: *The Evolution of a Novel* (The University of Tennessee Press, 1981). For other discussion of this novel see the articles dedicated to it in the special issue of the *Bulletin of the New York Public Library*, vol. 80, winter 1977.
7. Grace Radin, op. cit., p. 122.
8. These two 'enormous chunks' are reprinted in an Appendix to Radin, op. cit.
9. See Kirkpatrick, op. cit.
10. For example, Jane Marcus, in the *Bulletin of the New York Public Library* (note 6 above) says that *The Years* is 'a great novel . . . the pride of British literature of the 1930s' and that it is as radical in form as *Ulysses* or *The Waste Land*.
11. See Lynda Morris and Robert Radford, *The Story of the Artists International Association 1933–53* (Museum of Modern Art, Oxford, 1983).
12. Frances Spalding, *Vanessa Bell* (Macmillan, 1984) p. 291.
13. Woolf's less attractive attitudes, her xenophobia and racism in particular, are documented by Lorrie Goldensohn, 'Unburying the Statue: The Lives of Virginia Woolf', *Salmagundi*, nos. 74–5, Spring–Summer 1987, pp. 1–41.
14. Lynda Morris and Robert Radford, op. cit. (note 11), p. 41.
15. *The Times* (London), 28 April 1937.
16. Spalding, op. cit., p. 294.
17. E. M. Forster, 'The Last Parade', *Two Cheers for Democracy* (Penguin, 1965) p. 17; for Vanessa Bell's reaction see Spalding, op. cit., p. 340.
18. A slightly shortened version of this memoir is printed as Appendix C to QB II. The original typescript is now in MHP, Sussex University.
19. Julian Bell, 'War and Peace: a Letter to E. M. Forster', in ed. Quentin Bell, *Julian Bell: Essays, Poems and Letters* (Hogarth Press, 1938).
20. Quentin Bell, 'Bloomsbury and "The Vulgar Passions"', *Critical Inquiry*, Winter 1979, pp. 239–56, and QB II 256.
21. The cartoon is reproduced in the *Bulletin of the New York Public Library*, vol. 80, 1977, p. 157.

Chapter 9

1. See Raymond Williams, 'The Bloomsbury Fraction', *Problems in Materialism and Culture* (Verso, 1980), p. 148f.
2. J. M. Keynes, 'My Early Beliefs', in ed. S. P. Rosenbaum, *The Bloomsbury Group* (University of Toronto Press, 1975) p. 64.
3. Forster's 'Credo' was republished as 'What I Believe', a Hogarth Press pamphlet, in May 1939, and was later included with that title in his *Two Cheers for Democracy*.
4. *Two Cheers for Democracy* (Penguin, 1965) p. 79.
5. See Catherine Belsey, *Critical Practice* (Methuen, 1980).

6. See also John Mepham, 'Trained to Silence', *London Review of Books*, 20 November 1980, p. 21f.
7. Goldensohn, op. cit. (chapter 8, note 13) p. 32.

Chapter 10

1. Quentin Bell, 'Bloomsbury and "The Vulgar Passions"', *Critical Inquiry*, Winter 1979, p. 256.
2. Agnes Smith's letters to Woolf are in MHP, Sussex University Library.
3. Q. D. Leavis, *Fiction and the Reading Public* (Penguin, 1979) p. 179.
4. Sigmund Freud, *Civilisation, War and Death*, ed. John Rickman (Hogarth Press, 1939) p. 93.
5. Ibid., p. 12.
6. The history of the revisions of *Between the Acts* is given in Virginia Woolf, *Pointz Hall: The Earlier and Later Typescripts of Between the Acts*, ed. Mitchell Leaska (New York University Press, 1983).
7. The texts of two essays left unfinished at her death, 'The Reader' and 'Anon', together with introductory notes by Brenda Silver, are in a special Woolf issue of *Twentieth Century Literature*, vol. 25, nos. 3/4, Fall/Winter 1979. The quotation is from 'Anon' p. 403.
8. Ibid., p. 396.
9. 'The Reader', ibid., p. 428.
10. F. R. Leavis, 'After "To the Lighthouse"', *Scrutiny*, vol. 10, no. 3, January 1942, p. 295.
11. E. M. Forster, 'Virginia Woolf', *Two Cheers for Democracy* (Penguin, 1965) p. 250.

Chapter 11

1. See especially Phyllis Rose, *Woman of Letters* and Alex Zwerdling, *Virginia Woolf and the Real World*.
2. *Recollections of Virginia Woolf*, ed. Joan Russell Noble (Penguin, 1975) p. 62.

Index

DATE DUE			

Mepham   235397